THE RAISING

JERRY KORN

OF THE QUEEN

SIMON AND SCHUSTER

NEW YORK   1961

To Bobbie

Acknowledgments

The principal sources for the material in this book are the four partners of Queen Salvors, Inc.—Lloyd Deir, Beldon Little, Paul Brady and Alvah Sadler—their wives, and the following crew members and participants: Maurice Simmons, Henley Doughtie, Mack Duncan, Woody Crisp, Duke Morris, Kin Reed and Mrs. Reed, Bob Russell, who was a frequent visitor to the tanker, and Samuel Kahn of the Ocean Shipping and Trading Company. Technical and background information was supplied by Frank Braynard of the American Merchant Marine Institute, Lieutenant Commander Everett J. Mooring and Chief Journalist Robert Patty of the United States Coast Guard, Frank Oberle of Merritt-Chapman & Scott, Inc., Captain C. W. Randall and Paul Preus.

Special thanks are due to J. Lewis Rawls, Jr., for his untiring assistance and support. Valuable advice was contributed by Eugene Rachlis and Kathryn Morgan-Ryan. I would also like to thank Jerome Klapper for an inspirational assist and the Robert Murrays of Manchester, New Hampshire, and Limerick, Maine, for their kindness and help.

My deepest debts are to Cornelius Ryan, without whom the book would not have been started, and to David Maness, without whom it could not have been finished—and finally to my wife for her limitless contributions of patience, understanding and perception.

PROLOGUE

The Tanker

THE VESSEL ROSE abruptly out of the sea, half submerged and listing at a sharp angle. Her two superstructures leaned out over the water, rising over either end of the hull like disembodied islands. Between them, waves rolled up the sloping tank deck and broke hissing among the pipes and valves. Cables slapped vacantly against the cargo booms in the faint March breeze, and loose pipes snatched up by the surf clattered against the bulwarks. Somewhere in the aft island a door slammed in rhythm with the breakers.

All about the ship lay evidence of a violent end. Far forward where her bow should have been there was nothing but torn metal; some great force had ripped the stem away bodily, leaving only gaping compartments, open to the sea. The steel catwalk that had once bridged the tank deck lengthwise now extended over only half of it; the rest of the structure had been wrenched to one side and hung drunkenly over the port gunwale, with parts of its steelwork resting among the bitts and pipes of the deck.

The cylindrical tank hatches were open, their round covers missing. Some valves and pipe sections had been stripped away. Deck fittings had been removed, cables torn off, sections of rail cut out. Back on the boat deck, lifeboats were gone from their davits, preservers were ripped from the bulkheads, and portholes were without glass. Over everything that the waves could reach lay a heavy, slippery black film of crude oil.

The great wooden nameboard was missing from her bridge, the bow identification was gone with the bow. But her identity was still visible at low tide. As the water receded, her name and port of registry could be seen stamped in white on her stern.

AFRICAN QUEEN, the letters said. MONROVIA.

Three years before, she had been the object of admiring news stories and proud statistics. "The new supertanker," one newspaper had reported at the time of her launching, "is 590 feet in length, 74 feet in the beam, with a draft when loaded of 32 feet and a dead-weight tonnage of 21,500. She is powered by steam turbine and embodies all the latest principles of tanker design, being all steel welded with riveted gunwale bar. . . ."

She had been the size of a heavy cruiser, and almost as handsome. All the abrupt lines had been smoothed away by the designer, and the height of the superstructure carefully controlled so that the usual chunkiness of the tanker was avoided. Her hull was long and black, her islands a gleaming white, her smokestack buff and rakishly streamlined. At sea, cutting through the water at her cruising speed of seventeen knots and pulled low by a full load, the *African Queen* had the long, sleek grace of an arrow.

She was a striking ship and, for the short span of her life, a happy one. She had been built in 1955 at the Kieler Howaldtswerke A.G. in Kiel, lovingly and with Germanic attention to detail. Only high-grade steel was used in her construction, only the best available marine equipment installed on her bridge. Her engines were the finest that could be had in Europe. She was filled with pleasant surprises for her crew: deck and cabin fittings of unusual quality, a huge galley glistening with stainless steel, a machine shop in the engine room that took the breath of every engineer who saw it.

The *African Queen* had been built for a company of Norwegian investors who, like many of the world's tanker operators, had registered in Liberia for tax purposes, using the name African Enterprises, Ltd. The *Queen* was the company's only ship, and during her fitting out and in the months that followed the owners lavished attention on their tanker like the doting parents of an only child. She was furnished like a luxury hotel and maintained like a fragile piece of precision machinery. No flake of rust was permitted to besmirch her hull; each year $25,000 was spent on paint. Her engines, kept in superb condition, ran so smoothly that they could be only faintly heard and felt from topside. From stem to stern the *African Queen* was immaculate, glistening, comfortable.

There was more behind this concern than the simple affection of her owners for a beautiful ship. European tankers often offer their crews sumptuous surroundings to make up for the hard life the men lead. The voyages are long, the pay low, the time in port brief. The turn-around period has grown progressively shorter as oil pumping equipment has improved, and a tanker that pulls up to the pier at 5:00 P.M. may be ready to put to sea again before breakfast time next morning, off on another 8,000-mile trip.

At sea there is constant danger. A storm that is little noticed by other ships may create waves that break over a tanker's low deck, imperiling the men who must hurry from pilot house to stern on the spray-blown catwalk. The cargo is capricious and an endless source of worry. There are frequent fire drills. The crew may smoke only in quarters. A short circuit in the ship's wiring may bring on a major emergency. A loose pipe slamming against the steel deck may strike the spark that ends everything.

Unlike many other kinds of cargo, oil must be nursed constantly. Its expansion and contraction must be checked. It must be shifted from tank to tank as the vessel changes trim on a long voyage. Its temperature must be taken, and on frequent trips from the tropics to colder zones it has to be heated so it won't be a solid mass when the time comes to pump it out.

All this makes for a difficult life for a tanker's officers and men. Aboard the *African Queen,* everything conceivable had been done to make this life easier. The officers' quarters were richly furnished. The lounge just below the bridge was paneled with dark mahogany and teak. Its floors were covered with deep-piled rugs. Sandalwood chairs, upholstered in coral fabric, were clustered around a large-screen televi-

9

sion set. Heavy draperies curtained the portholes. The captain's quarters and the adjacent owners' suite duplicated that decor.

Aft, the crew's quarters were only slightly less luxurious. The tanker sailors lived in good-sized staterooms, with no more than two men to a room; they slept on foam rubber mattresses in hardwood bunks. Each cabin had built-in bookshelves and lockers, an electric fan, a washbasin, a medicine chest. Over each bunk was a night light. In front of the double portholes was a table that folded against the wall when not in use. Upholstered benches flanked the table.

On the deck above was the great galley with its gleaming counters and sinks, its mechanical potato peelers and dish washers, its huge electric mixers and ranges. To starboard of the galley was a large, pleasant mess hall; on the port side was the larder, filled with a vast and varied array of canned foods, including whole sides of mutton and beef in the freezer. No men at sea ate better; on a three-month voyage the food bill might run as high as $10,000 for the *Queen's* crew of forty-seven.

They were a cosmopolitan lot, largely German but with a wide sampling of other nationalities—Spanish, Italian, Scandinavian, Indian. The officers were Norwegian or Finnish. Among these men there was a surprising kinship. They were loyal to the *Queen;* she had fewer desertions than is customary among tanker crews. One seaman had worked in the Kiel shipyard where she was built, and had then signed on and stayed with her as part of the crew. They liked the policies of the owners. And they were fond of their skipper, a tall, gentle, sad-faced Norwegian named Kia Danielsen who had been at sea for twenty-seven of his forty-three years.

Liked by her crew and cherished by her owners, the *African Queen* was like a great yacht, gleaming, happy, well cared for. For three years she patrolled the seas, carrying her great cargoes of petroleum from the far-flung oil ports of the world, under blistering suns, through fierce storms, steadily, uneventfully, dependably. She seldom saw her three home ports in Germany, Norway and Liberia; instead, she ran from the Persian Gulf and South American ports to New Jersey or occasionally Rotterdam or the West Coast of the United States—thousands and thousands of miles virtually without incident.

In all this time only two small clouds darkened her existence. The first was that not long after she was built an abrupt and inexplicable world oil glut developed, depressing the tanker market, and limiting the cargoes available to her so that more than once her owners had to order her cruising speed cut in mid-voyage to avoid long tie-ups in port while awaiting new business. The second was that in the months since she had slid down the ways two ships of similar construction, running through punishing seas, had suddenly broken in two just forward of the pilot house.

Shortly after midnight on December 28, 1958, the *African Queen* pulled away from the dock at Cartagena, Colombia, her engines throbbing, and headed out to sea on a routine 2,100-mile trip to the Socony-Mobil refinery at Paulsboro, New Jersey, on the Delaware River. She rode low in the sea, heavily weighted by 21,000 tons of highly volatile crude oil, but still briskly responsive to the helm. By daybreak she was well into the Caribbean, making an easy thirteen knots.

In the officers' lounge forward and in the mess hall aft, Christmas decorations swung from the walls; aboard the *Queen* the holiday season was scrupulously observed. A special meal was served to all hands on Christmas day as they steamed up through the subtropics off Cuba.

As the ship started up the East Coast of the United States and into colder weather, the skies and the sea turned gray. At midnight of the twenty-ninth, twenty miles off the Virginia capes, Captain Danielsen got out of bed only an hour after going off watch, and returned to the bridge to keep an eye on the weather. The seas were now quite rough and it had begun to rain. He ordered the *Queen's* speed cut to eleven knots. At 1:30 A.M., nearing Maryland's Chincoteague Bay region, he reduced speed again, sharply, to ease the strain of the heavy swells on the tanker. She was making barely four knots now.

The rain was driving down hard and the seas were pouring

11

across the tank deck as the *African Queen* bucked the gale head on. The captain was a little worried about his navigation; the radar was not working, and it had been some time since the skies had been clear enough for star shots that would have fixed his position. Nevertheless, when the time came for the turn into Delaware Bay at around 4:30 A.M. he was pleased to see the lightship he had been waiting for, and without hesitation he called for a change of course, a turn to port that sent the *Queen* pounding westward, with the storm now on her stern quarter.

For another hour, as the ship headed slowly toward the land, he stood in the chartroom, growing increasingly anxious now as he failed to pick up the shore lights that should have been visible along the banks of the Delaware. When it was almost six o'clock, he decided that it made no sense to go driving forward in the darkness; in a couple of hours day-break would come and he could navigate visually. He would turn around and head back to sea, then wait offshore for enough light to see what he was doing. He ordered more speed so the ship would have steerage way, then gave the helmsman a new course.

The *African Queen* was about halfway through her turn when she ran aground.

There was no panic, on the bridge or anywhere else on the ship. Most of the men were asleep, and they slept on. Many who were standing watch were not even aware of what had happened, she slid onto the shoal so gently and so swiftly. The captain himself knew it only by the sudden, barely perceptible laboring of the engines.

But the chief engineer found himself inexplicably awake. Scarcely knowing why, he began to dress. He was on his way to the engine room before he really noticed the slight vibration of the engines that had awakened him.

One member of the crew was aroused from sleep by the wailing of his pet cat. He went sleepily out on deck to see what was happening. Another man, who, for reasons of his own, had chosen this hour before dawn to iron his pants, left them on the ironing board and stepped outside. Elsewhere on the ship all was quiet.

On the bridge, the captain, pale and tight-lipped, was trying to slide his vessel off the shoal. In quick succession he ordered the engines to full astern, half ahead and full stop. Nothing happened. He tried full astern again. Suddenly the second mate shouted, "She's off!"

At that moment there came a jarring *crack!* almost directly under their feet, and the horror-stricken captain saw the bow of the *African Queen*—the entire 110 feet of it forward of the bridge—slowly swing to starboard all by itself, as if on a hinge. Peering white-faced over the bridge rail, he found himself looking into the open ends of the bow tanks as they spilled their thousands of gallons of black oil into the sea.

If the broken bow of the *African Queen* had torn away completely in that first instant, and had then drifted away or sunk, the remaining four fifths of the tanker might have been on the way back to port under tow by nightfall. But for a few minutes the bow was held fast to the rest of the ship by the starboard plates, which bent and buckled but refused to tear. The result was disaster. As the wind and the waves kicked up by the dying storm played against it, the bow turned all the way around, the steel hinge protesting noisily, until it was facing the stern of the ship. For a moment the great prow loomed hideously over the tank deck. Then it struck, with a clanging slam that shook the tanker to the keel. The blow wrenched the bow loose, but the waves now had it pinned to the tanker's side. Instead of drifting off, the bow hammered again and again at the *Queen,* slipping a little farther along toward the stern after every impact and crashing into the ship each time at a new place.

Sparks flew high with each blow, showering down on the oil that now coated the sea. Desperately the men fought to prevent a fire. Some of them raced to pump fire-retarding foam into the tanks. Others lined up along the starboard rail and, standing right at the point of impact, jammed heavy rope, foam rubber mattresses and whatever else they could find into the gap between the hull and the wildly tossing bow. With each collision the whole ship jumped. One vicious slam buckled the inch-and-a-quarter deck plates, raising a bump in the tank deck a foot high. Ten-inch hawser was snipped as if by scissors between the grinding sides, and smoke rose from the mattresses. The spray coming over the deck was oily, and soon the steel underfoot was slippery and treacherous.

Relentlessly the bow traveled down the tanker's side. At last it reached the stern section—and there it struck to the very vitals of the ship. The men in the engine room heard an enormous crash; the side of the ship gave a mighty heave, and water began to run down the inside plates. Twice more the bow hammered through the engine-room wall before it finally drifted off astern. The men ran out to safety as the seas rose over the turbines.

On the bridge Captain Danielsen watched helplessly as the *Queen* settled heavily back onto the sand, her hull ripped open, her engine room flooded. The great danger was over, but in the space of a few minutes his lovely vessel had been transformed into a battered, truncated, half-sunken wreck.

He had ordered an SOS signal sent within minutes after the bow broke. Now in the gray dawn he could see U.S. Coast Guard airplanes and helicopters beginning to arrive. The tanker's crewmen slowly made their way to the sundeck atop the poop structure, the highest deck on the ship, and awaited rescue. Soon the helicopters began to move in, slings dangling beneath them, and the rescue operation got underway. Looking around him, the captain could see that he was not in Delaware Bay at all; he was ten miles from the nearest shore, faintly visible to the west.

By noon all the men but the captain and the mate had been airlifted off the tanker; the two officers stayed, waiting word from the owners that a salvage effort had been begun and that their departure from the *Queen* would not constitute legal abandonment. Not far off, the bow still floated, bobbing vigorously in the seas.

That afternoon a Coast Guard motor lifeboat arrived with the owners' message, and Captain Danielsen left the *African Queen* for the last time. It was only then that he found out where he was: off Ocean City, Maryland, twenty miles south of the river mouth he had been trying to reach.

The Merritt-Chapman & Scott salvage vessel *Curb* had put out from New York while the rescue operation was still underway; it arrived at midnight and anchored a few hundred yards from the tanker.

The next morning a full-scale salvage attempt was launched. It lasted, in all, forty-five days and involved the efforts of forty-three men and an impressive array of equipment. It cost more than $150,000, and there were times when it seemed likely to cost the lives of a few men as well. There were several injuries, and many bad scares. And when it was all over the broken tanker still lay out on the shoal, and the world's foremost salvage company had withdrawn in full retreat.

It was not the job that defeated Merritt-Chapman; it was the weather. The men working on the tanker rarely saw sunshine. It rained and snowed, the icy wind never relented and the waves hammered incessantly against the exposed ship, soaking everyone with freezing spray. The men lived aboard the salvage vessel and commuted daily to the wrecked tanker. Getting aboard was always a hazard in the foul weather—and there was one day when it took what amounted to a full-blown rescue operation to get the salvagers off at dusk. The simple loading of equipment became a complicated and dangerous project. Working on the dripping, oil-slicked, tilted decks was exceedingly risky; soon after the work started the salvage master fell and hurt his back and had to return to New York while another man came down to take his place.

At the end of six weeks the salvagers had anchored the bow, still floating nearby, had made one small wood-and-concrete patch on the tank deck, where the battering of the bow had buckled the deck plates, and had obtained a fairly clear idea of where the rest of the damage lay. It was small return for their investment of time and money, and it was obvious that they could not go on this way.

Early in February Merritt-Chapman & Scott informed the ship's owners that salvage operations would have to be suspended until spring, when the weather improved. The

New York salvage firm was fully prepared to return at that time and resume work on the tanker. But in the meantime, possession of the ship and the attendant responsibility—which had rested with the salvagers while they were aboard—would be restored to African Enterprises, Ltd.

This placed the owners of the *Queen* in a dilemma. There were still thousands of gallons of black, sticky oil aboard the tanker. For weeks, the coastal resorts of Delaware and Maryland had been living in dread of that petroleum; if it ever got loose and washed up on the beaches it might take months before the black scum could be removed. The two states' congressional delegations in Washington were beginning to fuss about it: the ruination of resorts like Ocean City and Rehoboth Beach would be a major catastrophe.

The owners could not stand the liability. Their once-beautiful *Queen* was now a smashed and oil-smeared wreck; the cost of getting her off and repaired now would scarcely be covered by her insurance—and no amount of insurance would protect them against the millions of dollars' worth of lawsuits that would result if the oil from her tanks swept across those Maryland and Delaware beaches.

On February 12 African Enterprises, Ltd., announced publicly that it was giving up possession of the *African Queen*—abandoning the broken vessel to Lloyd's of London, which held the insurance. The underwriters followed suit immediately. It would be cheaper to pay off the owners and take the loss than to risk a legal action over the oil. The tanker market was depressed, and it probably would cost more to get the *Queen* off the shoal and back into operation than the vessel was worth. Lloyd's too announced that it was surrendering possession.

Along the docksides of Maryland and Delaware the news that the tanker had been abandoned was greeted by a brief period of astonishment, followed by an even briefer period of discussion. Boatmen from Ocean City and Lewes, Delaware, thirty-five miles up the coast, had been hired by Merritt-Chapman & Scott during the unsuccessful salvage attempt, and word of the luxuries aboard the tanker had spread all along the coast. If she was now abandoned, who owned all that stuff out there? A few people said that it still belonged to African Enterprises—that in abandoning the ship the owners had not relinquished their claim to her furnishings. This opinion was widely and promptly rejected. Within hours after the abandonment was announced, the first small boats slipped up into the shadow of the port deck and a few figures climbed aboard the tanker. They were swiftly followed by others. At first the scavengers were furtive—but after awhile, when nobody came out to stop them, they stopped worrying.

The boarders found dazzling pickings. A few were so overcome with the luxury all about them that they wandered around like visitors to a museum, stopping to admire one delightful sight after another—until they discovered that while they were looking others were taking. Then they hurriedly got to work.

There were times in the weeks that followed when twenty or thirty men could be seen clambering over the listing hulk, pulling, sawing, unscrewing, hammering, arguing. They ripped up the deep, thick rugs and dragged them to the boats. They stripped the heavy draperies from the portholes, shouldered the coral-upholstered chairs and carted them off, tore the fixtures from the bathrooms, yanked up the wiring in the telegraph room and staggered out with the powerful transmitters and receivers. A man came out of the officers' lounge dragging the big television set. Others brought armloads of small radios from the crew's quarters. Someone went off with the big radar scope. Someone else climbed a mast and sawed down the radar antenna, which fell to the deck in a useless mass.

Seven men joined forces and lurched across the deck bearing the vessel's $8,000 gyrocompass. One fellow emerged from the captain's cabin whooping with delight; on his back was the skipper's uniform jacket, heavy with braid and a perfect fit. In the various corners of the tanker there was marine equipment beyond calculation: paints, ropes, engines, electric motors, running lights, hardware, life preservers and—a prize catch—several lifeboats, some of them with motors.

Inevitably, there were men who hated to see anyone else dipping into this treasure trove. Two burly fishermen would wrangle fiercely over a pile of rope, ignoring another pile just like it a few feet away. One man struggled futilely for some minutes to ease a sofa through a cabin door and suddenly found that there was a beefy clam digger pulling at the other end of it. "You hang on if you want," the clammer growled, "but this goddam thing is going in my boat and you're coming with it!"

One Lewes boatman saw an adding machine and hastily claimed it. Just then he caught sight of a typewriter and took that. Then he was distracted by a fine upholstered chair. He rushed it to his boat and rushed back to find the typewriter and adding machine gone.

On some days the boat traffic was so heavy on the port side of the ship, the only place where it was safe to tie up, that late arrivals couldn't even get close. Many went home empty-handed.

One boatload of plumbers from the inland city of Salisbury went out to stock up on pipe from the miles of metal tubing aboard the *Queen*. By the time they arrived most of the best spaces by the port rail had been taken. Being plumbers and not boatmen, they proceeded to tie up anyhow—far aft, where the tank deck was at its lowest. At that point waves would sometimes come sweeping clear across and roar over the lip of the deck in a miniature Niagara. The plumbers' boat hadn't been there long when it suddenly filled up like a plugged toilet, then capsized.

Aghast, the plumbers sent in an urgent call with a passing boatman for Coast Guard help. A small boat was sent out from the Ocean City Coast Guard station. The Coast Guardsmen found the plumbers' craft almost completely submerged and weaving crazily in the choppy seas. They tried hard to seize and right it, but it finally slammed into their boat and sank it. The station's big motor lifeboat had to put out and rescue plumbers and Coast Guardsmen alike.

And still the pillaging went on. The ship's brass bell disappeared, followed by the helmsman's wheel and the wooden nameboard off the bridge. Hundreds of yards of costly hawser were dragged out of the lockers and thrown into the boats; so were thousands of dollars' worth of paint, which the tanker had aboard in vast quantities. Cartons of food were lugged out of the ship's pantry. Bags of unground coffee were grabbed up, and even big packages of half-soaked matches. Many men stocked up on crockery.

One fisherman attacked the ship's safe with a crowbar and pried the door open. Shortly afterward he was seen around Ocean City in an expensive new car. Another hunter was said to have found $250 under a crewman's mattress. In Lewes a boatman proudly invited in the neighbors to see his living room—entirely furnished, from divan to draperies, off the tanker.

When the furniture and other easily removable items had disappeared, the men went after metal. There was brass in the porthole frames, copper in the pipes and fittings, monel metal elsewhere, all of it valuable. Portholes were left to gape open—including, after a while, some that were submerged at high tide and half submerged at all tides. The lids of the hatches, called Butterworth covers, were heavy with brass, and scavengers laboriously removed them. One man undogged and lifted a Butterworth cover on the forward part of the tank deck. It happened to open into a tank that had been torn in half by the break-up of the ship, and mighty seas were pounding through the tear. As the cover swung back, a wave roared into the tank below, and a towering geyser more than a hundred feet high shot into the air over the tank deck, thoroughly scaring everyone in the vicinity.

Besides the quest for valuables, there was a certain amount of senseless vandalism. Expensive bathroom fixtures that couldn't be removed were smashed with sledge hammers. Mirrors came crashing to the decks, windows were wrecked, bulkheads were stove in. The contents of drawers and lockers were dumped out and strewn around. Ship's papers were scattered all over the bridge, and a great pile of message forms, enlistment contracts and message files rose in one corner of the radio room.

The Coast Guard at Ocean City watched all this activity with growing anxiety. Officials feared it was only a matter of time before someone got killed. One man already had fallen fifteen feet; scores of others had fallen lesser distances. Practically everyone who was a regular visitor to the ship had experienced some kind of narrow escape. Concern intensified as the raiders began to turn to the bow.

It was more dangerous by far than the stern section. It was noticeably unstable—the only part of it that rested on the ground was a small area of the torn bottom. The rest was afloat. The nose pointed sharply into the air at an angle of perhaps twenty degrees, rhythmically riding up the anchor cable and back with every sea. The waves broke over the slanted deck; there was almost always white water where the deck disappeared into the ocean. Many a scavenger who slipped on the plates went skidding madly down the deck, grasping desperately at obstructions, and ended up with a tumble into the roiling seas below. Fortunately it never happened while a man was out there alone; each victim was eventually dragged, shivering, out of the water.

One day a party of boatmen who tried to board the bow found that the rope ladder they had used previously was missing from its accustomed place on the starboard side. They shouted up, and a head appeared at the rail. "You can't come aboard," the man called down. "This bow is gonna be salvaged."

After a while he relented and let them board the bow to get some metal they had piled up there the day before. His name, he said, was Lewis Bertrand, and he had been hired by some men in Lewes who planned to beach the bow and sell it for scrap. Bertrand was to stay aboard until the salvagers were ready. His visitors looked around at the steep, bobbing bow. "You're gonna stay on here all *night?*" one of them asked.

"Sure," Bertrand said. "It don't bother me."

The boatmen gathered up their gleanings and started back down the ladder. "You're sure you don't want to come back in with us?" they asked Bertrand.

"Naw. Thanks, anyhow."

The storm struck that evening with speed and fury. By nightfall it was a full-blown gale. At 7:45 P.M. the Ocean City

Coast Guard station got a call from the station at Lewes. An anxious woman named Bertrand had phoned in to say that her son Lewis had gone aboard the tanker and that she hadn't heard from him since. The Ocean City station commander promptly ordered the motor lifeboat made ready. Before it could leave, an even more disturbing report came in. A man who had just made a scary trip in from the tanker in a small boat reported that flashing lights were visible from the bow. "It was a regular S.O.S. signal," he said. "Three short, three long, three short."

Ocean City quickly queried Lewes: "Find out which part of the tanker that man was on."

In the driving rain, without waiting for the answer, a crew boarded the thirty-six-foot lifeboat and headed out into the violent seas. By now the storm was at its peak, and it was apparent almost immediately that any rescue effort was foredoomed. Several times the lifeboat came near to swamping. Finally it headed back in.

Word of the boat's inability to reach the tanker was hurriedly passed along to Fifth Coast Guard District Headquarters down the coast in Norfolk. Shortly afterward a helicopter took off from Elizabeth City, North Carolina, and headed north through the storm, followed within a few minutes by an amphibian plane. They let down over the tanker and sent up a series of flares. The tanker itself was still there, although it was sometimes hidden in spume. But the bow, which had been anchored 1,500 feet off, was now a mile and a half away. It had capsized, and only a tiny corner of its prow was visible above water.

As this word reached the Ocean City station, a report came in from Lewes: the missing man had been aboard the bow.

At midnight the Coast Guard called off the search until morning. The next day and for a few days longer the fruitless hunt for Bertrand continued. At last it was halted. His body was never recovered from the sea.

As for the *Queen* herself, she was abandoned by the scavengers. She had claimed a life, and the boatmen were reluctant to go near her now. Along the water front in Ocean City the general feeling was that no one in his right mind would set foot on the hulk again for a million dollars.

The *African Queen* lay out on the shoal alone, her decks washed by the seas, her cabins abandoned, the cables slapping against her cargo booms in the soft March wind. She rested on the bottom, tipped grotesquely, ravaged and desolate, a sad wreck of a once handsome ship, now doomed to rot on an unmarked shelf ten miles out in the Atlantic.

ONE

I

SHIP SALVAGER BELIEVED LOST

NORFOLK—Lewis Bertrand, placed aboard the derelict Liberian tanker *African Queen* in connection
with a salvage claim on the ship, was the object
of an unsuccessful Coast Guard search early today. . . .

As Lloyd Deir read the first paragraph of the news story
the chatter of children and the clatter of dishes faded from
his hearing. His fork slowly descended to the kitchen table.
He read the story through, stared blankly across the tiny old-
fashioned kitchen for a moment, then read it again. He put
the paper down beside his plate and got up from the table.
He could feel the excitement rising in him.

"Is that all you're going to eat?" his wife asked. He nodded
abstractedly and walked through the bedroom and into the
front room. The rooms were big and clean, but the walls were
cracked tongue-in-groove board, and the paint was chipping
everywhere. He seldom saw this evidence of age and dis-
repair in the old former schoolhouse without flinching, but
this time he paid it little attention. He sat down on the old
sofa, then got up again and went out the front door into the
chilly night. He picked his way through the yard, with its
orderly litter of derrick booms, chains and engine parts, and
opened the door to his workshop. Inside, he started a brisk
fire in the stove. Then he seated himself on a can of gasoline,
leaned back against the wall, and gave himself up to heavy
thinking.

He was contemplating the opportunity to make a million dollars, and he scarcely knew how to think about it first.

The idea of salvaging the *African Queen*—the whole ship, not just the bow or whatever loose fittings and furniture could be carried off in small boats—had been simmering in Deir's head for three weeks, ever since it was planted there by Beldon Little. Little had read a news story about the scavengers one day and had scarcely been able to contain himself. He had sent the paper home with Mrs. Deir, who was visiting that afternoon, and in half an hour Lloyd Deir had turned up, bouncy as always, eyes agleam with the thought of salvage. The two men had talked half the night.

"Nothing could stop the two of us from bringing that ship in," Little had said urgently. "Great God, Lloyd, she must be worth two or three million. The paper"—he slapped it with his hand—"says they spent more than six million dollars building her, and that was only three years ago. The bow was broke off, but hell, even forgetting the bow, most of that six million is right out there for someone to step right up and take it!"

"But it must belong to someone," said Deir. "Nobody goes off and leaves a ship sitting out there like that for anyone to come along and help himself."

"It's all right here in the story," Little said. "That tanker was *abandoned*. That means that anyone that wants to can claim her. She's laying right on that shoal, so most of her is bound to be above water. That way, everything is right where a man can get at it. A diver wouldn't need to go down more than thirty or forty feet. That's nothing; I could do that. I did lots of diving in the Navy. Patch her up, pump her out, haul her to port"—Little struck his hands together—"and that's a million each for you and me!"

"We'd have to go out and look her over," said Deir. "She may be worse damaged than you think. Oh, we could get her if anyone could. But let's not push along here too fast. There's a lot of problems connected with a thing like this. A lot of problems. There are things we'd have to do and a lot of tools and equipment to get—I don't know what all.

"But I tell you what worries me most. There are people *on*

that tanker. You can't take over a ship that's already taken over, just go on out and say, 'Sorry, fellows, she's ours now, you run along.' They'll be mad, and I wouldn't blame them. They won't get off. Not for us. If we just walk aboard that daggone ship and say it's ours, why, man, they'll throw us *both* overboard!"

"Not if we go armed, they won't," Little replied promptly. "It isn't their ship. They're just stripping her. They have no more right there than we have and they know it. And anyone who's been to sea knows the law of salvage: a ship that's been left belongs to whoever claims her. If we go out there and take her, and post her and all, that makes it *our* ship, and we can damn well do what we please with her. Those guys will have no right to be there at all. We'll have the right to keep them off—by force, if we have to."

"No," said Deir flatly. "That's no way to do things. We can't chase people off with a gun. That's the way trouble starts. Somebody would get hurt, sure."

The subsequent discussion had lasted for hours, without producing a solution. They had refused to give up the idea, however. Despite his objections, Deir was as fired by the thought of salvaging the tanker as Little was. The two men had, in the past, talked of someday "doing something big"— something that would lift them to the level of financial security dreamed of by so many other hard-working, hard-pressed Americans. Both felt strongly that it was possible for a small man to become a big man in the United States if he had the wit, the energy and the good sense not to let his opportunity pass unheeded. This obviously was the opportunity, and they didn't doubt for a minute their ability to handle it.

They had known each other for about two years. They worked together, and they lived not far apart in the pleasant little Virginia town of Holland—Deir in the ramshackle old rented schoolhouse, Little in another rented house owned by Deir's father-in-law. They had gone bowling together once or twice; their children played together; their wives were fast becoming good friends.

The two women actually were better acquainted than were Deir and Little. The men were friendly without being close; they were perhaps too unlike to develop a deeper relationship. Little was a slender, curly-haired, mercurial Alabaman of thirty-five with an engaging grin and a trigger temper, slow spoken but tense, and almost feverishly anxious to make a mark in the world. Deir was a short, wiry man, lean, hard-bitten and authoritative. It was his custom to think long before reaching a decision and then, having reached it, to embrace it wholeheartedly. Emotionally, Deir was a curious mixture of coolness and enthusiasm. This made him an excellent worker who brought to every job a combination of eagerness and indomitability that was, in his business, an invaluable and much-sought-after asset.

His business—and Little's—was metalwork of all kinds. Both men were skilled mechanics, riggers, heavy equipment operators. They could weld, use an acetylene torch, operate a chain fall or a crane, take an engine apart and reassemble it, build anything made of metal. Deir, in particular, had earned a reputation around the Norfolk area. He was a worker of rare ingenuity, a natural engineer who stubbornly refused to be stumped by any problem, a man who, starting from scratch, had repeatedly built devices that had won the admiration of graduate engineers—a great metal shed for a farm equipment distributor, a hydraulic-powered freight elevator that an astonished federal inspector approved after a painstaking and unbelieving examination of its innovations, an $80,000 metal press on which the closest other bid—by an expert construction firm—had been ten times higher.

But most of the time the two men had worked for the scrap-and-salvage yards that dot the tidelands around the Hampton Roads–Norfolk region. They cut and piled scrap metal, restored damaged engines and other equipment for resale and improvised solutions to unanticipated problems. Often this work involved the recovery of small vessels which had run into trouble in the coastal waters. Shipping and boating is big business in southern Virginia, and as much scrap is recovered from marine wrecks as from old automobiles. Having done a good deal of work on broken and sunken small craft, Deir and Little accepted as a matter of course their ability to move on to larger things. The fact that scrap salvage is a far cry from true marine salvage involved a semantic distinction that didn't occur to either of them. They had pulled ships out of the water and salvaged their parts for sale or saved the whole hull for future restoration; that was salvage in any dictionary. They felt they had broken into the business; now they were ready to graduate to the big time—on their own.

But the long meeting in Little's kitchen had produced nothing better than a decision to seek legal sanction for a salvage attempt by wiring the owner's agent in New York, asking permission to take over the tanker.

They had drafted the telegram that night, Little had sent it the next day—and that was the last of that. They had never received an answer. The ship that Deir and Little wanted to salvage was still being raided by every boatman for fifty miles up and down the coast; there was no way to take control of her short of force.

Or there *had* been no way until now. Deir shifted restlessly on the can of gasoline and felt the excitement stirring in him again. The death of that man on the tanker would scare off the local boatmen; he was sure of it. The scavengers would stay off the ship, at least for a while. Anyone who wanted to claim her would have to move now. He and Little had talked of going out there and having a look. This was the time.

But though the most pressing immediate problem might be solved, there were plenty of problems left. Deir wasn't even sure how big a tanker was. And how badly would this one be damaged? Suppose he and Little went out there to stay and live and work; who would take care of their families? A full-scale salvage attempt would take money; where would they get it? And, most important of all, what were their rights? Could they actually take possession of that ship and claim it as their own? It hardly seemed likely.

But he knew one thing. If it was humanly possible to find solutions to those problems, he would find them. He did not often fail—that was a simple statement of fact—and he certainly was not prepared to be licked on the biggest thing that had ever come his way. Salvaging the tanker was not only desirable in terms of the promised rewards—money, plus adventure of a kind most men only get to dream of; by his personal standards it was *essential* that he do it.

He put more coal on the fire and settled back once more against the wall. His life so far had been one great, long struggle. He had no complaint; everyone else he knew could say the same. But he had put more into his life than most men—an investment of time, courage, energy and talent that should have produced a substantial return by now. It never had; he didn't live in that broken-down schoolhouse because he wanted to. But he was a man working with his hands in a region where manual labor came cheap, and the fact that Deir's head was more important in his work than his hands had never seemed to make much difference. More and more, as he had passed his fortieth year, his station in life had galled him. He was not living up to his potential. Without any touch of immodesty, he knew he was a better man than was reflected in his way of living. And now he was facing a chance at last to do something about it. That tanker could be the equalizer—and more.

It could make up for everything—for the Depression years, for the grinding unpleasantness of jobs taken strictly for sustenance, for the dangerous work of his youth, the only kind he had been able to get when times were bad.

He had lived with danger of one kind or another for most of his life; staying on a half-sunken tanker ten miles offshore shouldn't really bother him at all. And every experience, as the saying goes, had taught him something.

Twice, as a boy, he had had narrow escapes from death. The first had resulted from a swimming miscalculation that almost led to his drowning; he had made his way across a broad river all right but had almost gone under, exhausted, on his way back. Halfway across on that return trip, he had known that he could not lift his arms again, yet he had gone on swimming with a doggedness he couldn't help—and afterward, as he lay panting on the bank, he knew that he had discovered in himself a resource of resolution whose existence he had never suspected. (For this he had paid a price: a morbid fear of water that was still with him, and that he had to conquer almost daily as he worked around the Virginia water front. It was not the best trait, he thought wryly, with which to take on a major salvage job at sea.)

His other brush with disaster had occurred not long afterward: his back had been broken in an automobile crash when he was fifteen. He had spent five months in a cast, and the doctors had told him he would never be active again but must spend the rest of his life as an office worker. It would not be fair to say that from this experience he had learned never to trust doctors; what he had learned was never to depend on anyone but himself for the final verdict on anything. A few months later, at sixteen, he had gone to work as a steeplejack, and he had made his living chiefly at that until he got into the army at twenty-five.

Steeplejacking, then as now, had little relationship to steeples, but involved any work whose main requirement was a willingness to ascend to dangerous heights. And he had always had a liking for heights. Doing work like that, he reflected, you get a different slant about what constitutes a risk; you come to realize that everything in life is a risk, but that some things are simply more risky than others. You learn to accept the consequences of the risks and, when these consequences are unpleasant, to come back for more because the alternative may be hunger and, worse, shame.

That freezing New Year's Eve in 1936 when he and his brother (who had followed him into the work) had been called by the New Jersey radio station to repair its 300-foot-high antenna, he would have given anything right then for the privilege of turning his back on the job and going back to a warm bed. But the thought had never really entered his mind—not seriously. He and his brother had gone to the roof of the tall building on which the two sixty-five-foot poles were erected and had shinnied to the top of those bare rods because there was no other way of getting there, hands numb, faces aching, bodies shivering. They had affixed a new wire between the towers and had then let themselves down and had gone home. They hadn't really warmed up again for hours.

There had been a number of close calls steeplejacking—there are bound to be, in that work. And each time, as soon as the danger was over he had had to make the decision anew: get the hell out of this lunatic business and into something else, or stick to it because it was his craft and because, of all the reasons for quitting, self-preservation was the least acceptable.

Once, soon after he had started at the work, he had been painting a factory building from a scaffold forty feet high when it suddenly gave way. He plummeted down, bounced off an open swinging window, and landed on the lawn below. Instantly he had leaped to his feet and gone racing back upstairs to rescue a colleague who was still hanging there. Then they had restored the platform and gone back to work.

Another time he had been cleaning the inside of a smokestack, sitting in a boatswain's chair fifty feet down, when the tackle at the lip of the chimney began falling to pieces, showering parts down on him and threatening to let the whole rig drop to the bottom, ninety feet below. He had carefully pulled himself to the top, hand over hand, and repaired the damage. Then just as carefully and steadily he had let himself back down again and finished the job.

That was another thing he had learned: let factory workers worry about time clocks; when your life depends on the quality of your work you take things slow, you think and think and think before making a move, and then when you make it, you make it right. He liked to tell himself that he had never in his life made a mistake at his work. If nobody else in the world believed it, that was all right with him. He believed it; he had to.

For nine years he had climbed to the top of just about every kind of structure built by man, and then he got into the army and his steeplejacking days were over. The army, at last, had given him a crack as his real love, mechanics, and he had never done anything else since. He had been assigned to an automotive maintenance unit, and had done well. The change was welcome, not only because it gave him an honorable discharge from his nine-year war against the law of gravity, but because it offered a chance at a stable, steady life—and midway in his army career that had suddenly become important to him.

Doris Parker had been fifteen and Lloyd Deir twenty-eight when they met. He had been stationed at Crittenden, Virginia, and she had been working as a waitress at the Suffolk bus terminal near Holland when he had stopped in on his way through to get a cup of coffee. They had scarcely exchanged two words that day, but he had returned the next day and asked for a date. She had refused him. A day later he was back, and that time she accepted. He did not know then how young she was—only that she was slender and pretty and sensible—and he was in love with her before he found out, and then her age made no difference. She accepted his proposal of marriage that first week, and they were married a few weeks later by a justice of the peace who operated a marriage mill just across the border in North Carolina. (The wedding was a fitting conclusion to a whirlwind courtship: they arrived by bus at 9:00 p.m. and were on their way back to Virginia, man and wife, twenty minutes later.) Doris' father, who on one occasion had actually driven Deir away with a shotgun when he found that the soldier was seriously courting his young daughter, had quickly accepted his new son-in-law after the marriage, and the two men had become good friends.

In a lifetime which had seen few failures but equally few smashing successes, Deir could count his marriage as the best thing he had ever done. He and Doris had been married for fifteen years now, and they had three handsome, well-mannered children. He addressed her as "Sweet"; she called him "Deir"—which was what the soldiers were calling him when they met. She was still a slender, lovely woman, with some of the childlike quality that had been part of her original attraction for him; she was not above playing a lively game of basketball with the kids in their cavernous living room, and at such times she seemed scarcely older than they were.

Most important of all, she understood perfectly her husband's need to control his life, to make his own decisions, to trust in himself, the only person he had found completely dependable. She had never openly questioned one of his decisions; when she tried to guide them it was always gently and usually by indirection. This was generally quite effective —as Deir was perfectly well aware.

All things considered, Deir thought, as he sat in his workroom, he had had a good life. Perhaps, given a second chance, he would have done some things differently, but he was not dissatisfied with the past. The one thing he had missed out on was the chance to turn his professional aptitude into cash, to be as good as he knew he was, to give his family the better existence that could be bought only with money.

And now, after all these years, the chance had turned up. And he knew, sitting there and thinking about what he had done and what he had missed, that his decision was almost made. He would have to do a lot more thinking—as always, there were still all those questions to be answered—but it would take some mighty discouraging answers to stop him now.

For hours he sat there on the gasoline can, lost in thought, occasionally getting to his feet to feed the fire. At last he dozed off. When he awoke it was after midnight, and the fire had gone out. He got up, shivering, and went into the house.

2

IT WOULD BE at least a week before Deir and Little could get away to visit the ship in Maryland. Both men were working, and they couldn't just walk off their jobs. That meant that they would not have to commit themselves to the adventure, even tentatively, until the weekend. Deir welcomed the chance to do some more thinking, but this feeling was mixed with another.

Suddenly, somewhat to his own amusement, he found himself on edge, obsessed with the thought that someone else would beat them to the *African Queen*. It was completely illogical—the tanker had been lying on that shoal for two and a half months, and it had been three weeks since Little had first talked of salvaging her, and in all that time Deir had scarcely given the tanker a thought. But now that he had begun to take the salvage talk seriously he couldn't stop worrying. He was working that week for the Portsmouth Salvage Company, a scrap firm in Portsmouth, overseeing the reconditioning of a storm-damaged surplus landing ship which the company had bought, but his thoughts were never far from the *Queen*. He scanned the newspapers anxiously for some indication that another salvager had claimed her first—and then became irrationally concerned when the tanker wasn't mentioned in the papers at all.

Yet he did not permit his anxiety to cloud his judgment. He had a week in which to reach a fairly firm decision regarding the tanker, and he intended to use it all. Of course, the final commitment would not come until he had seen the wrecked ship. But the very act of driving to Maryland would be a decision of a sort; he knew that once he set eyes on the *Queen* he would be a lot like a little boy setting eyes on a puppy, and the decision would be out of his hands. So far as was possible, he had to answer all the questions in his mind before seeing the ship.

Certainly there were questions enough. How accessible was the tanker? Could they get out to her without difficulty? Would the local boatmen help—especially after Deir and Little broke the news that the old treasure-hunt days were over? (Even if they were scared off by Bertrand's death, the scare probably wouldn't last forever—not if there was any valuable gear left on the ship.)

What shape was the *Queen* in? Could they live on her? Was there a place to work? A place to sleep? Would it be safe to cook aboard a wrecked petroleum tanker, or would they have to subsist out there for weeks on cold food? How long would a repair job take? Who would keep them supplied? Who would pay the bills?

One question alone kept his mind occupied for hours. It was the key question of the entire project, and the fact that he couldn't possibly answer it without seeing the ship didn't keep him from speculating. How badly was the tanker damaged? Was it possible that the whole side was torn away? He wondered what conclusions could be drawn from Merritt-

Chapman & Scott's abortive salvage attempt. If the damage was really bad—hopeless—the big New York salvage company never would have stayed on the job for fifteen minutes, let alone forty-five days. But then why had they given up? Sure as hell the damage must have been bad.

He tried to picture how it must look, and then imagined himself planning the salvage job. If the damage was extensive, they were in trouble. It might require a single large patch—cumbersome, extremely heavy and hard to lock into place. Perhaps, he thought, they could use a dipper stick, a jointed boom like the elbow-angled crane on a power shovel, to hold the patch against the ship while divers worked on it. How would they make a big patch watertight? Could they make it conform precisely to the contour of a damaged hull? There would probably be big gaps; could they be sealed with some kind of sponge rubber? Step by step he went through the whole job in his mind. And then he wiped the slate clean, imagined a whole new set of circumstances, and started through the entire procedure again.

Finally, there remained a question he couldn't answer himself at all, because it was completely remote from his experience. Characteristically, he fretted more about it than about any of the others: it was the one area in which he felt he had no control, and that made him uneasy. It was the question of the law. It simply didn't seem reasonable that they could just go out to a ship worth millions and take it over without permission. Beldon Little was sure they could. Little had served in the Navy and the Merchant Marine and he knew some sea law, the way most seamen do. But when Deir sought confirming opinions from equally knowledgeable people around Portsmouth Salvage, carefully masking his reasons, he was disturbed to discover that no two self-styled experts agreed about the legality of a salvage claim on an abandoned ship.

At last Deir paid a call on the one man he knew who might really have firsthand knowledge—Captain Duff Porter of Norfolk, who had recently retired after forty years with the U.S. Army Corps of Engineers. Deir knew that the Engineers, charged with the care of rivers and harbors, occasionally get involved with salvage problems. In strict confidence, Deir told Porter what he and Little had in mind. As Deir talked, the old officer's eyebrows rose.

"I think we can do it all right," Deir said steadily. "What we need to know is, will we get the chance? Will they—the law—let us out on that ship? Can anyone stop us? Can two people just go out and claim a ship that nobody else seems to own?"

Porter pondered, "It's my understanding," he said at last, "that a ship is never really abandoned—not entirely. I think it has to be abandoned *to* someone, like the Coast Guard or the Corps of Engineers. Someone has to be responsible. I can't say for sure, of course—I'm not a lawyer—but I would guess that your ship has an owner somewhere."

Deir nodded bleakly. "Then those boatmen have no right on her and neither have we?"

"That would be my guess," said Porter.

"Thank you," said Deir. He had his answer now. But he had scarcely reached the street before he decided to ignore it. Damn it, the boatmen *were* out there and nobody had stopped them. Nobody would stop Deir and Little, either. Still, the conversation with Porter had clarified his own thinking. He was glad he had asked.

Shortly after seven o'clock on the night of Friday, March 13, Lloyd Deir arrived at Beldon Little's house. Deir had done his thinking, had answered all the questions that could be answered without visiting the ship, and now he was ready to go. He walked in on Little and proposed that they start for Ocean City.

Months later, Little would recall that he had been ready to go immediately—had, indeed, thought all along that this was the night they planned to leave—while Deir's recollection would be that Little had needed convincing. But there was no disagreement whatever about Mrs. Little's reaction. She hit the ceiling.

Hazel Little was a tall, high-strung, pretty woman who fifteen years before had been a waitress in a little town in North Carolina when Beldon Little, then in the U.S. Navy, had walked into the coffee shop where she worked and asked her for a date. This curious parallel with the Deirs's romance was carried a step further when, after one of the brisk courtships typical of wartime, Little and Hazel had hurried off to be wed by the same marrying judge who had performed the breakneck ceremony for Lloyd and Doris Deir.

For many years afterward life for Hazel Little had had a hectic quality as her husband cast about restlessly for a way to improve his lot and that of his family. He had shipped in the Merchant Marine, served again in the Navy during the Korean War, attended diesel school in Tennessee, worked for a brake relining company, spent a year in West Virginia building coal processing plants, tried the Merchant Marine again, and worked briefly as an organizer for the maritime union. At last he had settled down in his present work. He had been at it for a couple of years, and Hazel was enjoying the first stability of her married life. They had three nice children and a good home—and now, just when she was beginning to know a little security, here was Little suddenly planning to go off on some crack-brained scheme. She was stunned and angry and frightened.

"You're not to go!" she cried. "I don't know what you can be thinking of, going off and leaving me and the children for nobody knows how long. For what? It's stupid, stupid." She began to weep bitterly.

"You've heard us talking about this," said Little, bewildered. "You've known right along we were thinking of it. Why this now? Don't you see it's a chance we'll never get again? We could wind up rich, honey, with more money than we ever dreamed of."

"You *could* wind up dead!" she sobbed. "Why? Why? We're all right now, the way we are. Now you want to go off to that thing and you could drown, you could fall off something and kill yourself, you could get hit by something, you could be killed by one of those boatmen—I heard you talking about them, how mad they'd be."

She turned a tear-stained face toward him. "Think of us. Where will we be without you? What will we do?"

Deir tried to reassure Hazel, secretly congratulating himself on having a wife who in all the years of their marriage had never once raised serious objections to a project of his.

"We're gonna be all right," Deir said. "There's no danger out there we can't handle. If you're careful, nothing ever hurts you. It isn't as if either one of us is going out to that daggone thing alone. We'll be watching out for each other. Nobody will get hurt."

But in the end, of course, it was Little who finally soothed her.

"Honey, we won't be gone long, and we won't be running a risk," he said gently. "I *am* thinking of my family. I'm doing this for all of us. I've dreamed all my life of someday finding something where I could make a stake and change our whole life. Now it's here. I can't let it pass."

He was talking now about the great motivating force of his life, and Hazel, knowing it, knew she was defeated. Beldon Little had been a poor boy in Alabama, and he had been fighting the consequences of that ever since. Being poor in the South is a lot different from being poor in the North. In the North you can fight your way clear—you may even be encouraged to do so. In the stratified white society of the Deep South you're supposed to stay where you are. All his life, Little had battled doggedly against the limitations imposed on him by his origins. Every move he and Hazel had made, every job he had tried, had been aimed at improving their life, at forcing people to respect them. The key was money, and for an honest man of limited education the only chance of ever getting any real money was to work hard, watch sharp, and never let that one big chance pass by. Always he had talked of "the big chance," of someday "doing something important," of the need to listen alertly for the knock of opportunity. He was a man obsessed by the desire to rise, and if he saw his big chance in the *African Queen*, his wife knew that nothing she could say would stop him.

After a while Hazel stopped crying and got up to make a pot of coffee, while the men began, with mounting excitement, to make their plans.

The main thing they would have to do, after looking the ship over and deciding whether they wanted to take on the salvage job (although by now anything else was inconceivable) was to lay permanent claim to the vessel, to make her indisputably theirs. To do this they would have to remain aboard. This consideration raised a number of problems. After they had talked for a while Deir put the chief difficulty into words and proposed a solution.

"We're going to need money," he said. "There's no sense going out there until we do something about that. I've been giving this a lot of thought. If we try to fix up that ship and stay out there to work on her, we'll run out of money in a week, and that's the end of our salvage. And how about our families? They'll starve, with nothing coming in. We've got to find someone to come in with us as a partner and finance the deal as his share.

"You know Paul Brady? I think we ought to go talk to him. I think he might be game for something like this."

And so Paul Brady was nominated, without knowing anything about it, as the third member of the salvage team. He would, as Deir outlined it to Little, serve not only as their banker but also as a purchasing agent and keeper of the home base while they were out on the ship. All that remained was to talk him into accepting.

Brady owned an appliance store in Suffolk. That town, which bills itself as "The Peanut Capital of the World," is a community of about 12,000, the biggest in the region until you get to the sister cities of Portsmouth and Norfolk, twenty-five miles away. Brady was an eminent Suffolker, a pleasant and popular man of forty-six with a solid reputation for honesty and dependability. Some months before, Deir had helped build a commercial boat basin—a marina—for Brady on the bank of a stream near Brady's house, and he felt sure that Brady had some money to invest, plus a substantial appetite for adventure. He seemed like a natural for such a project as this.

The more Deir and Little discussed Brady the better he sounded to them. Their enthusiasm soared as they thought how perfectly he seemed to fit their needs. At last, at ten o'clock, they hurried out of Little's house and drove the eleven miles to Suffolk.

They found Brady working late in the woodworking shop at his home. By now the two adventurers had so stirred each other up with the fantastic prospect facing them that they burst in on Brady like a whirlwind, and it was some time before he could even figure out what they were talking about.

"Look," Deir began, pacing about the shop, "we're going out to salvage that *African Queen*—at least we're pretty sure we are; we're going up to look at her tonight—and we want you to come in with us on the deal. What do you say?

"We'll do all the work; you put up the money. It won't cost much, I'm sure of it, and God *knows* there's a mint of money to be made there. It's the chance of a lifetime. A million dollars. Two million. We'll split three ways, everything even. We're going to claim her and bring her in, but we need financial help. I thought of you right away—"

"Hold it, Lloyd, stop right there," Brady begged. "I can't tell what in the world you're talking about. You have me all confused. *What* is it you're going to salvage?"

"The *African Queen*," Deir said impatiently. "That tanker."

"*What* tanker? Lloyd, if you don't slow down I'm not even going to listen to you. What's the *African Queen,* and what are you going to do with it and where do I come in? Start from the beginning."

They told him. "Man," said Deir, "that ship is worth millions! All we've got to do is go out there and bring her in. But we need someone to help us. We haven't got much money. We want you to come in with us." He paced the room, ducking around piles of lumber. "It shouldn't take more than five weeks or so once we get started," he said. He stopped and stared at Brady, an excited grin on his face. "God *knows,* there'll *never* be another chance like this!"

Brady stared back, nonplused. Now that he understood the proposition he was more confused than ever. It had an irresistible appeal, but it also had a wild-eyed unconventionality that was enough to ring alarms in the head of any conservative small-business man. He wanted to know how much it would cost. Deir couldn't tell him. He wanted to know precisely what their plans were, but Deir had to admit that precise plans would have to wait until they had seen the tanker.

"I've thought about this a long time, though," Deir said earnestly. "Sure, maybe we'll get out there and it'll all be impossible. Okay. That's a chance we take, but it doesn't cost us to look. We *have* to look. Little and I are going out there, absolutely, no doubt about it. We'd just feel a lot better if you were in it with us."

"So help me," Brady said, "I think you guys are nuts. How can a couple of ordinary men even hope to get a ship like that off the bottom? My lord, it'll take an *awful* lot of money. I can see myself sticking some dough in now, and some more later, and then more and more and more. Hell, it could go on forever. And I'll tell you the truth, Lloyd, after what I invested in that marina I don't have much left." He shook his head. "No fooling, fellows, I just don't see how I can help you."

"Look," Deir said. "Suppose we do it this way. We'll go out there and go aboard the ship. We'll lay claim to her legally and keep everyone else off. Then we'll strip enough scrap off the top of her to raise what we need to help finance us. We can keep doing that till we're ready to start the real salvage part of the operation. You stay ashore, keep the books and sell the scrap we bring in. You won't have to lay out any money except whatever costs we have over and above the value of the stuff we bring off the ship. That way it won't really cost you much."

Brady offered more protests, but his heart wasn't in them. He wanted to join Deir and Little, and at last join them he did. The project seemed foolproof as Deir had outlined it, and the returns in both cash and excitement would be fantastic.

"When are you leaving?" he asked them.

"Right now," said Deir.

But it was midnight before they talked themselves out. In the process, Brady's enthusiasm mounted steadily. When Deir and Little left at last, they carried with them a couple of armloads of essentials which Brady had provided: life-jackets, a Coleman stove-lantern that burned gasoline, a kerosene lamp, a paintbrush. The brush was to paint a "Keep Off" sign once the men were aboard the ship.

40

"I'll meet you here in twenty minutes," Deir said as he left Little at his house. "You pack some things."

A few minutes later Deir unlocked the door to his house, slipped into the bedroom where his wife lay sleeping, and gently shook her shoulder. "Sweet," he said in a low voice. "Wake up. You have to help me. Sweet?"

He waited as Doris sat up sleepily in bed, and then hastily began to tell her of his plans.

"Little and I are going out to that tanker, the *African Queen*. We're going to start a salvage operation on her, I think, but first we've got to look her over, and we've got to move fast so someone else doesn't beat us to it. You have to help me pack."

Doris looked puzzled. "What?" she asked uncertainly. "What tanker? What time is it, Deir?" She got out of bed.

"The *African Queen*," he said. "I told you about it." As he spoke he began pulling clothes out of drawers. "It's that tanker up by Ocean City that got grounded. We're going aboard and claim her. We're going to salvage her. Sweet, she's worth millions, I don't know exactly how much, but a lot, an awful lot. We've decided . . ."

He stopped, surprised. His wife's eyes had grown large and her cheeks were flushed. Suddenly she turned and got back in bed. "You are not!" she said flatly. "You're not going to do any such fool thing." She pulled the blankets up around her and glared. "You come to bed!"

He stood there, a shirt in his hand. In fifteen years of marriage nothing like this had happened. Doris began to cry. The more he tried to explain, the more tearful and angry she became. She put her hands over her face, weeping, and again ordered him to bed. She refused to listen to anything he said. And she refused to get out of bed herself and help him pack.

"I don't care how much money you're going to make on that old thing," she kept sobbing. "It's dangerous and it isn't worth it."

When Deir tried to talk to her she shook her head. "That ship frightens me," she said. "Deir, please don't go. It's such a long way off, and you'll be gone so long, and we're doing all

41

right the way we are. It'll be dangerous. I know. Stay home. Please. Come to bed."

It took him half an hour to calm her. "Look," he said at last when she would listen to him. "This is a chance we'll never have again. I've *got* to go. This house we're living in"— he gestured at the warped wooden walls—"isn't what we want. This is a chance to do better, and there'll never be another like it. Going on like we are, we're not getting anywhere. I don't want to live like this forever. If we can bring up that tanker, there'll be lots of money. We can get a new house. We can send the kids to college. We can live the way we *ought* to live."

He began packing again. "I've just got to go out there," he said. "I want you to be for it, but whether you're for it or against it I'm going."

After a while she silently got out of bed and helped him pack. By the time he was ready to start, it was after 1:00 A.M. Before leaving he went to a closet and took out a shotgun; he and Little had decided to take along some protection after all. As he tucked the gun under his arm he grinned briefly at his wife. It was the same shotgun his father-in-law had once pointed at him.

"Now don't you worry about a thing," he said at the door. "We'll be all right."

3

ALTHOUGH DEIR and Little had been thinking and talking of the *African Queen* as if she were located within easy reach, she was in fact a long way off. The road distance from Suffolk, Virginia, to Ocean City, Maryland, is about 125 miles. The trip also requires a ferry crossing of twenty-five miles between Norfolk and the eastern shore of Chesapeake Bay. The total travel time, with good ferry connections, is about five and a half hours. There would be times in the months that followed when the partners would shuttle over this route with scarcely a pause at either end. They would come to know every crossroad, every gasoline station, every village.

But on this first night, driving in a borrowed pickup truck, it was all new to them. This newness added spice to an adventure that was already almost unendurably exciting. As the hours passed and they sped through the flat coastal country in the darkness, they alternately chattered nervously and subsided into silence. Now that they were actually on their way, they were more than ever seized by the fear that someone might beat them to the prize. The idea was unbearable. They thought of the *African Queen,* which neither of them had ever laid eyes on, as their ship.

They were planning on a stay of about three days—long enough to accomplish their initial mission of taking off the metal and equipment they would need to finance future salvage work. Then perhaps one of them would remain aboard the *Queen* to hold the claim while the other raced back to Suffolk and handed the stuff over to Brady for sale. They were bringing along a minimum of equipment, most of it from Deir's shop: hand tools, 500 feet of rope, a block and tackle, a couple of flashlights and some bedding, plus the things Brady had supplied and Deir's shotgun. In addition they had an inflatable rubber life raft. The raft would do them little good in really bad weather, but it still seemed worth having along.

It was shortly after dawn when they finally pulled into Ocean City. There were few people about. The size and emptiness of the town astonished them, and they spent some time driving around, familiarizing themselves with the place. The main part of Ocean City is built on a long, slender sand spit about a quarter of a mile offshore, connected to the mainland by a bridge. Between the spit and the mainland is a fine little harbor, with boat moorings on both sides; the harbor has access to the open sea through a channel where a 1933 hurricane tore away a section of the spit.

The *African Queen* had placed its stamp all over the town. Relics of the grounded tanker were on docks and piers and piled beside houses: ship's lights, great coils of oil-stained hawser, fire extinguishers, piles of copper pipes, stacks of fine plywood. Just to remove any doubt about the source of this stuff, in front of one house was a huge, handsome mahogany bridge sign sixteen feet long by about three feet high. It was standing upright so the giant lettering was clearly visible: AFRICAN QUEEN. Propped against one side of it was a smaller sign: *For Sale*.

Their first task was to find a boatman who would ferry them the ten miles to the tanker—and, later, back to Ocean City. Their future relationship with these men was a great source of worry to Deir and Little. They could not imagine working on the *Queen* without at least the sufferance of the Ocean City boatmen; if this hard-fisted brotherhood should turn against them the whole project might be threatened.

Early as it was, a few men were out working on their boats. The first one they asked about a ride to the tanker glanced curiously at the equipment in the truck and said, "What you want to go out *there* for?"

They had decided there was no point in ducking the question. "We figure to go out and stay aboard," said Little. "We were thinking of salvaging her."

The man's eyebrows shot up. "You gonna *stay* out there? All *night?*"

"That's right."

He looked at them scornfully. "You boys been out to that ship? You seen what it's like? You better go take a look at her before you talk about staying there." He turned back to his boat.

They tried one man after another. All turned them down, some brusquely, some pleasantly. Most of them, it was clear, had no desire to go anywhere near the tanker; just as Deir had expected, Bertrand's death had thrown a scare into them. But a few obviously did plan to do additional scavenging; to them, Deir and Little were interlopers. Almost without exception the boatmen greeted the word *salvage* with disbelief, derision or resentment.

One man, however, a short, peppery, balding man of about fifty, actually seemed concerned for their safety. His name was McKinley Reed (known to the boatmen as "Kin"), and Deir and Little were to get to know him and like him. But at this first meeting they could hardly wait to get away from him. "You could get hurt out there," said Reed. "I'd have to consult the Coast Guard. That other feller got hisself killed."

They left him hastily. "Man," Deir said, "the Coast Guard's the *last* thing we want. They might tell us to stay off."

In the end they rode out to the ship with a burly, good-looking, straight-talking man in his mid-thirties named Paul Russell. It was fairly late in the morning by the time he agreed to take them in his motor launch, and a little crowd of boatmen gathered to watch them load their equipment. Most of the onlookers were silent, but there were a few open scoffers. "Easy to talk about staying there when you ain't seen it," said one man. "I'm betting you'll be with Russell when he comes back in."

Russell himself was scarcely more encouraging. "I've been on ships all my life," he told them as the boat started out of the harbor, "and the condition that tanker's in I wouldn't stay on her overnight for ten thousand dollars. She's already heeled away over. It wouldn't surprise me if she went all the way."

There had been a brisk wind earlier that morning, and the seas were still rough as they emerged from the channel. It was the first time in his life Deir had been on the ocean, and he was frankly nervous. Besides suffering pangs of his old fear of the water, he was uneasy about what lay ahead. If even a small part of what the boatmen said was true, it was sure to be dangerous.

Little, too, was tense. The rough seas didn't bother him, but the attitude of the boatmen did. Russell, in particular, was obviously a man who didn't scare easily. If *he* said the tanker was hazardous, it certainly must be true.

When they had been out about forty minutes, Russell silently pointed at the horizon. There she was, tiny in the distance. As they drew closer they could see her two deckhouses towering over the tank deck. A couple of miles off was the bow, upside down, with a dead man inside it.

In another twenty minutes they were approaching the derelict. Deir was flabbergasted. It seemed to him that he had never seen anything so enormous in his life. Little, too, although he was familiar with ships, was filled with awe at the size of this hulk they were planning to raise. Up close, the project seemed audacious almost to the point of absurdity.

Russell pulled up to the port side in businesslike fashion. A number of boats had passed them on the way out and were now tied up beside the tanker. The sound of hammering could be heard from the deck above. Apparently not everyone was afraid of the broken vessel.

Russell boosted his passengers aboard and clambered up after them. "I'll stay here for three hours," he said. "Then I'm going in."

Little and Deir looked around wordlessly. They had come aboard close to the pilot house, and it rose over them three stories high, with a great forty-foot radio mast atop it. In front of them was the catwalk. Once it had run the full length of the deck. Now it was twisted crosswise just past the two cargo masts, cutting right across the deck and over the side. A storm must have done that, possibly the one that had killed Bertrand. All around them were pipes and valves and great hatches. Deir, staggered at the spectacle, thought there must be a fortune in valves alone. At the far end of the tank deck was the aft superstructure, still a gleaming white, topped by the big buff smokestack.

As they stood there, a wave slammed into the broken tanks in the front of the ship and a great tower of water suddenly rose with a roar through the open hatch right in front of them. They jumped and gaped.

Under their feet the deck slanted away at a sharp angle toward the sea on the starboard side. There was also a slight slope toward the stern. A heavy film of grease coated the deck plates, and they found that the only way to walk was to edge along the seam where two plates met; there was an inch-and-a-quarter ridge there, surmounted by bolt heads that provided some traction.

Gazing about them in awe, they began their investigation of the pilot house, staying close together, silent except for an occasional exclamation. The rooms were stripped to the walls, and there was evidence of vandalism everywhere, yet even in ruins the pilot house was an impressive sight. Much of the beautiful wood paneling remained, and the hardwood floors were intact. A handsome wrought-iron rail ran along the top of the stairwell. The bathrooms still had the stamp of luxury, although many of the fixtures were smashed. They were incredulous at the luxury all about them. They stopped in front of an electric panel in the pilot house and read some of the labels on the cutoff switches: STORE, PANTRY, BATH, DINING SALON, OWNER'S BEDROOM, OWNER'S DAYROOM.

"Great God," murmured Little, "she must have been something!"

"If they spent like this up here," said Deir, "she must have a fortune in machinery—good stuff—down under the water."

They crept to the lip of the break, just forward of the pilot house, and looked at the torn steel there. In the port corner they could see where the awful wrench had stretched the inch-and-a-quarter plates until they were barely half an inch thick.

After a while they started back toward the stern, where the aft superstructure loomed, a brilliant, incongruous white, over the oil-blackened deck. There was less evidence of extravagance here, but what they saw interested them even more than the pilot house had. Lurching unsteadily down a slanted corridor, they stopped and peered through the engine-room door. The room was huge. Even more impressive, the equipment that was visible above water seemed in superb condition. Deir and Little, machine-minded men, gazed at the surging water in the room, reaching almost to the doorway they stood in, and thought of the wonders that must lie beneath it. Whatever machinery was hidden there, it was certain (as Deir had said) to be worth a good deal of money.

As they mounted the decks, they found a great trove of usable equipment—stuff that hadn't been worth the scavengers' trouble but that would prove invaluable in a salvage effort: cable, blocks, winches, cargo booms, boat davits. Not until they reached the topmost deck did they see signs of damage. A part of this sun deck, which consisted merely of wood-and-canvas flooring set on a framework of two-inch pipe (it was more a wooden awning for the deck below than an actual deck in itself), had been battered away by the hammering of the seas. Right now the swells were slamming against the ship perhaps fifteen feet below them, but it was clear that in bad weather the biggest waves must come almost all the way to the base of the smokestack.

Their swift inspection completed, they stood by the rail and discussed what they had seen. It was impressive, but it was also somewhat disheartening. There seemed no doubt at all that the ship was worth millions—maybe even more than they had first thought. But nothing they had read or heard about the *Queen* had prepared them for anything quite this scary. The slope of the deck was alarming. Russell had said the ship was listing about twelve degrees. That didn't sound like much, but when you actually stood on the slippery deck it seemed downright precipitous. A man who lost his footing where there was no rail could easily skid over the side, and once he was caught in those starboard swells there would be little hope of rescuing him.

The seas were slamming against the hull relentlessly, rising up onto the tank deck one after another. Every time one struck, the tanker gave a little jump, like a horse under the whip. What would happen when a storm swept in? That capsized bow and the twisted catwalk were evidence of the ferocity of the Atlantic gales that hammered this coast. Would the listing ship roll over in the next severe storm that struck her? Neither man was afraid of taking normal risks, but it would be stupid to stay out here if the odds were heavily stacked against them.

Deir had estimated the dimensions of the engine room—boiler room, and now, standing at the rail, he computed the volume of this huge well that went clear to the bottom of the ship and tried to figure out how much water there was in it, plus the amount of water and oil there must be in the tanks up forward. Just how much weight was there inside the ship?

"Let's see," he said, half closing his eyes. "That room goes down pretty near forty feet underwater, and it's about seventy-five feet across and maybe a hundred feet long. Figure the space a gallon of water takes up. . . ." He was silent a while. *"Daggone,"* he said. "There must be thirteen million gallons in this thing. Say six pounds to the gallon . . .

seventy-eight million . . . Man, that's forty thousand tons!"

They began to feel better. All that weight was helping to keep the tanker pinned in its present position, plus its own weight of perhaps ten thousand tons or so. Furthermore, the ship's center of gravity was relatively low: in the tank section the hull stood only about forty feet high from keel to deck, but it was seventy-four feet wide. In the circumstances, capsizing seemed less likely than one might suppose when standing on the sloping deck. They looked about them dubiously.

"Well, I reckon she'll stay a while," Little said. "Just the same, if she can tip this far, she can tip some more. . . ."

There was also another problem, and it was more perplexing (though considerably less vital) than the first. They had promised Brady they would return to Suffolk with valuable material that could be turned into ready cash. It now looked like a rash promise.

There still were things that could be sold off the tanker; indeed, while they were going over the ship a number of men had been gathering stuff for just that purpose. (One of them was Kin Reed, the man who had declined to take them out without checking with the Coast Guard.) But it was apparent that the cream had been taken—that there wasn't a chance in the world of getting the several thousands of dollars' worth of material they had hoped for. Deeply troubled, Little and Deir tried to decide what to do. Now that they were on their ship at last, they hated to leave. How could they doubt that someone else would take over the moment they were gone? But how could they stay? They had provisions for only three days. They could expect no support from Brady; his backing had been contingent on their finding salvageable material in these first few days.

"There's nothing for it but to go back," Deir said grimly at last. "We'll go see Brady and try to talk him into backing us all the way. We'll come right back out."

They talked about it a little longer, so reluctant to leave that at one point they actually considered tossing a coin and abiding by the result. But finally, greatly depressed, they rejoined Paul Russell and told him they were going back with him. He offered no comment.

49

But the reception party of dockside loungers that met them in Ocean City had plenty to say. "Boy, that night passed fast, didn't it?" chuckled one man. "Find it a little *rough* out there?" There was an appreciative laugh from his audience.

"Sure isn't the way we imagined it," Deir agreed.

"Yeah, that's right," said Little. "You guys will never see us again."

A few hours before, they had loaded their equipment in Russell's boat with a sense of great excitement. Now they unloaded it, visibly crushed by the anticlimax.

When Deir and Little drove off that evening, they left behind them the definite impression that they would never be back.

4

THEY WERE on their way back to Ocean City the next night.

It had been a hectic thirty hours. They had arrived in Suffolk at 9:00 P.M. Saturday. Not at all certain that Brady would stick with them once he knew the facts, they had spent the homeward drive discussing possible alternatives. Both Deir and Little were acquainted with a Suffolk scrapyard owner named Leon Familant. They were fond of him and thought he might make an acceptable partner. Little also had friends in North Carolina, just across the border, who might be interested in investing in the project.

They checked in with Brady first. His expression grew thoughtful as they told him what they had found. At last he shook his head. If the ship could not help pay for its own salvage, then the cost was simply going to be too much. Half regretfully, half relieved, Brady pulled out of the deal. Deir and Little accepted the verdict gracefully; it was no more than they had expected.

But on Sunday when they went seeking substitute backers they were dismayed to find that nobody was interested. Most people seemed to feel that they were tackling a job far beyond their capabilities. Nothing they could say made any difference. That evening, troubled, they went back to Brady.

"You won't have to pay for everything we use," Deir urged. "I have a lot of the tools we'd need—we'll save money that way. If we shop around we can pick up the rest of the gear without spending too much—scrap yards, junk shops, second-hand places. Besides, if we spend time enough out there we'll be able to get some scrap off her—not as much as we thought, but enough to help.

"Paul, you ought to see that ship! She's worth millions, easy. Man, she's the biggest thing I ever saw! You don't want to back out on a deal like this. We can get her up. Stick with us."

It was not an easy decision for Brady. It was apparent now that this was going to be an expensive operation, and his resources were limited. But Deir's enthusiasm was infectious. Brady had seen him work and respected his judgment. If he was like this *after* seeing the tanker, it really must be worth going after. In the end he agreed to stay with them.

"My limit is five thousand," he said slowly. "That won't be enough to finish the job, but it's the best I can manage."

Deir leaped to his feet. "You'll never regret it," he said.

At 11:00 P.M., Little and Deir started back to Ocean City. This time they rode in Deir's own truck, a sturdy cab-over-engine vehicle with a large open body. They had loaded up for a long stay. Besides all the things they had taken with them the first time, they had cans of paint, chainfalls, rope, crowbars, hoisting equipment, pipe wrench, sledge hammer, a kerosene stove, flashlights, cooking utensils and food. They also took one more shotgun.

On the ferry between Norfolk and the eastern shore that night, crossing the mouth of Chesapeake Bay, they put their heads together and drew up an official-sounding newspaper notice of their intention to take over the *Queen*. "The salvage crews aboard the *African Queen*," it said, "ask the full co-operation of all concerned. For your safety and for the safety of the salvage crew aboard this vessel we ask everyone to stay clear. This is also to notify that we . . ."

"There ought to be a name in there," said Little, "not just *we*. What name does our salvage company have?"

"How about the one I'm operating under in Holland?" suggested Deir. "Industrial Maintenance."

". . . that we, Industrial Maintenance of Holland, Virginia, are on board and have taken possession and reserve all rights and liabilities to said vessel, the *African Queen*."

On the road again, they began to worry about interlopers, just as they had on the first trip. "We've been lucky so far," said Deir. "Someone sure as hell is gonna get the same idea we have and go aboard that ship. If I find someone out there I don't know what I'll do."

"I know what I'll do," said Little. "Throw him the hell off."

They drove so fast that the heavily loaded truck set up a fearful vibration. It felt as though the whole vehicle actually might fly apart. But they didn't slow down.

And then, when they got to Ocean City, they found weather conditions so bad that they couldn't get out to the *Queen* anyhow. A whole day passed before they could make the trip. Paul Russell tried to console them. "If you can't get out there, nobody else can either," he said. That night they slept, fitfully, in the little cabin of Russell's boat.

It was still dark when they heard his footsteps on the deck above them. "Wind's died down," he called. "Let's go."

Just as dawn was breaking the two salvagers boarded the *African Queen* for the second time. They had her all to themselves now. For a moment they stood there in the chill gray morning and silently looked about them. But Russell didn't give them much time. He began tossing up equipment. "I have to hurry back," he said matter-of-factly. "Help me get this stuff off." It made a respectable pile on the deck when they had finished. They handed Russell the newspaper notice they had prepared, and he promised to see to it that it was published in the Salisbury *Times*. They watched him get ready to leave.

"Take care," he said. "I guess you know what you're doing. But just remember one thing. If it storms out here, you're stuck. In bad weather nobody can come get you." He hesitated, watching them sharply. They said nothing. "Okay," Russell said. "I'll be out from time to time. So long."

The two men stood at the rail until his little boat was out of sight.

The very first thing Deir did was to find a piece of wood about five feet long and three feet wide. On it he painted a neat sign in big black letters against a white background: PRIVATE PROPERTY—KEEP OFF. They posted it high on the port side of the aftersection, where it would be clearly visible to anyone who approached.

Then they began to put away their equipment.

They had decided to make their living quarters in the stern. The pilot house, towering over the broken midships section, had certain advantages that tempted them for a while: it was higher and cleaner and out of reach of all but the most mountainous waves. Deir advocated it at first. But Little held out for the after deckhouse, and logic was on his side. Aft was where the damage was, and where the work was. It was also where the weight—and therefore the stability—was, and that made them feel a bit safer: it was always possible that the vessel would break again someplace along the tank deck, permitting the pilot house to capsize. Finally, if the whole ship should roll over (and they had never stopped worrying about that) there were plenty of portholes in the aftersection through which they could climb to safety. In the pilot house they would be trapped.

They selected a small cabin on the same level as the tank deck, overlooking the port side of the ship (the comparable cabins on the starboard side were underwater). A long corridor ran lengthwise through the aft deckhouse, and all the cabins opened into it; in addition a short passage led off the corridor at right angles, opening onto the narrow portside deck. Deir and Little picked a cabin at the junction of these two passageways. They chose it because of the easy access it gave to the port deck in the event of an emergency. But it also had the one touch of frivolity they had observed on the whole ship, and that somehow made it a more desirable place to live: the walls were plastered with magazine pictures of pretty girls, apparently European actresses.

Otherwise the quarters were Spartan. It was a tiny room, about eight feet square, with just one bunk in it. Disturbed by Russell's warnings of danger, they were determined to stand watches all night for safety's sake, so they figured that only one man at a time would be sleeping anyhow. There were two porthole openings, but the glass, along with the brass frames, had been removed by metal-hunters. They got a couple of portholes from elsewhere on the ship and installed them in the openings. They didn't quite fit, but the two men patched the cracks with rags and lashed down the ports with ropes to keep them closed. The door also was missing, and since the corridors outside gave evidence of being inundated in high seas, its absence was dangerous. They replaced the door too from another part of the ship.

A stray piece of mahogany plywood six feet by two furnished a table. They tried leveling it in the sloping room by raising the legs some five inches at one end. When they had finished they stepped back—and stared in amazement. They checked by placing a drinking glass on its side atop the table; the glass rolled—apparently uphill! There was something terribly wrong about a table that tipped one way, within a room that tipped another. The illusion was so powerful that it literally made them dizzy.

They had been having trouble walking, particularly along the ship's longitudinal axis. The list forced them to proceed, in Deir's words, "one foot short and one foot long." But it seemed incredible to them that their room could actually be slanted this sharply. They had brought along a plumb bob, and now they suspended it from the ceiling, where there once had been a light fixture. It hung at a crazy angle—but it showed that the table was approximately level. They looked at each other and grinned.

They put up a shelf against one side of the room, set at the appropriate angle, and put the kerosene stove on it. With its sloping furniture, the cabin now began to resemble something out of the fun house at an amusement park. Next to the stove they moved in the little store of food they had brought. Their wives would have been appalled at their larder: several cans of Vienna sausage, six cans of soup, some canned pork and beans, a can of condensed milk, a jar of instant coffee, some tea bags, four loaves of bread, two boxes of soda crackers, a box of cream-centered cookies (Little's favorites), a couple of cartons of candy bars, a jar of peanut butter, a jar of mayonnaise (Deir was addicted to plain mayonnaise sandwiches), some oranges and bananas, and finally four jugs and a couple of vacuum jars, all filled with water. They figured this food and water would last them about ten days if they used it sparingly. Little, in addition, had a carton of cigarettes. Deir, having quit smoking cigarettes five years before, had taken along half a dozen cigars.

To complete their preparations, they inflated Deir's rubber life raft to its full size—twelve feet by seven—and lashed it high above the railing on the port deck, just outside their cabin.

This work had consumed most of the day. Several times boatmen had appeared off the port side. Most of them had read the sign, hesitated briefly, then turned back in toward Ocean City. A few had hailed them and asked to come aboard, but Little and Deir had politely turned them down. However, when there was something special a visitor wanted on the tanker, one of the partners would obligingly get it for him. The two men wanted no trouble from the boatmen, and the loss of a piece of pipe didn't mean much to them when they were after a couple of million dollars. One fellow told them he had a customer for a six-inch valve. That was too much trouble to take off themselves, so they let him come aboard and get it. He left gratefully.

Finally, there had been one visitor they had welcomed. Kin Reed, small and perky, had shown up during the day and they had invited him aboard. For a while they had talked, and then they had come to an arrangement with him. "Now, I'll tell you," said Little. "We'll be getting a boat of our own, but we don't know when. We'd like to hire you to be our shore contact in the meantime—carry out supplies and all."

Reed was still dubious. "I don't know if you fellers have any right out here," he said. "Besides, there's some things on here I might want—like for instance that plywood up in the pilot house."

"It's yours!" Deir said immediately.

So Reed had agreed to make frequent visits—daily ones if

possible—until they could make other plans. He had stayed a while longer, chatting and eagerly inspecting his plywood, then left.

Now it was getting late. All day long they had worked to the constant roar of breakers coming up on the tank deck; because of all the splashing and spray both men were thoroughly soaked despite the oilskins they wore. As it grew dark it seemed to them that the swells were getting heavier. Neither man mentioned it, but each caught the other glancing at him covertly from time to time.

They moved into their cabin, lighted a lantern, opened a can of beans for supper, dried themselves and got ready to settle down for the night. They left the kerosene stove lighted, for heat. It was very cold.

They were now beginning to get frankly uneasy. The great ship was lurching noticeably under the impact of the seas. But there was something even more unsettling. For hours they had been half aware of a variety of noises coming from all over the ship—the rush of water, the groan of straining metal, the whistle of the wind. They had been too busy to pay much attention. But now, with nothing else to occupy them, they began to listen more closely to the sounds. They were getting worse, much worse—and somehow strange and otherworldly. Some were shrill and vibrant. Others were low and dull. Sometimes they were staccato, sometimes long and drawn out, sometimes so faint that the two men found themselves straining to hear them. Sometimes they resembled familiar land sounds, oddly hideous in this place.

By tacit agreement, they avoided speaking of this bizarre racket. For a while they tried to talk about other things, but it was useless. Repeatedly they would halt in midsentence as a new sound caught their attention. Soon they didn't even try. They just sat there grim-faced and anxious, assailed by a grotesque cacophony.

Whistles screamed. Horns tooted. There was a great clanging of bells. Suddenly they both started, astonished to hear distinctly the lowing of a cow. A train roared by underneath them. A trumpet blasted out a long, piercing note. Abruptly and horribly there came the sound of a great many people chattering a short distance down the corridor. White-faced, Little and Deir stared at each other. An automobile horn brayed outlandishly from someplace deep inside the ship. The clanking of chains was clearly audible in the next cabin.

And all the while the waves grew worse, and the ship bucked in agony as the breakers smashed against her. They were coming down from the northeast, slamming directly against the flat of her broken midships section. With each collision the *Queen* rose slightly in the little sand trough she lay in, then settled back heavily. The two men eyed the plumb bob. It was dancing madly at the end of its string. Deir reached out and steadied it. It still hung over the same spot on the table. That was a tremendous relief: the *Queen* hadn't begun to roll over.

They sat there, flinching as the noises assaulted them. Once in a while one of them would get up and stare out a porthole. The waves were coming all the way up to the deck, washing past their cabin, occasionally wetting the life raft hanging high above the port rail.

It was a long, long night. Neither man slept, although both were very tired. This was Tuesday, and they had had little sleep since Deir had appeared at Little's house the previous Friday. Among the noises they heard repeatedly that night was the blast of ships' horns. They knew this was no more real than anything else in the mad compendium of sounds, yet it was scary. The possibility that some ship might ram the *Queen* in the darkness worried them; they were out there without lights.

Daylight came at last, and as it did the waves began to subside. The noises died down. Gray and haggard, the two men went stiffly out on deck, shivering in the morning cold, and checked the raft. Then they went in and had a breakfast of instant coffee and Vienna sausage.

In the prosaic light of day it was not hard to figure out where all the noise had come from. During a month of scavenging, various hatches, ventilators and ports had been opened all over the ship. The water was rushing into these openings, forcing air ahead of it, and then sucking the air back as it receded, playing on the ship's ventilators and pipes as if they were part of some gigantic organ. In addition, cracks and crevices that could not be reached by the seas were open to the wind, and the repeated jarring of the vessel by the waves was shaking all the loose fittings and making unattached pipes roll around on the metal decks.

So all the noises had a perfectly rational explanation. That fact had not kept them from being utterly nerve-racking. But Deir and Little would never again let themselves be bothered by the noises as they had this first terrible night.

5

FOR MOST OF their second morning aboard the *Queen*, Little and Deir went around dogging down loose portholes and tightening hatches—less to stop the noises than because it was necessary to start tidying up in preparation for salvage operations. They set aside some items of equipment that might be useful to them later. Much of the stuff had been lying out in the open getting rusty; they greased and oiled it and put it away. While they were about it they made a special pile of choice metals that might prove salable, in accord with their promise to Paul Brady. There wasn't much of it.

"You know," said Little thoughtfully at one point, "I'll bet we could cut off that whole pilot house, cut it up into sheets, and sell it for thirty-five thousand all by itself, and no need for a big salvage deal. Fast profit."

Deir answered shortly. "That's not what I came out here for."

A salvage plan was already beginning to take shape in Deir's mind. He was not sure it would work, but it was a daring approach, and one that appealed to him greatly. Why not get hold of the severed bow, bobbing away out there, pull it in next to the port side of the hull, and sink it? It would make an almost immovable anchor. They could then lash the hull to it with cables, draw the cables up and tip the whole hull up on its side. The damaged area, which presumably was someplace on the starboard side, would then be exposed, and they could repair it without difficulty. As he worked, he kept turning this plan over mentally, examining it for flaws.

At 11:00 A.M. Kin Reed showed up, and the two salvagers welcomed him warmly. He had a copy of the Salisbury *Times* with him and he was bubbling with the news: the *Times* had carried a story about them based on the paid notice they had run plus an interview with Paul Russell.

To their dismay, the story made much of the two shotguns they had brought aboard. In addition it mentioned that another man, a fellow named Gifford Warner of Connecticut, had also had salvage designs on the *Queen*. He was claiming that he had been there first, and that they had no right to the tanker. They looked at each other jubilantly. If Warner had been planning to seize the ship, they had come aboard none too soon!

For a time Reed worked in the pilot house, getting off plywood. Once he mislaid a tool and asked their help in finding it. He had done the same thing their first day on the *Queen*. They were beginning to find this highly amusing. After a while Reed had his boat loaded high with wood, and he left. "See you fellers tomorrow probably," he said.

That afternoon they had less welcome visitors; for a while it looked as if the shotguns were going to come in handy.

This boat, unlike the others they had seen, approached from the north, from the direction of Lewes. That in itself disturbed them. They were beginning to feel that they knew the Ocean City boatmen, but they knew nothing of those from Delaware. Furthermore, the strange boat was a good deal larger than the others had been. It was coming fast, and it somehow appeared ominous. As it drew closer they could see that it was a forty-foot dragger with five big, rough-looking men aboard. One of them, incongruously, was dressed in a business suit. The boat pulled briskly to the port side. Deir slipped into the cabin and then mounted the steel ladder to the second deck of the aft superstructure, the shotgun hidden by his leg. Little went down to the tank deck.

The man in the suit, young and powerfully built, threw a line onto the deck and said to Little, "Here, make it fast."

Little tossed back the line. "Sorry, buddy," he said. "This ship is now under salvage and nobody can come aboard her."

The man hurled the line up again. "I don't give a damn what she's under," he said. "We're coming aboard. Take that line!"

Little threw it back again. "Now I'll tell you, mister," he said, his neck turning red. "You might as well stay right where you are, because you're not coming on this ship."

"Slip the line through the hawser port, Al," said one of the men in the boat. "Don't let that son of a bitch bull you."

Little once again threw the line off the tanker, harder this time. On the aft deck Deir watched intently, prepared to shoot if Little's defense required it.

"Mister," said the burly man in the business suit, "you throw that goddam line back here again, I'm gonna come up there and bust you. You hear me!"

Little struggled to control his anger. "Now look," he said. "We can't let you up here. This is a salvage operation"—he thought fast—"and our insurance doesn't cover anyone who comes aboard except the salvagers. We don't mean to have trouble with anybody, but we don't make the rules."

There was a brief conference on board the dragger. Then the young man addressed Little again. The group from Lewes had obviously decided on a change of tactics. "Only thing we wanted was a small souvenir," the man said in a more moderate voice. "We been out here before. I don't know who you are or what you're doing here, but we ain't looking for trouble either. You let us on and I'll get my souvenir and we'll leave. All I want is a small light I saw up on the pilot house there. I got a nephew visiting and he'd sure like a light like that." He waited for an answer.

"Well," said Little exasperatedly, "why didn't you say that? Why come around threatening? We don't mind you coming on board if you got a reasonable errand. But we'll ask you to leave once you got what you came for."

He made fast the dragger's painter and then moved back to the aft deckhouse and joined Deir. Four of the men climbed up to the tank deck, leaving the fifth to look after the boat. For a time they fussed around the pilot house. Then the burly young man picked his way along the sloping tank deck and started to mount the ladder to the aft superstructure. Little quickly stepped to the head of the ladder.

"I'm sorry, friend," he said. "You said the pilot house. You can't come up here."

"Why the hell not?"

"Because our tools and living quarters are back here and we don't want them disturbed."

"Well, I'm coming up anyway. And you better not stop me."

Little picked up a piece of inch-and-a-half pipe. "I don't think you're coming anywhere," he said grimly. He was getting angry again. He wasn't at all sure that he and Deir could hold off four big men—five, counting the one in the boat—but he was fully prepared to try. Deir was still standing off a short distance, reluctant to show the gun.

"Listen," said the man at the foot of the ladder, his voice hard. "I'm coming up there and nobody's gonna stop me. And when I get up there I'm gonna kick your tail good."

Deir moved quietly up beside Little. "You're not gonna kick both our tails," he said. "Now why don't you just leave, and let's not have any trouble."

The man peered through the rails. "You got a *gun* there?"

"Never mind the gun. You come up here and we'll handle you without the gun, I guarantee you."

But the gun made a difference; it obviously argued far more convincingly than the two salvagers could. The threat suddenly subsided. The invaders retreated and worked around the rest of the ship briefly. Before they left they returned to where the partners were standing and solemnly shook hands. "No offense," they said.

Just as they were boarding the dragger, one of the men called to Deir, who had come down to the tank deck. "You fellows better be careful, though. We'd hate for you boys to get killed out here. It was over the news that the government's gonna come out here and blow this thing up. We'll take you in if you want to come."

"Thanks," said Deir. "We appreciate it. But we figure we'll stay."

61

"Suit yourselves," the man said. They left, to the great relief of the partners.

"You figure they were right about the government?" Little asked Deir.

"Naw."

They spent the rest of the afternoon surveying the ship, trying to estimate the scope of their salvage project. They were standing in the engine room a few hours later, watching the surging of the water there—Deir estimated that it was rushing in and out at a rate of 65,000 gallons a second—when suddenly they were rocked by a shattering blast. They gaped at each other in consternation. "My God," said Deir, shaken. "Do you suppose those guys *were* right?"

They turned and raced for the deck. Another explosion occurred while they were tearing along the corridor. They burst out on deck and looked frantically about them. There was nothing to be seen. Then Little pointed to the sky. "Look," he said. "Way, way up. Could it be those two planes?" There was a double condensation trail slashed across the sky, so high that the airplanes making it were not visible.

"They couldn't be dropping bombs—not from that high, I don't think," said Deir dubiously. Suddenly he snapped his fingers as a great light burst on him.

"The *sound barrier!*" he exclaimed. "That's what it was! Those explosions were those two planes passing through the sound barrier. We heard the sonic boom."

They looked at each other and grinned weakly. "My lord, what next?" said Little.

The fact is, the next crisis was almost upon them. Brady had decided to pull out, once and for all.

6

THE NIGHT BEFORE, Brady had decided to go out and visit the ship for the first time. He had made the long trip to Ocean City, uncertain what he would find when he got there. Arriving in the morning, he had chartered a boat to take him out to the tanker. The seas which had so bothered his partners during the night were still running high. As the boat passed through the channel and into the Atlantic it began to roll violently. After about three quarters of an hour it had been forced to turn back to Ocean City. That gave the boatman, one of the many in the area who opposed the salvage project, a chance to work on Brady. He made good use of it.

"Couple damn fools," he confided. "What do they know about ships? You think they'll ever get that tanker off of there? Two men? Hell, no. You think them two can do what Merritt-Chapman can't? That's the biggest outfit there is, friend, and they had to quit on her. I tell you, I know a little about the sea, I guess. Them amateurs are gonna fall right on their faces."

To a degree, he was only voicing doubts that had been in the back of Brady's mind right along. Every once in a while, the full scope of the operation Brady had let himself in for would dawn on him suddenly, and he would be aghast. It wasn't just the size of the ship, and the inevitable problems in repairing and refloating her. He was worried to the point of sleeplessness by the thought of what it would all cost and how close to financial ruin he might be skirting. A fantastic amount of equipment would be needed by Little and Deir; it was all very well for them to make light of it, but he couldn't. If he stayed with the partners, there was another consideration, too. No matter how much he was out of pocket, whatever happened by way of profit and loss, his appliance business in Suffolk was bound to suffer. That business was his life. He had started it with two other men before World War II, had ultimately bought them out and had struggled to build it up. While he was in the Army his wife had cared for the store. Since his return he had devoted six days a week to it, and more. He had seen it grow into a thriving business. He was enormously proud of it, and of the place it had won him in the community. If something happened to it he didn't know what he'd do.

He sat in the pitching boat, listening half to the boatman, half to his own doubts. Deir and Little weren't really risking anything, it occurred to him. He knew they weren't thinking of it that way, but the fact was that the risk was all his, and the dimensions of the risk were looming larger and larger.

When they got back in to Ocean City, Brady said to the boatman, "You going back out there tomorrow?"

"Yeah, sure. Anything you want me to tell them?"

"Yes. You tell them to come in and talk to me. I think I'm through with this thing."

The next morning, a worried Deir traveled in to Ocean City to telephone Brady. He and Little had spent a fairly good night. The noises had not been so bad, and they were beginning to get used to them. The only difficulty had been in getting to sleep. They had now abandoned the thought of standing guard all night; it seemed unnecessary. So the two of them had slept in the one bunk. That posed certain problems. The bunk, located opposite the portholes, ran parallel to the longitudinal axis of the ship and was slanted accordingly. That meant that anyone lying in it tended to roll in toward the starboard side. The man sleeping inside stayed good and warm but was half crushed by the weight of his partner slipping down on top of him. The outside man froze. Neither slept well.

When the message was received from the boatman in the morning, it had been decided that Deir should speak to Brady. He was, after all, the one who had first known him. Deir hated to leave Little alone on the *Queen;* indeed, he considered staying there an act of considerable bravery on Little's part. But there had been no alternative. Somebody had to stay; it would never again be safe to leave the ship unguarded.

Deir's phone conversation with Brady was highly unsatisfactory. He marshaled every argument he knew—including the fact that he and Little had made the second trip out to the tanker only after receiving Brady's assurance that he would be backing them up at home. What were they to do now?

Brady was understanding but adamant. "I know," he said.

"I know what a pickle this leaves you boys in, and I feel responsible. But, Lloyd, I just don't see what else there is for me to do. I'd like to stick with you on this. Sure it's exciting and everything, but it's just too big for me. I just can't swing it. I haven't got the money; I should never have joined you in the first place. I just didn't realize. But I've been thinking: we're going to need boats, we're going to need pumps, we're going to need tools and machines and food, we're going to need this and we're going to need that, and damn it, Lloyd, there's just no end to it. This is just beyond me, and I don't know any other way I can say it."

When the conversation was over, Brady had done most of the talking; there really wasn't much Deir could say. But Brady sat there in his little store, looking at the phone and feeling terrible. There hadn't been any alternative, and yet his conscience was bothering him. He could see the two of them, alone out there on that beat-up tanker, trying to decide what to do now that their one financial prop had been yanked out from under them. It was a melancholy picture, and Brady, a man who had gone through life trying hard never to hurt anyone, was responsible for it.

That evening, still depressed, he unburdened himself to his wife. Lib Brady, an attractive, dark-haired woman, had, like the other wives, been opposed to the venture from the start. But as Paul spoke now she became troubled. At last she shook her head.

"Paul," she said, "you just can't do that. It just isn't right. You can't send them out there, and then pull out of the deal by phone. I don't want you to have any part of that ship, but you can't duck out on them this way. Why don't you go out there and talk to them? Tell them why you have to quit. Make them understand that you just *can't*. But this way, somehow it's still up in the air. They know you've left them but they don't know why. It just doesn't seem the right way to do things." She looked at him anxiously.

Brady's face cleared as she spoke. He grinned at her. "You're absolutely right. I can't just send some stranger with a message I'm quitting. It isn't the decent thing to do. I'll go out there again tomorrow. I'll tell them face to face that I can't stick with them, and why. It'll mighty sure make me feel better that way."

Brady arrived at the *African Queen* early the next morning, a day of brilliant sunshine. The size of the ship startled him; I'm well out of this, he thought. His boatman tied up on the port side and waited for him there. Brady clambered aboard.

Kin Reed arrived shortly afterward, was introduced to Brady, and then got ready to go forward to the pilot house and get more wood. "Either of you fellers see a crowbar I left out here the other day?" he asked before he headed forward. "Looked for it all yesterday afternoon and I swear it must have dropped over the side."

They grinned. "Before you go to looking for it over the side," Little said, "try the bridge, starboard wing."

The three partners had barely launched their discussion when they saw a large boat bearing down on them from the north. They broke off their conversation and eyed it narrowly. But before Deir could go back and get the shotgun Little leaned forward and peered. "That's some kind of government boat, I believe," he said.

It was a motor lifeboat with forty Coast Guard officers and men aboard, resplendent in brilliant yellow life jackets and crisp khaki uniforms. Reed joined the salvagers. "Here's where you fellers get bounced off," he said anxiously. "I been expecting this."

"Not a chance," said Deir stoutly. But he wasn't at all sure, and neither were the others. It still seemed too much to hope that they could just come out here like this and help themselves to a multimillion-dollar prize.

The Coast Guard boat purred up to the port side, and Little went down to meet it. A tall, handsome officer looked up at him. "Commander Maynard Young, United States Coast Guard Headquarters in Washington," he said pleasantly. "Request permission to come aboard."

Gooseflesh broke out all over the old Navy enlisted man. Little gulped, and his voice broke as he answered: "Permission granted."

Some of the Coast Guardsmen stayed with the boat. The rest—including one civilian—climbed aboard. Commander Young and another commander joined the group of salvagers on the deck.

"We've come out here," Young said, "because the states of Maryland and Delaware are afraid the oil in your tanks may escape and ruin their beaches. We'd like your permission to examine the vessel and sound the tanks."

"You're welcome to do anything at all you want to," Deir said.

Commander Young motioned his men to work, and they scattered, some of them bearing long rods with trigger handles at one end and lidded cups at the other. The cups would be dipped into the tanks and snapped shut with the triggers to trap the contents at various levels and see how much was oil and how much water.

There were introductions all around. Reed had been jumping from one foot to the other, and as soon as the introductions were over he broached the question that had been bothering him since the first day he had met the salvagers.

"Tell me one thing," he said to the commander. "These boys came out and they took over this ship and said it was theirs. Well, I believe it is, all right." Reed hesitated. "At least I think so." He peered anxiously at the officer. "Well, is it or isn't it?"

Young grinned. "Absolutely," he said. "This ship was abandoned on the high seas. She was open to salvage. Anyone who was serious about getting her off could come out and claim her. These men did it; now all they have to do is show progress. As long as they do that, no one can take the ship away from them. They have a perfect right to be here."

"And they can keep anyone else off?"

"They certainly can."

Reed, visibly relieved, grinned broadly. "Sure," he said. "That's what I figgered." Little and Deir, who had never been sure about their legal position, found themselves smiling foolishly.

The rest of that morning the salvagers conducted the Coast Guard officers around the ship. As they stood looking into the restless engine-room flood, Commander Young commented, "I envy you. It's a great challenge—one of the very few ways nowadays an ordinary man can start from scratch and make himself a million dollars."

Brady listened thoughtfully.

The civilian who had accompanied the Coast Guardsmen was a shipyard engineer, brought along to provide expert opinion on the ship's tanks. As the others went about the ship, Deir took him aside for a moment.

"I won't ever pin you down to this," he told the man, "but I'd sure be thankful if you could give me some idea what you think the tanker is worth. We have a hard job ahead of us, lots of work and lots of expense, and we have no real idea what we'll have when we're finished."

The engineer pondered briefly. "Well, don't hold me to it," he said, "but I should think any shipyard would be glad to pay you a quarter of a million dollars for her right where she is, once you have her afloat. In port, of course, she'd be worth a lot more."

"Thank you," Deir said, his eyes bright.

The Coast Guard officers were fascinated by everything about the salvage operation—what problems the partners faced, how they were living, what their intentions were. Deir explained his tentative plan to use the bow to roll the hull up on its side, and was pleased to see that nobody seemed inclined to scoff at the idea.

After a time, Brady, Deir and Little excused themselves to resume their discussion of the future. Brady's boatman was waiting impatiently to take him back to Ocean City, but before he left there were a few things to be settled.

A great deal had happened to Paul Brady's thinking since his departure from Suffolk that morning. Like everyone else seeing the *Queen* for the first time, he had been impressed by her size, her grace and her obvious value. His first thought had been that she was just too big to handle, but then the Coast Guardsmen had arrived and had somehow changed everything, less by what they said than by their attitude. They had listened respectfully to Little and Deir, they had seemed impressed with their plans, and they had not once questioned the practicality of the project. If *they* thought it could be done . . .

"I'll tell you," said Brady to Little and Deir. "I'm going to stick. We'll go ahead with this thing." He hesitated. "Someplace we're going to have to find us another partner to help take the load. But I think it's going to work out all right."

Deir and Little made no secret of their pleasure. They assured Brady once again that he would never be sorry. Then they shook hands all around, and Brady climbed down the ladder to the boat and started home.

While they were talking, men had been inspecting the tanks. In two of the tanks, away aft, were the *African Queen*'s own fuel supplies, a kind of oil called bunker C. It was so thick, so tarlike, that the sailors couldn't plunge their rods into it; it probably could be depended on to stay put forever. The Coast Guardsmen checked all the other tanks—and found every one of them empty.

"Well, no problem there," Commander Young said cheerfully. The Coast Guardsmen got ready to leave. Their uniforms, spotless when they had come aboard two hours earlier, were now filthy. Deir and Little got some paste detergent and tried to clean them off before they left, but they only succeeded in smearing the oil further. Commander Young grinned. "Don't let it worry you," he said. As he walked down to the tank deck he asked if he could have a sample of the steel plate from the forward section where the bow had broken off, and Deir promised to send him one as soon as possible.

Then, as the commander was about to leap into his boat he turned for a moment and smiled. "One last thing," he said. "It's my duty to ask you this: May I take you ashore?"

Little answered. "Thank you, sir. We'll stay aboard."

"Right. Good luck, then."

There was one more party of visitors that day—a newsman and a photographer who had come out from the Salisbury paper to get another story on the salvagers. The photographer seemed interested in only one thing: he wanted a picture of the men with the two guns in their hands. Deir and Little, who couldn't understand this press fascination with firearms, turned down the request, although they did pose for other pictures.

After a time the reporter and cameraman left, and their boat circled the *Queen*. The salvagers kept an eye on it, not because they expected trouble from the two newspapermen but simply because in their anxiety they had fallen into the habit of watching all boats that came near. They were still shaken by the experience with the Lewes boatmen. As the press boat swung around the tanker's stern, the photographer caught sight of Little and shouted something. Deir, standing on the port deck some distance away, called to his partner, "What did they say?"

There was a brief pause, then Little turned and shouted, "Get the guns!"

Deir hesitated not a moment. He wheeled and plunged into the deck house. Little, after an instant's startled irresolution, hurried after him, his feet pounding on the deck. At the entrance to the passageway, Deir met him, carrying the two shotguns, and thrust one into his hand. Then the two men raced back up the deck toward the fantail, their faces grim and purposeful. When they got there Deir turned to Little.

"What's wrong?" he asked, breathing hard.

Little stared at him, puzzled. "I don't know," he said. "What did you run for?"

"Well, hell, man, *you* said, 'Get the guns!'"

It began to dawn on Little. He grinned and pointed to the press boat. "That's what *they* said," he explained.

For a moment the two men looked at each other, and then suddenly all the worry and tension of the past week burst out of them in an explosion of laughter. Leaning against the rail of the *Queen*, they roared helplessly.

At last Deir said weakly, "Well, we sure gave that photographer a show. He said get 'em and we got 'em. By now he must have his picture; I guess we might as well stand up straight and pose right."

And they did. The picture was in all the next day's papers.

7

WHEN KIN ARRIVED the next morning he called out, "Hey, I got something for you here!"

Deir and Little looked over the side. "What is it?"

At that moment two heads popped up in Kin's boat. It was Hazel Little and Doris Deir.

For the two women it had been quite an adventure. A few days before, Hazel, nervous and worried about her husband, had become sick, and her doctor had ordered her to stay in bed for a few days. Too upset to follow his orders, she went to see Doris Deir. "Let's go up there and visit them," she urged, and Doris agreed immediately. They made arrangements to have their children looked after and left Suffolk before midnight Friday. They were in Ocean City before 6:00 A.M.

They had heard of Kin Reed from Brady, so they headed for his place and arranged to ride out to the tanker with him. Once they had made this arrangement, both women became uneasy. Neither could swim. Like her husband, Doris had an abiding fear of water. Hazel was not afraid of the sea, but she was ill at ease among strangers. And Kin Reed, bluff and outspoken, did not win her over. As they walked to his boat Hazel watched him narrowly, wondering if he was to be trusted. Then, when Doris hesitated before getting into the boat, her fear of the sea welling up within her, Reed spoke sarcastically (or so it seemed to them). "You want to go or don't you?" he asked. They climbed unhappily into his boat, and Kin headed out to sea.

In the boat, they huddled in a corner, as far from Reed as they could get. Hazel was physically ill, Doris was badly frightened, and both were chilled clear through. Furthermore, the sea was rough, and the boat tossed alarmingly.

"Don't you think," Doris suggested in a small voice, "that we should wear life jackets?"

It happened that Kin had a deep-rooted aversion to life jackets, which he called, for reasons no one ever heard him explain, "cart jackets." He wouldn't wear them, and he tried to talk everyone he knew into following his example. Now he growled, "You don't need them cart jackets. If anything happens, just put your arms around my neck and"—he gazed solemnly out at the horizon—"we'll all go down together."

The women edged farther into their corner.

The seas grew increasingly rough as they left the shore behind. Soon the spray was whipping back over Kin's windshield, hampering his visibility. He decided to prop up the windshield. "Here," he said to Hazel, pointing to a stick at the far end of the cabin, "hand me that club." The choice of words was unfortunate. Hazel, all her suspicions confirmed, asked sharply, "What do you want it for?"

He stared at her. "What do you mean, 'What do I want it for?' I want it 'cause I *need* it. *Hand it up!*"

"No!"

He snorted. "Look here," he said, "if I could leave the wheel I'd get it myself. I gotta push up this window."

Embarrassed, Hazel handed him the stick. He propped open the windshield and, now that things were pretty well under control, began to chat with the women—about the sea, about the tanker, about their husbands. Hesitatingly, they responded. The trip out took more than an hour. By the time they got to the tanker they were all chattering away like old friends. When Kin elfishly suggested that the women duck out of sight and surprise their husbands, they complied with conspiratorial delight.

The women found their husbands' appearance shocking. Both were black with oil and heavily bearded. Equally appalling was the appearance of the ship itself, tipped at what to the women was a clearly perilous angle, smeared with grease, strewn with wrecked equipment. As for living conditions aboard the *Queen,* they were simply beyond belief: a tiny, gloomy room decorated with girlie pictures, the walls and floor dirty with oil, the bed unadorned by sheets of any kind, primitive food cooked on a primitive stove. When the men showed their wives around the ship, Doris Deir found it was impossible to grasp Lloyd's arm; his sleeve was so coated with oil that her hand kept slipping off. She finally wrapped a rag around his arm and held onto that.

Before leaving Suffolk, Hazel and Doris had packed a feast, little anticipating how badly their husbands needed it. Now, sitting in the tiny cabin, the four ate fried chicken and roast beef, potato salad and garden salad, lima beans, buttered rolls and coconut pie. The men gorged themselves.

Doris Deir, looking about her afterward, was concerned about her husband's health. Was he eating out here at all? Normally he was an exceedingly finicky eater. Accustomed to working with dirty hands, he had developed an idiosyncrasy about food: he would not swallow anything his hands had touched. When he ate sandwiches or cookies or fruit, the last little morsel held by his fingers was always thrown away. Now his wife wondered how he could possibly down anything amid all this filth.

Deir shrugged when she asked. "We eat out of cans," he said. "It's clean."

Not much work was done that day. For the first time since taking over the *Queen* the men took things easy, playing host to their wives. They showed the women around, proud of their ship and still a little staggered that it was all theirs. They guided them through the pilot house, and were pleased when Hazel and Doris reacted with housewifely amazement at the evidences of luxury. In the stern deckhouse the big attraction was the great kitchen, which extended all the way between the port and starboard boat decks, with one end dry and the other tilted toward the sea so that waves came splashing in through the starboard doorway. The big stainless-steel counters remained, as did a few pieces of equipment that could not be removed.

After the rigors of the preceding days, having the women on board was a wonderful restorative. But at last it was time for them to go. Before they left, the men discussed with them a problem that was becoming increasingly pressing. The two partners had no intention of staying on the *Queen* indefinitely. For the time being, they had done all they could— which was little enough. They had prepared for future operations by sealing the few portholes and hatches they could reach, making minor repairs, and collecting and cleaning all the tools and machinery that might prove usable. They had also gathered up a small supply of metal to sell for cash—although far less than they had once hoped for. Now they needed a vast assortment of equipment before they could proceed with the next steps in the salvage operation. While they shopped for these essentials, someone would have to be hired to come aboard and stand guard over the crippled ship. In short, they were ready to hire their first employees.

They had spoken of this to Brady the previous day. He had agreed that someone was needed, but beyond that he was at a loss. Nothing in his business experience had prepared him for that kind of recruiting. With the Coast Guardsmen aboard the tanker, it had been impossible for the partners to reach any conclusion, and the matter was left hanging. Now Deir and Little had thought of a couple of candidates, unskilled but trustworthy. They asked their wives to seek them out, and the women agreed to do so.

And then, reluctantly, they left. They could delay no longer, because the seas were getting rougher and Kin Reed was impatient. Before he went he said quietly to the men, "I think you got a blow coming. You better batten down."

The waves that afternoon grew steadily in size and force. Deir stood at the rail for a while and watched them. The sea was still strange to him and he found the size of the swells astonishing. They seemed at least twenty-five feet high, with troughs correspondingly deep. Peering down the side of the tanker, he could see, for the first time, the curved plates that formed the ship's belly, and a couple of times he thought he could actually see the sandy bottom itself.

The wind had been freshening gradually, and the thermometer was dropping. Abruptly the storm was upon them, and the noises of the ship were as intense as that first night. The motion of the ship was severe, too. The swells that normally rolled in from the east, striking her low starboard side and rushing up the tank deck, were now coming down in an ominous gray parade from the north. Since the tanker was facing northeast, the waves were striking from the port quar-

74

ter, some of them slamming hard against the exposed mid-ships bulkheads and the rest pouring down the hitherto protected port decks. They watched anxiously. Their cabin was on the port side. So was the life raft. So were a number of other things which they had stored in the lee of the deck house for safekeeping.

Fighting the rising wind, the two men checked the lashings on the raft and decided to leave it where it was, so it would be accessible from their quarters. They cleared what other equipment they could off the port decks, secured everything else as well as possible, and went to their cabin for the night.

Supper was a gloomy meal. They missed their wives, they were worried by the weather, they were again assailed by terrible noises, and—perhaps worst of all—they could not get the stove to work. They dined that night on cold canned beans—a depressing contrast to the banquet they had enjoyed at noon. The lurching of the ship was so bad now that as they sat eating side by side on the bunk, with their backs against the cabin wall, they found that their heads snapped sharply in beat with the pounding of the sea.

When they had finished their meal, they improved the rough calking around the portholes, poking the rags in tight and pulling in the ill-fitting windows as hard as possible. Outside, the waves were now rolling heavily along the port deck, splashing up as high as the portholes and occasionally shaking them vigorously.

For several hours after that they just sat there in the vibrating, dimly lighted cabin while the storm grew in ferocity. It was now very cold, colder than they had yet known it to be aboard the *Queen*. Little pushed himself off the bunk and tried once again to get the stove working.

Suddenly a giant swell slammed into the side of the ship, striking the portholes with tremendous force. They flipped open and two huge jets of water gushed in and roared across the room. The two men were inundated. There was water everywhere, calf-deep on the floor, dripping down the walls, soaking into the bed, washing into a deep pool at the low end of the cabin. Deir leaped to the door and threw it open to let the water out, only to find that the corridor was also flooded.

He waited until the water subsided, then ran out and slammed shut the door between the passageway and the deck. Inside the cabin, Little flew to the portholes, closed them and lashed them down again. Deir helped him replace the rags around the edges. Then, sodden and shivering, the two men set about swabbing up the floor and wringing out their clothes.

By now the tanker was reeling so violently that objects were tumbling off the table, and the plumb bob was swaying in yard-long arcs.

"Look," yelled Deir over the noise, "we better run a line out through that passageway and fasten it to the port rail. We've got to have some way of pulling ourselves out of here if this thing goes over! She's sure shaking something fierce."

They found a length of rope, anchored it inside the cabin, and ran it out into the long corridor and around the corner into the shorter passageway. Outside, the deck was coated with ice, but between waves they leaped out and, despite the slippery footing, managed to lash the line to the rail. Then they ran back in.

Both men prayed that night. As the hours passed, the storm grew steadily worse, the movement of the ship more frightening, their discomfort and anxiety more acute. Although the portholes did not blow open again, several times waves struck with sufficient force to push out the rag calking, and every time that happened fifty or seventy-five gallons of water poured in.

What worried them most was the fact that the ship, which had apparently been so firmly fixed to the shoal, was now being slammed so hard by the waves that she was off the bottom as much as she was on it. Worse, she was being hit on her high side. Would she roll all the way over? They could no longer doubt that it was possible. At last Deir slid off the bunk and crossed to the other side of the cabin, where there was a patch of wet bare wall under the portholes. With a pencil, he drew a cross section of a hull in outline on the shaking wall, roughly four inches high by seven and a half inches wide, to correspond to the dimensions of the *African Queen*. Then he carefully figured out an angle of twelve degrees off the horizontal—the angle of the *Queen*'s list—and drew the new line across the hull to indicate the sea. He now had a fairly accurate cross-section picture of the tanker as she sat in the water. With the eye of a natural engineer, he studied the drawing for several minutes. Finally he said, "I don't see how she can go over. I just don't see how." But his face remained grim.

By now Deir had run out of cigars. He borrowed a cigarette from Little. By the end of the night he had borrowed several more.

At dawn the storm, which had been raging for twelve hours, seemed to be growing worse. And now they found something new to worry them. In the light of early morning the life raft was visible for the first time since the night before. The towering seas were yanking at it relentlessly, sweeping over it again and again, causing it to bob and jump against its loosened lashings. The only path to the raft was along the deck, which itself was under water about half the time.

"Oh, man," said Deir. "God *knows* we're gone if we lose that!"

There was only one thing to do: duck out between waves, snatch the raft from the threatening sea, and pull it back into the passageway where it would be safe. They put on several layers of clothing, then moved tensely out into the passageway. The danger was great. If one of those waves caught them while they were on deck it probably would sweep them overboard.

They cracked the passageway door and stood poised as a great swell rolled by. Then they leaped out onto the deck.

Slipping and sliding frantically along the ice, they pelted down the deck to where the raft was tied. Hastily, with fumbling fingers, they untied it, racing to beat the next wave.

And then it was too late; they were under tons of icy water. Little grabbed desperately at the rail. Deir, clutching the raft, lost his footing. In an instant he had disappeared from Little's sight.

The wave dragged Deir along the deck. Bumping, scraping, flailing, choking, he held on to the raft with one hand and tried to grab hold of something with the other. At last his fingers snagged a piece of piping, fumbled an instant, and held. There was a tearing pain in his shoulder as it caught the full weight of his body, still hurtling down the deck. He hung on. Minutes seemed to pass before the water freed him. When the wave retreated, he was prone on the deck, soaked and half stunned, but still holding the raft. Choking, he struggled to his feet. Little ran to his side. Dragging the raft, they fought their way back up the deck in the face of the wind. They just made it before the next huge sea came down on them; they were halfway through the doorway when it roared by, soaking them both again. They fell inside with the raft, and slammed the door shut. For a long time they leaned against the walls of the passageway, panting.

One compartment of the raft had collapsed, but it was still serviceable. They tied it down in the passageway, then stiffly made their way back to the cabin.

Shortly after 8:00 A.M. the storm began to abate, and then it died swiftly. By ten the sun was out, and the two partners, scarcely able to believe it was all over, went out on deck.

For the rest of the day they sat in the sun, performing only unavoidable small chores like repairing the raft. They were too exhausted to do more. Deir was nursing his aching shoulder. But somehow they felt good, too. The storm had been the climax to a wild week; if they were ever going to quit the *Queen,* now was the time. They didn't give it a thought. They had endured the worst; there was no point in quitting now.

By nightfall they had dried out pretty well. They ate and went to bed. The sea outside was as placid as a mountain lake.

The next day, Monday, March 23, replacements arrived to spell them, and Deir and Little went ashore.

8

THEY NOW BEGAN perhaps the most vital, difficult and time-consuming—if least dramatic—part of the entire salvage project: a massive and painstaking shopping operation which was to require many weeks and, ultimately, many thousands of dollars. For almost two months the two men worked ashore, returning to the *Queen* only to deliver equipment and to put new shifts of guards aboard. It was a hectic, exhausting and frequently frustrating period. The right equipment proved hard to find, and money to pay for it even harder. Again and again the project was threatened by apparently insurmountable obstacles, and only an indomitable refusal to face facts kept it alive.

The number and diversity of items they needed was extraordinary. They were starting a salvage company virtually from scratch, and although Deir and Little still were not sure just how badly their ship was damaged it was clear that repairing it would be a major task. They would need materials for patching, more hoisting equipment, pumps, hoses, generators, batteries, compressors, fuel, miles of wire and hundreds of yards of cable, covers for portholes and hatches, an almost infinite variety of small parts, tools and electrical gear —an endless and staggering list.

As they planned their purchases, they made, as a matter of course, an assumption which was to fix the pattern of the entire salvage job. They would patch with steel. They were experienced metalworkers; any other course would have seemed absurd. They were unaware that the veteran salvagers of Merritt-Chapman & Scott had decided against using steel on the ground that any burning or welding of metal on a vessel filled with oil fumes could be suicidal. To be sure, the two men had a clue to the decision of the professional salvage experts—they had seen the wood-and-concrete Merritt-Chapman patch that rose in a strange bump on the starboard side of the tank deck. But they were so unfamiliar with standard marine salvage techniques that they were not sure what that block of concrete was, and during all their subsequent months on the ship they never were entirely certain. They were, however, fully aware of the danger of working with fire and electricity aboard the reeking ship. They merely accepted that hazard as an unavoidable part of the job and determined to take all possible precautions.

Once the *Queen* was patched she would have to be pumped dry. A single new pump might cost several hundred dollars, not including hose. They would certainly need a dozen pumps, maybe two dozen, and possibly even double that—plus a source of power to make the pumps work.

Then there was another probable expense. Although Deir was still considering the use of the *Queen's* capsized bow as an anchor to roll over the rest of the ship, this approach was beginning to look more and more impractical. The problem was not so much that the method wouldn't work as that it would be expensive and time-consuming. So, while Deir still liked the idea, Little had already started to think of alternatives. If they could not expose the damaged plates by rolling the ship onto its side, they would have to examine the holes and apply the patches underwater. As Little had pointed out, he had had some diving experience in the past, and he hoped that he could handle whatever diving the salvage of the *Queen* required. In any case, he thought it likely that they would have to add diving equipment to their list of needs, although Deir didn't seem to think so.

Finally, there had to be some way of getting this huge array of equipment out to the scene of the salvage, ten miles offshore. Hauling it from Norfolk to Ocean City would be no problem: Deir's truck was fine for that, and Brady owned a light truck that could be used as well. But Kin Reed's boat was much too small to ferry heavy, bulky machinery out to the ship. They would need at least one large boat or scow, perhaps two.

To Brady, who would have to bear the expense of all this, the growing scope of the operation was stunning. Originally he had agreed to back Little and Deir in the belief that the job could be done at moderate cost. Even after he realized this error, he had felt that he could handle a large part of the expense. Now, however, he quailed before the imposing list of requirements.

To ease the impact on Brady, Deir and Little agreed to buy at first only those items required for immediate operations, and to shop carefully for those. The two men were expert bargain hunters; they knew practically every scrap-and-salvage yard within a 100-mile radius, and they had a good idea of the value of the equipment they were seeking. Finally, in this initial phase of the shopping operation, the partners determined to spend no more than a thousand dollars. It was an unrealistic figure, and they all knew it, but at least it was a target that Brady could look upon without feeling faint.

In the final analysis, there was only one solution to this problem of costs, and Brady had mentioned it on his visit to the *Queen:* they must find a fourth partner who would help Brady shoulder the financial burden.

The equipment-purchasing got off to an inauspicious start. Little and Deir had brought back from the *Queen* a few hundred pounds of brass and other metal, and on March 24, their first day back, they took it to a local scrap yard. They received only two hundred dollars for it.

They spent the rest of the day traveling, moving from one scrap yard to another, walking through the yards, telling the owner what they wanted, examining the available merchandise, then moving on to another place, sometimes just down the road, sometimes a hundred and fifty miles away. They drove hundreds of miles that day, stopping and looking but never buying, and when they returned to Suffolk at dusk they were weary and depressed. They had seen little they could use, and that little was, by their lights, incredibly high priced. But the equipment was absolutely essential; if they couldn't find it the whole operation was doomed.

They stopped in to make their doleful report to Brady and found him in a state of great anxiety—more worried, if anything, than they were.

"Boy, am I glad to see you," he said. "The F.B.I. wants us."

He showed them a letter he had received from the Department of Justice. It stated that an agent would call on them that day; Brady said he had already spoken to the man, and he was on his way over. Like most Americans, the three men had a deep-seated awe of the F.B.I., and the thought of being questioned by a G-man made them thoroughly nervous.

When he showed up he was well dressed, quiet, self-possessed—a cordial, steely man who somehow succeeded in making them feel even more ill at ease. They sat in his car on Suffolk's main street, and he asked them a number of questions. Who were they? What were their plans for the tanker? Did they understand the liability they were incurring? He had with him a written statement. It said that they were taking over the tanker *African Queen*, that they were aware of the responsibility this entailed, that they agreed to assume full liability, that they intended to salvage the ship and get it off the shoal as soon as possible, that while it was there they would light it adequately. He was pleasant but firm. They would have to sign the statement. Quaking, they signed.

Afterward Brady was in a state. "Boy," he said, "this is bad! *I'm* the only one with any money. If the government finds us liable for damages, they could take everything I've got." A few days later, after a hasty trip to a lawyer, he asked the men to sign formal papers of incorporation. They incorporated as Queen Salvors Enterprises, Inc. Brady was still the only one with any money, but at least the responsibility was legally apportioned. It was agreed, among other things, that any partner who dropped out would lose his full interest in the venture.

A short time later they received a formal letter from the Justice Department, officially notifying them that they would be held liable for any damage done to the beaches by oil from the *Queen*. Similar letters, they were informed, had gone out to African Enterprises, Ltd., the original owners of the ship, and to Lloyd's of London, the underwriters. That wasn't much consolation. Neither was Deir's highly pertinent comment. "Hell," he said, "the Coast Guard just told us there *wasn't* any oil." Logic or no logic, all that responsibility was still a great worry.

The next day Brady joined Deir and Little, and all three partners carried their search for equipment to the yard of the Portsmouth Salvage Company, where Deir had been working up to the time of the salvage project. As they entered, Buddy Jacobson, one of the three brothers who owned the company, called Deir aside. He shook hands cordially, then said, "Is all that true about you and this big salvage job? How you making out?"

"Why, we're doing pretty good," Deir said cautiously. "Still a long way to go, of course."

"Isn't that a hell of a big job for two or three guys to try alone? What are you doing for equipment?"

"That's what we're here for."

"Well, I guess you know what you're doing, but it sure seems to me it's going to run into a lot of money." Jacobson looked at the ground for a moment, then said casually, "Looking for another partner? Looks like you need one, and we might be interested."

"Well," said Deir, poker-faced. "I don't know. I'll have to ask Little and Brady. I suppose they might be willing—if we could count on you for the right kind of help. We *are* a little short of equipment. Maybe if you could supply the stuff we need as your share . . ."

That day Jacobson took the three of them to lunch. Now that the deal was a possibility, he was the hardheaded businessman. He asked precisely what they were doing, how badly damaged the tanker was, how much equipment they were going to require, how expensive the operation would be, how much time they thought it would take.

Then he delayed a final decision. "I've got to see it," he said, not unreasonably.

The following day, Deir and Buddy and Freddy Jacobson flew out to Ocean City in a chartered plane and swooped down over the tanker. From the air the *Queen* looked small and pathetic. She was crazily tilted and half submerged, with white water foaming on her tank deck, and she appeared lost and desolate in the great blankness of the sea. Looking down at her, Deir thought that she bore less resemblance to a $2,000,000 prize than to a broken and discarded toy. But there was an advantage to that illusion. From the air she also looked less imposing as a salvage project—she looked, in other words, like something a couple of amateurs might be able to manage.

The Jacobsons said little as they flew back to Norfolk. They found the airfield there weathered in. The little plane circled a while, then, its gasoline running low, returned to Salisbury, not far from Ocean City, and landed there after an anxious trip. The three men rode home to Virginia in a rented car.

Deir reached Holland at daybreak. He was very tired, but he was jubilant. Before he left the brothers they had given him their decision. Portsmouth Salvage was in. If Brady would pay for food and salaries, the Jacobsons would supply the equipment. Now, certainly, the worst of the financial crisis was over. The last dilemma had been solved, and they could get on with the work.

The advantages of Portsmouth Salvage's participation were felt immediately. In a short time, two of the project's major needs were met. First, the Jacobsons helped locate twenty surplus Navy pumps. They were submersible and electrically operated, and therefore somewhat dangerous to use around raw oil, but they were inexpensive—and that seemed much more important under the circumstances. New, they would have cost at least eight hundred dollars apiece. These pumps were not new—indeed, each of them required virtually a complete overhaul—but they were bought for only thirty dollars each. It was a great haul, and the salvagers' spirits rose.

Later, feeling that they needed a couple more pumps of the same kind, Deir and Little visited a scrap yard in Newport News whose owner in other times had repeatedly tried to interest Little in a pair of brand-new pumps. The owner tried again this time, but Little and Deir, worried about what he might ask for them, professed disinterest. They paid elaborate attention to life preservers, cable, winches, tools—everything but pumps. At last he pleaded with them: he had been stuck with these pumps for months; wouldn't they take the pair off his hands? With a great show of reluctance, they finally bought the two of them—for fifty dollars. They were still in the factory cartons.

"Boy, I tell you," Little exulted on the way home, "things must be getting better! Hell, there's thirty dollars' worth of *brass* on those pumps!"

An even greater find was made right in the Jacobsons' own yard: a couple of surplus boats that seemed to be just what they needed. One was a Navy airplane-rearming boat, a strange-looking bargelike vessel of light plywood, thirty-three feet long, with a rounded bow and a padded canvas fender completely encircling the gunwales. It had a gasoline engine that gave it a speed of ten knots, it had plenty of cargo space and it promised to handle well. It was ideally suited to the peculiar unloading problems posed by the grounded tanker. Light and fairly maneuverable, the rearming boat could be brought up to the stricken ship even in heavy swells, butted up against the port side, and held there firmly, protected from damage by the fender. The boat was in good condition, and they quickly shipped it to Ocean City by truck.

The second vessel was an LCVP—a landing craft for vehicles and personnel—which they felt might be valuable for ferrying heavier loads. It was thirty-six feet long and ten and a half feet in the beam, with a high freeboard and a diesel engine that enabled it to travel at a speed of about eight knots. It was a clumsy, ungainly vessel in considerable need of repair, but they couldn't be choosy. It would do.

Finally, the partners' association with Portsmouth Salvage brought a new and valuable addition to their crew, the man who ultimately did most of the diving required by the salvage operation.

As a matter of fact, by this time, in early April, the *Queen* already boasted a fair-sized complement: four men in addition to the partners who owned her.

The first crewmen, brought out to the ship by Hazel and Doris to relieve Deir and Little after their first week there, were a burly young ex-serviceman named Mack Duncan and an older man, Howard Hill, who had once been a Merchant

Marine seaman and now made his living as a hunting guide in North Carolina.

Duncan had been knocking about Suffolk between jobs when he was approached by Deir's father-in-law, an old friend of Duncan's family, and offered a job guarding the tanker. It sounded interesting, and it paid better than the grocery-store job he had been considering, so he promptly accepted.

Hill had been suggested as a possible crewman by Little, and the women had driven to his home to sound him out. He was a slight, pleasant man who had readily agreed to go aboard the tanker; it was the off season for hunters and he could use the employment. He eventually did a couple of one-week hitches on the *Queen* and then quietly returned to North Carolina.

During the last week of March it had become necessary to relieve Duncan and Hill, then completing their first week of guard duty, and the salvagers set about finding two more men. Once again, Robert Parker, Mrs. Deir's father, had turned up a candidate. The man he suggested was Henley Doughtie, who was to become indispensable to the salvage operation.

Doughtie was a huge, crag-faced, red-haired man with the powerful but slightly bulbous physique of an overage athlete, the alcoholic capacity of an oak barrel and the limited but violent vocabulary of an old-time Army drill sergeant. It was said around Holland, where he lived, that he often consumed a half-dozen quarts of liquor in a day, without regard to kind or quality, that he never uttered a sentence that could be repeated in the presence of a clergyman, and that he had never known a man two weeks without insulting him atrociously. This was something of an exaggeration. It was also said that he had not an enemy in the world. This was true. He was a man of terrible aspect and gentle disposition, a man both fierce and inoffensive, with the bare-muscled strength of an Atlas and the capacity for work of a steam engine. He had an immense store of bad jokes, most of them astonishingly dirty. In spite of this he managed, in a way no one could ever quite explain, to be very funny.

Deir and Little called for Doughtie at his cluttered shack in Holland. It took him a long time to get ready. He puttered around the one room, swearing amiably and ferociously, searching for the things he wanted to take with him. They included a cast-iron frying pan—"I don't travel no place without that goddam sonofabitch," he explained to Little—several other cooking implements and a pint of cheap whisky which Little saw him slipping surreptitiously into his small suitcase between a couple of shirts. As Doughtie packed, he muttered obscenities to himself and made small talk. Suddenly he turned to Little.

"I ain't been feeling so goddam good," he said. "My wife done left me."

Little, surprised, said inadequately, "Well, I'm sure sorry to hear that."

"Yeah," said Doughtie, watching him sidelong. "Her goddam husband come and got her." A pleased smile flickered briefly across his face and he hoisted up his bag and said, "Well, let's go. Ain't gonna get to no damn ship layin' around here."

They hired another man at the same time. He was named, by the sheerest coincidence, *Tom* Doughty and he was also a drinking man. Tom was about thirty-five, a hard worker who quickly became Henley's constant companion and the chief butt of his insults and jokes.

At this time both Doughties were strange to Beldon Little, and the more he thought about them the less certain he was that they were suited for the job. Little, like Deir, did virtually no drinking. Like many another nondrinker, he worried a good deal about alcohol's effects on others. And he was disturbed now at the thought of placing the valuable tanker in the keeping of a couple of swillers. He thought of the two loaded shotguns on board and winced. Before starting out for Ocean City he quietly removed the whisky from Henley's bag, later telling Deir what he had done.

On the road that night the four men stopped at a diner, and Deir, Little and Tom Doughty went in for coffee. Henley chose to remain outside.

After half an hour, the three men emerged from the diner

87

to find Henley on his knees behind Brady's pickup truck. Strewn on the ground all about him were his clothes. He was feverishly pawing them, looking inside the shirts, shaking out spare pants, peering under piles of socks.

"Lose something?" Deir asked innocently.

Henley jumped to his feet. "No," he said. Then: "Well, yeah, I had something in this here goddam suitcase and now the bastard is gone and I'm damn if I know what become of it."

"What is it? We'll help you look."

"Naw," he said hastily. "It was nothing. It'll turn up, I guess. Don't bother."

He rode the rest of the way in the back of the truck, occasionally searching furtively in his bag, while the two men in front chuckled appreciatively and Tom Doughty watched in bewilderment.

In time Little learned that Henley was an absolutely dependable crewman, always. He also came to understand the older man's need for alcohol; after a while he actually began to bring Henley liquor whenever possible—taking great care that no one else knew about it. Deir did the same. They never hid a bottle from Henley again.

The sea was rough when they reached Ocean City, and they had trouble getting aboard the tanker. Kin's boat bobbed violently alongside, and to fend it off Deir braced his back against the smaller craft and his feet against the *Queen*, walking up and down along the tanker's side as the boat rose and fell with the swells.

Henley, no seaman, tried boarding the ship in two moves, stepping first into a convenient porthole. Halfway, he got a surprise assist from a wave and clambered aboard half soaked and furious.

"Did you *see* that sonofabitch!" he bellowed. "Picked my goddam ass up and like to throw me *over* the bastard!"

Howard Hill and Mack Duncan, after a solid week of guard duty, were delighted to see their replacements arrive. All during their stay on the ship the weather had been so terrible that not a single boatman of any kind had come near the *Queen*—Reed or anyone else. After three days the two men

88

had run out of food. Worse yet, they ran out of cigarettes. Desperately, they had dug around in odd corners of the tanker until they had found some cigarettes of doubtful origin in a soaked package, probably left behind by the original crew. These they had dried over the stove and smoked.

The seas had been awful. Several waves had broken clear over the tanker. Duncan, with virtually no sea experience, had not been bothered by the swells, but Hill, a former sailor, had scarcely slept. Both had been troubled greatly by the noises. Eventually, they became more or less accustomed to them, but never so much so that they weren't occasionally fooled. Toward the end of the week, when they had been without food for two days, Hill, rereading a magazine article for the third time, had suddenly leaped to his feet and had shaken Duncan, who was sleeping. "Mack!" he said urgently. "Wake up! A boat's coming!" They raced out on deck. There was nothing in sight but the same high gray waves. Puzzled, they returned to the cabin. In a little while they both heard the boat. They turned and sped back outside. Nothing.

"Damn them noises, anyhow," Duncan told the partners after the greetings and introductions were over. "I don't want no more of them!"

Henley glared about him balefully, listening. "Don't you worry," he said. "Miz' Doughtie's boy ain't gonna stay out here with no damn noises. I'll get them mother-lovers."

And he did. A week later when Hill and Duncan returned to the *Queen*, most of the noises were gone. By the time Henley had spent a few weeks on the tanker, he had conquered all the strange sounds but a few. He spent all his spare time—and there was plenty of that during his first stay—tramping grimly about the ship, tracking down every squeak and rattle. He threw pieces of loose pipe overboard, tied down flapping porthole covers, chinked up holes, blocked ventilators, tied squealing doors and hatches. One especially bothersome noise ran him a long chase. It was a kind of multiple whistle, very provoking, and it was days before he traced it to a door in the engine-room paint locker. The door was full of holes, and air was blowing through them as the sloshing water in the engine room rose and fell. Triumphantly, Henley plugged the holes and stepped back to listen. There was still one mocking whistle. He uttered a mighty oath. Then, struck by a thought, he leaped forward and jammed his last plug into the keyhole.

Not a sound.

During their first week on the *African Queen,* the two Doughties too, ran out of food, although they had brought an ample supply on board. Somehow, it was hard to ration oneself; there was nothing much to do but eat. When they ran out of cigarettes they, too, tried drying out old ones. It was like smoking red pepper, but it was better than not smoking. The worst thing that happened to them, though, was that they ran out of drinking water. Just when they were wondering if they would die of thirst, along came a tug, making its way up the coast. They hailed it and begged five gallons of water from the skipper. It lasted them until April 6, when their stint was up, and Hill and Duncan returned.

All during this time Deir and Little, and occasionally Brady, were working away on the LCVP, trying to get it ready to travel to Ocean City under its own power. The battered landing craft was up on a cradle in the Portsmouth Salvage yard, and the partners drew a daily audience of workers and idlers from the yard. They got plenty of advice.

"If I was you," offered one man, chewing on a toothpick, "I wouldn't bother with no tow for that tanker once I got her up. Hell, all in the world you got to do is get on your radio and give a call to the Coast Guard. Once she's afloat she's a ship adrift—right? Well, a ship adrift is in trouble—right? You send out an S.O.S. call and just wait for the Coast Guard to come rescue you. They'll pull you in." He flicked the toothpick away triumphantly. "Wouldn't cost you a nickel!"

Brady, who was there that day, grinned briefly. "Sure," he said. "The Coast Guard would come pull us, all right. They'd pull us right out to sea and sink us in deep water!"

That week Buddy Jacobson got a call from a man named Maurice Simmons. Simmons was a sheet-metal worker by trade, but this was the off-season and he wasn't making any money. His hobby was skin-diving or, more accurately, scuba diving, in which the skin-diver carries his own compressed air in a tank. He had been calling various scrap-and-salvage yards all day; did Jacobson know anyone who could use a diver?

"Come on over," Jacobson said.

When Simmons arrived, Jacobson introduced him to Little, Deir and Brady. The newcomer was a bright, cheerful fellow in his early twenties with crew-cut hair and a broad grin. They liked him immediately.

Maurice Simmons was a Navy veteran, married, with two small daughters and a third child on the way. His engaging, clean-cut appearance and constant high spirits gave an impression of extreme youthfulness; in fact, he was a highly perceptive adult, steady and capable of solid judgment. He was devoted to his family and any desire he may have had for adventure was amply satisfied by his hobby. But the opportunity to work on the *Queen* salvage appealed to him. For one thing, there was sure to be plenty of diving. For another, he could use the money, and the terms sounded good. He was offered ten dollars a day for each day aboard, plus a thousand-dollar bonus upon the successful completion of the venture, which they thought would take about five weeks. At that time the partners were under the impression that any earnings acquired outside U.S. territorial limits were tax-free (they did not learn until later that income remains taxable until the taxpayer has been outside the country for at least eighteen months). This error made the deal seem even more attractive to Simmons: a minimum of $1,250, tax-free, for five weeks' work (assuming the salvage was successful), after which he would be able to go back to his sheet-metal bench at the height of the season. He accepted.

The next day he helped them raise the LCVP off its cradle and into the water, ready for the trip to Ocean City.

9

Getting the LCVP safely to Ocean City was vitally important to the salvagers, and they planned the voyage with great care. She had a crew of four for the trip: Little, acting as skipper, Deir, Simmons and Tom Doughty, who was on his way back to the *Queen* for another spell of guard duty. Henley was booked for the voyage but roared off on a great binge at the last moment and couldn't be found at departure time.

Besides the crew, the vessel was to carry a cargo of diving equipment and assorted other gear. To get this stuff aboard the landing craft it was necessary to tie up to a dock, since there were no loading facilities at the Jacobson brothers' yard. The partners arranged to load up at a private pier a short distance away; the only stipulation the dock owners made was that they must clear out before seven the next morning because a large ship was due to tie up there at that time. After the loading, the LCVP was to pause briefly in Norfolk while Little did some grocery shopping to replenish the *Queen*'s larder and Deir hurried back to Suffolk to pick up a tarpaulin they had forgotten. They would all come together at Little Creek, on the seaward side of Norfolk, and proceed on the journey to Ocean City.

It was an efficient plan, calling for nothing more difficult than the split-second timing of a rocket launching. At the Portsmouth Salvage Yard a multitude of last-minute problems arose, and the hours ticked away as the men struggled to get their ungainly vessel ready to sail. It was dark when the LCVP finally groped uncertainly out into the Elizabeth River and headed for the pier to be loaded. She promptly ran onto a tidal flat. As soon as they got her off, her engine cut out. At last, close to midnight, she limped up to the dock, and the four men started back to the Portsmouth Salvage Company to get the equipment. Blundering through the yard of a large industrial plant in the darkness, they were almost shot by a night watchman. "We're just cutting through, for *God's* sake," Little said hastily. "Show us the way out, and we'll leave." The watchman finally let them go.

All night they worked at the loading. Before dawn the LCVP was ready to cast off again. Deir bade the others farewell and started off to Suffolk to get the tarpaulin. They had neglected to arrange for Deir's transportation, so he had to hitchhike home.

Deir's journey took hours, and he fretted anxiously, wondering what the others were thinking. In Suffolk he hastily gathered up the tarpaulin, borrowed Brady's truck to carry it in, and hurried back to Little Creek, where he was to meet the LCVP. He fully expected to be greeted by a fiercely impatient and possibly mutinous crew. It was mid-afternoon before he arrived.

They weren't there.

Long after dark, the cranky mutter of a diesel engine announced the arrival of the landing craft. She came panting up to the dock at midnight, having traveled twenty miles in roughly that many hours, counting in the stop at Norfolk. On the way, her engine had cut out repeatedly. Disgusted, the four men tied her up. Tom Doughty volunteered to remain on board, with a small bottle for company. The others went home for a couple of hours' sleep.

Early on the morning of April 11 they reconvened at Little Creek, turned the LCVP's blunt nose to the northeast, and headed hopefully across the mouth of Chesapeake Bay, bound for Ocean City at last. They planned to remain well out to sea, following the coast. To their left as they traveled would be the eastern shore of Virginia and Maryland, speckled with sand spits and creeks. Somewhere in that mosaic of tiny islands there was an inland waterway which might have afforded a safer route, but it was inadequately marked and of uncertain depth, and Little decided not to chance it.

Dawn found them chugging across the bay. The engine was still acting up, and no one could figure out why. On the other side of the bay they pulled into an inlet, and Simmons

93

went over the side in his diving suit to see if the propeller was fouled. It was not. They started up the engine again and pushed on.

As the sun rose in the sky, it got warmer, and they all relaxed. The trip began to be fun. They watched a large school of porpoises that churned up the water all around them, and they told stories and matched lies. Toward midday they lunched—on canned beans and Vienna sausage. They had traveled about fifty miles but had roughly twice that distance to go. Though the voyage seemed destined to set some kind of mad endurance record, nobody worried much except Deir.

He was not pleased with the way things were going. He had had misgivings about taking the outside route from the beginning. The LCVP had scraped across shoals a couple of times, so Little had moved still farther seaward, into the marked shipping lane several miles offshore. They were doing all right, and the seas were only slightly choppy, but Deir was worried about the engine. If it cut out this far out to sea they might be in real trouble. Besides, Deir was afflicted with a congenital distaste for any action that he had not originated. As the afternoon wore on he began to suggest to Little that they turn into one of the inlets along the coast and try the inland waterway.

"Lloyd, I tell you," said Little, "that inland waterway is not marked. A man can't see where he's going. I don't want to run aground in there and never get her off."

They were still discussing this question—and the discussion was growing somewhat heated—when it became academic. The engine stopped.

Both men leaped to its side. Little hit the starter. The engine grunted once and subsided. Little looked startled and tried again. There was no reason for the starter to fail; the battery was brand new. Again the engine turned over just once. A hasty check disclosed the trouble. Someone had left the electric bilge blower on, and it had drained the battery. On this boat ventilation of the bilge was totally unnecessary, but a bilge blower had been required by government specifications during the war. A few unkind words were said about the government.

In the silence they looked around them. The porpoises had disappeared. The sea, which had been choppy, was now glassy. The air was breathless, expectant. "Man, oh, man," said Deir. "If ever I saw a calm before a storm . . ."

The only thing to do was anchor and let the battery rest a bit and revive. They sat there uncomfortably, feeling the LCVP buck against the anchor line under the impact of the stiffening wind. Soon the boat was yanking at the anchor so fiercely that it scared them: another few minutes of this, they thought, and the snapping anchor line might rip out the side of the craft. With tremendous difficulty, all pulling together against the wind, they managed to draw their vessel up over the anchor and then pull the anchor in. Then they flopped down exhausted, still with nothing they could do except wait out the battery.

But now they were drifting—and fast. They were headed back for Norfolk, making much better time backward in the wind than they had forward under power. What was more, they were not traveling exactly parallel to the shore—the wind was carrying them inexorably toward the beach.

It began to rain. The waves were now running several feet high and extremely rough. The LCVP was not built for heavy weather, and her motion was becoming very strange—an ever-changing combination of roll, pitch, yaw and skid. Her bottom kept slamming against the water as the seas slipped out from under her. Simmons and Tom Doughty crouched under the tarpaulin, trying to stay dry, while Deir and Little hovered over the engine.

At last they dared try the battery again. While Deir held a can of ether to the intake (diesels, which often have trouble starting, thrive on this highly combustible fuel, so they had brought along several cans of the stuff), Little pressed the starter. The engine caught on the second cough. The motion of the LCVP changed as the propeller bit into the water. Slowly the vessel reversed direction and began to creep forward.

They sighted a fishing boat after a while and thankfully followed it into an inlet. They stayed behind it as it threaded its way up a half-hidden creek, and late that afternoon they were rewarded by the sight of a little village with a small dock. They tied up there and wearily climbed out.

It was too late to go on. The best course would be to sleep on the LCVP that night and push for Ocean City Sunday morning. They would take the inland waterway; there was no longer much point in arguing about it.

The town was Oyster, Virginia, a one-pump community consisting entirely of a few ramshackle houses and a general store, to which they repaired for supper. They ate standing up at a counter, dipping into cans which the store owner obligingly opened for them. The menu was cold pork and beans and Vienna sausage.

The rain was still pelting down, and by nightfall the weather had turned bitterly cold. Back aboard the LCVP they all had trouble falling asleep. Deir and Little finally started up the engine (perversely, it was now working fine) and climbed on top of it for warmth. Simmons and Tom Doughty huddled in the bow, but it was too cold there to sleep. After a while Doughty lighted a bucketful of diesel oil and he and Simmons crouched down near it. At last they all dropped off. Over them was the tarpaulin, covering the landing craft from bow to stern.

They awoke Sunday morning coughing and snorting. Under the tarp, the LCVP was filled with a blue, noxious fog.

"Hey, man, put out that damn fire," Deir gasped.

They pulled back the tarpaulin and stared at one another in astonishment. From head to foot, they were coal black. Their eyes glared grotesquely out of their pitchy faces; their teeth gleamed brilliantly as they talked. There was oil soot in their noses, and the taste of diesel fuel was in their mouths.

That ended the voyaging for the day. It was clear that they couldn't go farther looking like this, and there was no way to get cleaned up. The weather was terrible anyhow, and it had been a jinx-struck voyage. They voted to go home and try again Monday.

They scraped off some of the soot and Deir scouted around Oyster until he found a telephone. He called a cab from the town of Cheriton, a few miles away. When it got there the four wild-looking travelers piled in gratefully and started home. The LCVP, well covered and securely tied up, was left overnight in Oyster.

From his home in Suffolk that night Beldon Little put in a call to Kin Reed in Maryland. Reed had been raised in this clam- and oyster-digging country; would he come down and pilot this jinx ship through the inland waterway to Ocean City? "Why, sure," said Kin. "Jinxes don't bother me none."

And so it was that, as the LCVP putted glumly away from Oyster on Monday morning, Kin Reed was at the wheel, with Little beside him and Simmons and Doughty in their accustomed places up forward. Deir was missing. He had had enough of a sailor's life for a while. He was back in Suffolk, making better use of his time, getting some equipment ready to take out to the tanker.

The landing craft's troubles were not over. Repeatedly they lost their way or scraped over humps in the unmarked channel. And then, twenty-five miles up the waterway, at a point where a stream crossed the channel on its way to the sea, the LCVP ran aground. Kin backed her off and tried again to go through—and again at another place, and then at every conceivable deep spot in the intersection. In all, they spent an hour there. Nothing worked. Chagrined, they turned around, with no alternative but to go all the way back to Oyster and then head out to sea again.

A couple of miles along the return trip they saw an old clam-digger on the bank. They pulled over and explained their problem, and he nodded. "There's a way through, all right," he said, "but you got to know it."

"Well, how about taking us through?"

He pondered, then shook his head. "Can't," he said. "That ain't rightly my work. Don't like to get messing around such things. Besides," he said, eying them, "I'd lose all that time. I could be making money clamming."

In the end they agreed to pay him for what he would lose in clams—two dollars—and he came aboard, tying up his boat at the stern of the LCVP. "This really ain't my business," he complained.

As they neared the shoal he took the wheel. "Somebody

97

stand by that engine," he ordered, "and do like I say."

They watched, fascinated, as he drove the ungainly craft head on toward the shallow place. Abruptly he turned the vessel hard to the right, running straight down the creek toward the sea. "Now!" he commanded. "Gimme speed!" Little poured on power and the old clam-digger rolled the wheel hard over in a tight U-turn to the left. "More power," he cried. "More power!" Little winced, but shoved the throttle full forward. Suddenly they were across the shoal and running back up the opposite side of the stream, still under full power. When they reached the waterway the clam-digger spun the wheel again and put them back on course. It was a masterful performance.

Little reached into his pocket and handed the old man a five-dollar bill. "Keep it all," he said in a strained voice. "It was worth it."

As the clam-digger was climbing back into his boat, he paused, then remarked, "Corps of Engineers is dredging all through here. Come summer they'll have this channel all marked." He shook his head sadly. "Gonna take a deep bite out of my income. Summers, I get as many as three boats a day over that bar."

The rest of the trip was more or less without incident. They chugged up the waterway, backing and filling and feeling their way, and late that afternoon they finally pulled into the Ocean City inlet.

But they had not heard the last of that ill-starred voyage.

10

ON THE SAME Monday on which the LCVP reached Ocean City, Paul Brady got a telephone call from Buddy Jacobson. Jacobson sounded angry.

"Paul, one of my men went to Maryland yesterday to visit the tanker. Somebody told him the LCVP was at some little town on the eastern shore so he stopped off on the way back. And you know what he found? That landing craft was tied up there without a soul aboard to guard her! They'd all gone off and left it sitting there, just like that!"

His voice rose.

"Now look, Paul, I hate to say this, and I know it isn't your fault, but this is no way to do business. I can't go along with it. I'm through! I'm not putting maybe fifty thousand dollars into this job and then they go up there and leave the boat, with all that stuff on it, unprotected among a lot of people they don't know. That's a fishing town. All those people can use this kind of gear. Those guys will be lucky if there's anything left when they get back. If they're *going* back. I've had enough, Paul. I'm sorry. I'm finished."

Brady was aghast. He tried to remonstrate, but Jacobson was in no mood for talk.

"I'm getting out of this," he said flatly. "It's a crazy deal. Those guys don't know what they're doing. They have no responsibility. If you take my advice, Paul, you'll get out, too, while there's still time."

He hung up.

Deir had walked into Brady's store while Jacobson was on the phone. Brady, still stunned, told him what had happened. He shook his head bleakly.

"Lloyd," Brady said, "I'm licked. There's just no way in the world I can do this alone. I've already sunk more into this thing than I should. There are a lot of expenses coming up, and they're more than I can handle. Without the Jacobsons I've got to pull out, too."

"Now, wait, Paul, you *can't* do that!" Deir protested. He began pacing rapidly about the shop. "Paul, I tell you, *we'll get her up!* You can *believe* that! God *knows*, we'll get her up. There's nothing that can stop us. Nothing!" He stopped.

"I tell you," he said levelly, "*I'm going to get that ship off*. I've never seen a job I couldn't handle once I started, and I'll handle this one. With Jacobson or without him. Paul, I tell you, man, there's nothing to *worry* about!"

"Lloyd," said Brady in exasperation, "that's easy for you to say. You're not sitting there watching your bank balance sink like a rock. Look, I'm a businessman. When I look at my checkbook I like to see some go out, some come in. This way

99

it's all going out! It's been a month now, and we're still buying stuff. I can't do it alone, Lloyd, I just can't."

They were sitting there looking at each other in glum silence when a customer walked in. Brady waved listlessly.

"Hi, Mr. Sadler," he said. "Don't you want to get in on this ship deal of ours?"

"I might," said Mr. Sadler.

Alvah E. Sadler, portly and dignified, was a prominent Suffolk businessman. He was bluff, soft-spoken and pleasant, with a thick crop of graying hair and a marked air of prosperity about him. Sadler may not have been the richest man in town, but he was known to be very well off. He had made most of his money by backing his judgment on prospects that other men often considered wildly speculative. Currently he was engaged in a major way in real-estate promotions, in which his poker-table instincts served him well, and he had half a dozen other thriving enterprises on the side. He had never had anything to do with salvage or shipping.

But Sadler had been wistfully aware of the *African Queen* salvage for some time. It was exactly the kind of project that appealed to him: challenging and a trifle uncertain, but with a big payoff if successful. He would have given a good deal to have been part of it. But he hadn't been invited, and his Virginia-gentleman code made it impossible for him to raise the matter himself.

The fact is that Brady had at one time thought of approaching Sadler with an offer of partnership—he obviously was a likely prospect—but had been forestalled by the entry of the Jacobson brothers. Lloyd Deir, on his part, had actually discussed the *Queen* project with Sadler a few days before during a chance street-corner encounter; it had been only a casual conversation, and nothing more had come of it.

Now, in Brady's store, the two partners exchanged exultant looks, well aware that Sadler's fortuitous appearance (he had come to pay a bill) could mean a complete turnabout in their fortunes. They told him more about their plans—and their plight. That night the three met again in Sadler's office.

By the end of the day Sadler was fully briefed, and almost committed.

As it turned out, some weeks passed before he became the fourth and final member of the partnership; he wanted to see the tanker first, and a succession of unforeseen circumstances delayed his visit. But in the meantime Deir, Little and Brady felt justified in counting on him. It made all the difference in the difficult and exciting weeks that followed.

With financing apparently assured, the partners were able to wind up their preliminary shopping operation. They had an amicable parting with Portsmouth Salvage after all, during which it was agreed that they would buy the LCVP and the rearming boat at cost. They picked up the pumps they had arranged to buy, and also got a small generator with which to test them (it was just large enough to run one pump at a time). The pumps proved to be badly fouled, and Deir and Little spent some days painstakingly overhauling them.

The one major item of equipment still lacking was a large generator. They needed a tremendous amount of electric power—enough to run all the pumps at once, to light the tanker internally, and to provide the outside lights required by the Coast Guard to warn off shipping (they were now using lights powered by batteries). All this was a substantial order, calling for a hundred-kilowatt generator. Brady, who was still paying the bills pending Sadler's final decision to join up, began to worry about money again—and with good reason. He had already gone well over the thousand-dollar limit they had originally set for this first phase of equipment-buying, and a generator that size might cost several thousand alone.

"But not if we pick up the parts secondhand and put them together ourselves," said Deir.

The parts in this instance consisted primarily of the generator itself and the engine required to run it. By dint of the most careful kind of shopping they found a workable marine diesel engine (cost: $600) and, in the same scrap yard, a generator, still attached to a useless engine (cost: $750). Putting them together would be no problem. But getting the generator off the old engine proved problem enough.

The generator was covered by a three-quarter-inch cast-iron bell housing that had to be removed before the bolts would be accessible. The only way to remove this housing was to smash it. Accordingly, one morning Deir, Little and Henley Doughtie—then enjoying a week off the tanker—showed up at the scrap yard with a sledge hammer and attacked the housing. Deir, a tough, wiry man, led off. For some minutes he pounded at the cast iron. The damage he did was negligible. He paused, winded, while they all looked at the housing with surprise and respect. Then Doughtie reached for the hammer with one huge hand. "Let Miz Doughtie's boy get a crack at that goddam thing," he said.

Henley was fortified that morning by approximately half a quart of liquor—just enough to make him feel like beating sense into a recalcitrant hunk of iron, but not enough to prevent him from doing it. He hefted the hammer lovingly. "Your trouble," he said, leering at Deir, "is you didn't have a *man* hittin' at that sonofabitch."

He raised the hammer above his head, paused, and brought it down with a thunderous crack. A great chip of cast iron flew off in one direction, and the hammer and part of the handle hurtled in another. Henley tossed aside the fragment of handle and beckoned grandly to the yard foreman, who was watching in amusement from the sidelines. "Let's have us a decent goddam hammer here," Doughtie said.

His second blow with the yard hammer broke its handle, too. The foreman got him another. "Don't break it," he said.

"*I'm* doin' this goddam job," Henley rumbled, aggrieved. "Please get away. You annoying the ass off me."

He aimed a ferocious blow at the housing. It hit fair, smashing off another large chunk of iron—and also the handle of the sledge hammer. The foreman produced another, but not without protest. "You'll have us out of business," he complained, half amused, half annoyed. "What are we going to do around here for sledge hammers if you break them all?"

"Why don't you put *handles* into your goddam sledge hammers where a *man* can use 'em?" Henley bellowed, enjoying himself hugely. "You got a goddam *man* using these goddam sledge hammers this day!"

He broke another. A small audience of yard workers had gathered to enjoy Henley's performance and the foreman's discomfiture, and Deir and Little were now laughing so hard they couldn't have lifted a sledge hammer with both hands. The foreman, grinning helplessly, kept supplying Doughtie with hammers; Doughtie kept breaking them. The two men maintained a constant exchange of protest and insult until the yard resounded with laughter.

"We can't keep you in handles forever!" said the foreman. "How many of those things do you think we carry here?"

"You irritating me bad," said Henley. "I don't give a goddam about you to start with. You keep messin' around me I gonna kill myself a man!"

He broke five sledge hammer handles and one hand hammer handle (after the yard had run out of sledge hammers) before the housing was demolished. He complained bitterly all the while about the quality of equipment "you got nowadays."

"Brother," said the foreman, gathering up the fragments ruefully, "it'd take two men putting on handles just to keep up with you. Take your damn generator and get it out of here before I start charging you for sledge hammers."

Muttering and grumbling in great good spirits, Henley helped Deir and Little move the generator away. It had been one of the most pleasant mornings of his life, and in later weeks he regaled his crewmates on the *African Queen* with highly embellished accounts of how he had simultaneously bested the scrap iron with his muscles and the yard foreman with his mouth, while wrecking vast numbers of hammers in the process. It made a great story, and as often as it was told everybody laughed—but Little and Deir took care thereafter never to let Doughtie swing a sledge hammer of theirs.

At last one day late in the spring Brady drove to Ocean City with Sadler. They met Deir there at daybreak, and the three partners boarded the rearming boat, with Kin Reed at the tiller, and started out to see the *Queen*.

It was a murky morning, and Reed missed the tanker entirely and had to grope for it in the fog. They beat on oil drums to signal the ship—but when the men on the *Queen* signaled back by pounding on the vessel's great smokestack, nobody on the rearming boat could figure out where the sound had come from. They found the tanker at last by blundering into it on the starboard side; Reed had to act fast to keep the small boat from running right onto the sunken tank deck.

The fog cleared rapidly after they went aboard, and Sadler took a conducted tour of the big wreck. Like everyone getting his first look at the tanker, Sadler found it extremely impressive. He went back in that night and stayed with the Reed family. The next day, a Sunday, he spent sitting in the sun on the stern section, fishing.

That night he and Brady drove back to Suffolk. Before he left he confirmed his decision to join the three partners, and he bound the agreement by making an immediate contribution of two thousand dollars to pay pending bills.

In the weeks that followed, many more such contributions came from Sadler. For a time Brady tried to match him, but at last he had to stop. Profoundly depressed, he told Sadler that he had reached the end of his rope. The salvage project had cost far more than any of them had anticipated, and Brady could no longer raise money. Since it had been agreed that anyone who dropped out before the completion of the operation would lose any investment he had made, Brady was heartsick. Nevertheless, he felt that he had no alternative. He would have to quit.

"I won't hear of it," Sadler said quietly. "You've made your contribution. From now on you just stop worrying about money—you hear? You let me take care of it. But there's a lot you can do, and I don't see how this operation could get on without you."

So Brady stayed, gratefully. Ultimately, Sadler bore almost the entire financial burden of the salvage project. Though it was understood that he would get his full investment back before there was any division of profits, the arrangement still left virtually the whole gamble on his shoulders. But then, he was a man who liked to gamble.

Yet he did one thing that made it clear he considered this a far greater gamble than any he had ever been involved in before. He kept his participation in the *Queen* salvage a complete secret from his friends and business associates—and even, until the last few weeks, from his wife. He had a reason. He was involved in many business deals with many people over a wide area, and he felt he couldn't let word get around that he was so deeply committed to anything so risky.

The first phase of the salvage program was now over. The partnership was complete, the project was on a firm financial footing, the necessary material—insofar as they could predict their needs—was on hand. More would be required later, but, in general, operations would now move from the land out to the stricken ship itself. The actual salvage work—first inspection, then repair—could begin.

TWO

II

WITH THE SALVAGE operation entering a new phase, Maurice Simmons found himself at center stage. Before anything else could be done, the salvagers had to know the extent and nature of the damage to the tanker's hull. Were there just a few small holes that could be patched easily with separate plates of steel? Or was there one gigantic hole that would require an equally gigantic patch—or even the unthinkable: a hole so big that it would utterly defeat efforts to patch it? Was the damage restricted to the vessel's side or did it extend to her bottom? If there was bottom damage the tanker probably would have to be rolled up on one side with the bow as anchor as Deir had originally planned, although Brady and Sadler felt this method might be prohibitively expensive, and Little was not sure it would work. How wide an area did the damage cover? And what was the profile of the damaged sections—did they extend down into the curved part of the hull in such a way that the patches would have to be tailored into an odd shape? There were countless questions, and no one could find the answers but Simmons, the man who would do the salvagers' diving.

Simmons, as the weeks had passed, had proved himself to be a willing and valuable worker. He had done a couple of tricks of guard duty on the *Queen* and had busied himself repairing portholes, shifting equipment and generally making ready for the operations to come. He had also shown himself to be an excellent companion, cheerful and co-operative, with a quick intelligence and ready wit. By the beginning of June he and Deir, in particular, had become good friends.

During those early weeks he had dived only twice, not counting his inspection of the LCVP propeller shaft back in April. The first of these dives had most unfortunate results; the second was brilliantly successful.

It was in mid-April, just after Simmons' arrival on the *Queen,* when Beldon Little asked him to go down and see if he could close some portholes that were swinging open underwater. When the time came to pump out the vessel, all such openings would have to be sealed. Simmons was reluctant to go down. He didn't feel the same confidence in the tense, hot-tempered Little that he felt in Deir. But Deir was in Virginia, and Simmons could not refuse to do the job he had been hired for. He put on his rubber suit—which was intended for use in much warmer water but was all he owned—and, with Little as his tender, slipped into the sea by the stern of the tanker. The result was a fiasco, made all the worse by the fact that Simmons became too rattled to figure out what had gone wrong until it was too late.

When he entered the water he was completely unable to submerge. Instead, he floated near the surface, struggling. When he tried to swim down, his feet remained visible above the water. Duncan and Reed and the two Doughties, watching from the rail, were highly amused. Little was not. Their reactions served to confuse Simmons further.

He finally climbed out of the water, whereupon he was lectured by Little ("If you weren't an experienced diver you should have admitted it and not tried to fool us") and unmercifully ribbed by the others ("*You* got down all right; it's just that your feet ain't good divers"). He was humiliated and hurt. It occurred to him only after he had changed back into his work clothes that on this first dive of the day he should have carried sufficient weight to make up for the air bubbles that always remained trapped in his suit until he was under a while. By then it was too late to say anything.

The most important aftermath of the episode was that it brought about a bitter exchange between Deir and Little a few days later.

"You shouldn't have talked to him like that," Deir said. "He's gonna be all right if he's left alone. But how do you expect a man to do his best when you jump on him like that?"

Little's temper flared. "You can't tell me a man's a diver, been down a hundred and ten feet, and then he gets out here and can't even get underwater. If you want to school him where he can get down and learn to dive, okay. But a job like this is no place to hold school! I've been telling you we need hard-hat equipment"—he meant the pressurized suit with helmet used by most professional divers—"but no, you wouldn't listen. Well, I know one thing: I'm gonna get a *diver* out here!"

Relations between the two men were not improved when Deir, in chastising the other crew members for riding Simmons, commented, "One thing you've gotta remember. A diver is as good as his tender."

But then came Simmons' second dive, which more than made up for the first.

The assignment itself was enough to curdle the blood. Simmons was to go down *inside* the ship, through the half-submerged pantry, filled with spoiled and rotting meat and vegetables, and from there proceed by a dark and cluttered passageway into the food lockers deep on the starboard side of the ship. There he was to close some portholes that were gaping open. He would then be perhaps fifty feet from the point at which he had started.

This time Deir was on hand—as well as Little and the two Doughties. Although the water was icy cold Simmons was, of necessity, wearing the same warm-weather suit. On his back were the scuba tanks. He had a rope around his waist so he could find his way out again and a battery-powered battle lantern in his hand.

Simmons looked with distaste at the garbage-filled water, then grinned briefly, slipped the glass mask over his face, and waded into the room. In a moment he was submerged (there was no problem this time) and a second later he was gone from sight. Deir and Little stood on the slanted floor of the outer room with the dirty water lapping about their feet and watched the line paying out as Simmons moved ahead somewhere deep inside the ship.

The corridor in which the diver found himself swimming

was a scant thirty inches wide, and pitch dark. It was lined with bins for sugar and flour, and these bins, hinged at the bottom, had swung open, impeding his passage. He clawed his way along, reaching back occasionally to unsnag his line, ducking around obstructions that were barely visible by the occasional flashes of the battle lantern. Strange shapes floated in the water—unrecognizable lumps of food that had been submerged now for more than five months. Simmons was very buoyant—too buoyant—but it was too late to go back. He kept drifting up to the ceiling and having to scramble for leverage so he could keep moving.

There was a sudden, brief glare of light, and he leaped back, startled. Moving closer, he saw that he had come to the storeroom, and that the light was caused by the flapping of the metal porthole covers, blown in and out by the sea. The water outside the ship was almost as bright as daylight.

Simmons was now terribly cold, shivering uncontrollably in his thin rubber suit. He was also worried. The portholes were back behind some deep shelves, and he would have to crawl through the shelves to reach them. Water was gushing in and out of the room; he could feel a powerful back-and-forth surge every time the porthole covers swung open and shut. He would have to be careful not to get sucked into the open port and stuck there. Worse, the covers were slamming shut with enormous force. If one of his hands got caught in there, he would certainly lose it.

He edged warily forward, into the room. He had trouble remaining upright, but he grabbed hold of a shelf and stood for a while, watching the swinging porthole covers. Then, very carefully, he slipped between the first set of shelves, hanging on tight. The cover flipped open and a great current swept over him. Then the direction of the flow changed and the cover whacked shut. Instantly, Simmons grabbed for the locks and dogged the cover down tight. One finished.

Shaking violently, he backed into the room again and looked along the shelves. Two portholes to go. His lifeline kept getting tangled; exasperated, he had to keep reaching back to flip it free.

As he approached the second porthole he was suddenly

hurled back by the surging water. It slammed him across the room, scraping him against the ceiling, twisting and turning him until he was wrapped in his line, completely disoriented. His flailing arms banged against shelves and pipes and open doors. At last he grabbed one of these obstructions and held himself fast. Then he slowly disentangled himself, paused a moment, and crawled doggedly to the porthole.

Lying between the shelves, he braced himself against the next surge, and then pounced as the cover whipped shut. Two done.

The last one was easy; he had the hang of it now. He waited for it to slam, dogged it tight, and slipped thankfully off the shelves. His skin was now so cold that it burned, and he was shaking so hard that he could scarcely control his movements. Still, he carefully examined the room before leaving, to make sure there were no more portholes: he didn't want to make this trip again. Then he painfully pulled himself back along the line—out of the room, through the long passageway with its open bins, and toward the light at the other end.

As he started out of the water his line snagged again—just as he was about to get his head clear of the water. Patiently he went back and cleared it. At last, blue with cold, he slowly came out into the room where Little and Deir stood. He had been under for twenty minutes.

They rushed him out of his suit and down the passage to the kitchen-bunkroom, where the stove was keeping things warm. Little found a bottle of liquor, and Simmons swallowed a bit. After a long time he began to warm up again. Deir peered at him.

"Get 'em?" he asked.

Simmons grinned. "Got 'em," he said.

"That boy surprised me," Little said afterward. "He really did."

With the food locker sealed up, Deir put in four pumps, hooked them up to the generator, and pumped the section dry. Brady had been protesting about the inaction on the *Queen*—it was more than two months since Deir and Little had taken over the tanker—and now at least *something* had been done. Also, there was in the back of Deir's mind the wisp of an idea: even if there were more holes in the ship than could be patched, perhaps her tanks could be blown full of compressed air and some of the water pumped out of undamaged areas aft—and maybe, just maybe, that would be enough to get her up off the bottom. It was, although he had no way of knowing it, a plan Merritt-Chapman & Scott had weighed months before. He mentioned it to no one.

As for Little, he could see no use in any of this. "For the Lord's sake," he said. "Fix her, *then* pump her. You're just sending dimes after dollars! It's all a waste of time."

Deir kept his counsel.

On June fifth, Simmons made his first dive outside the tanker. He was now wearing a so-called "wet suit," a sponge rubber affair better adapted to cold-water diving, which he had made himself back in Norfolk with his mother's help.

Deir was worried about the danger of diving near the damaged section, with its tons of water pouring in and out through presumably jagged holes. So Simmons' initial diving began far astern of the damaged area—in fact, nearer to the port side than the starboard. They now had a new life raft— a surplus Navy float consisting of a cork-filled rim around a floor of wooden slats—and they put this over the side to serve as a diving platform.

Simmons went down without difficulty again and again that day, covering a wider area with each dive, slowly making his way around the stern toward the damaged side. As he progressed he noted the first signs of damage: a number of rivet holes which had been sprung open by the battering up forward. On deck, Little began whittling pegs of broomstick to use as plugs; the wood would swell in the water and fix itself firmly in the holes. As Simmons moved slowly forward, plugging the holes with the pegs, he found more and more of them. Soon Little's hands were blistered from all the whittling.

When Simmons came up from his last dive he still hadn't

seen any real damage. "Not a peapickin' rip in her anywhere," he said.

"You'll find some," Deir answered. Just wait."

The next day Simmons went down again, starting at the point where he had left off the day before, but using the re-arming boat—otherwise known to the men as the "barge" or the "scow"—as a diving platform. He was now well along the starboard side, and there were rivet holes aplenty. He took to carrying a large supply of wooden plugs in his belt. He ran across other signs of damage now—great dents and wrinkles in the skin of the hull—and reported this to Deir, who was tending his safety line.

"Looks like somebody stood off with a maul and just pounded her," Simmons said.

"How about holes?"

"No holes except rivet holes."

Simmons continued diving until almost dark, taking it easy, moving slowly forward, plugging rivet holes as he went. Several times Deir asked about punctures in the ship's side, but when Simmons knocked off for the day he still hadn't seen any. "There's some kind of shadow up forward," he said, "but it was too dark to see what it was."

That night Deir worked by lantern light, constructing a contraption of pipes that could be hooked on the side of the rearming boat as a small platform for Simmons to rest on between dives. The side of the boat was too high for him to climb.

It was late when Deir got to sleep, but he was up early the next morning, as were the others. Considerable tension was developing aboard the *Queen*. During two days of diving Simmons had found no real damage. But the damage must be there. By now Simmons had examined a large portion of the starboard side of the hull. He was within forty or fifty feet of the tank deck, and still he hadn't found the holes through which the water was pouring in and out of the engine room. Did that mean the main damage was *under* the ship? That would be catastrophic; even rolling the *Queen* up on her side might not fully expose such damage. For many weeks now they had been expending money and effort, and risking their lives, and still they had no idea how big a project they had undertaken. That simply couldn't go on.

Shortly after dawn Kin Reed came out in the rearming boat. It was a Sunday, and Sadler was with him. Sadler joined Little and Henley Doughtie at the rail of the tanker, while Tom Doughty, Reed and Deir manned the rearming boat, which was serving again as a diving float for Maurice Simmons.

Simmons' forward progress had now carried him so close to the tanks that he was beginning to encounter the turbulent water that poured endlessly off the *Queen's* low midsection. The breakers that rolled up the slanted deck and hissed back into the sea were roiling the water for some distance off the tanker's side. As a consequence, before the new day's diving began it was decided that the rearming boat would have to be anchored at least seventy-five feet away from the hull of the *Queen*; Simmons would go down at that point and walk along the bottom, under the worst of the turbulence, until he was close enough to continue his inspection. As an anchor he would carry a small steel plate at the end of a rope; the day before he had had trouble staying upright in the increasingly rough sea.

"Now, look," said Deir. "It's getting dangerous down there, and I'm worried. If you get in any kind of trouble, give one sharp yank on the line and, man, I'll pull you up faster than you can think."

It was 8:00 A.M. when Simmons slipped over the side of the rearming boat, pulled down his mask, gripped his air hose firmly between his teeth, and disappeared below the surface for his first dive of the day. He was gone a long time, while they all waited anxiously. The safety line kept paying out as he moved along the bottom, and Deir held it tentatively, ready to haul away at the first twitch.

Then it grew slack. After a while Simmons broke the surface. Deir lighted a cigarette and silently handed it to the diver as he pushed up his mask. Simmons took a great drag, grinning. "Deir," he said, "I've got good news for you. I've found you a hole."

"Well, boy, that's great!" said Deir. "Tell me about it!"

"I can't tell you very much because I couldn't see much. I almost got pulled into the peapicker."

When he had reached bottom, Simmons reported, he had found himself in a great shallow depression in the sand, a wide pit blown out by the action of the water pouring off the *Queen's* tank deck some thirty feet above. The sea around this place was so murky with floating sand that he could see nothing as he plodded through it. Then he began to emerge from the sand cloud, and immediately he found himself staring at something that, to his hasty glance, resembled nothing so much as a relief map of the moon, with great gusts of water billowing in and out of it. As he moved closer he got caught by the suction of the water. He scrambled frantically back and finally got out of its way, but it had given him a good scare.

"All right, look," said Deir. "Don't worry about getting sucked in there. I've got you good. I want you to go back down, off to one side where you don't get in front of that stream, and look at it *hard.* Just stand there and look at it. Then come back and tell me."

Simmons tossed away his cigarette, pulled down his mask and disappeared once again beneath the water.

Again there was a long delay. While Simmons was gone Deir told the men on the *Queen* what the diver had found. Then they waited anxiously for his return. Suddenly he shot up again. He pushed up his mask and wiped the water from his face.

"Deir," he said, "let's go home."

"Okay, tell me," Deir said quietly. "What did you see? What did it look like?"

"It looked like hell. My God, Deir, the whole side of the ship is out! There's one hole down there as big as a house. It's kind of an oval dent, maybe eight or ten feet across, and right in the middle of it is a great big hole, about four feet. Like the hole in the middle of a funnel."

"What about the rest?"

"Well, it's just awful. I couldn't see it all, but it's all chewed up. It's damaged something fierce, no kidding."

"Okay, now we have to know exactly what's down there. Exactly, understand? You go back down and keep moving along, and every time you see a hole, stand there and look at it, and then come back and tell me what it looks like. We've got all day, Maurice. Take your time. Stand there and look. Look hard. One hole at a time."

For the rest of that day, Simmons bobbed up and down the side of the tanker. Each time he came up he would climb into the rearming boat and, with a piece of chalk, draw a new part of the picture on the boat's wooden engine housing. It was a long, hard day and an anxious one. Aboard the *Queen* nobody could tell what was going on. There was some shouting back and forth across the seventy-five feet separating the two groups of men but it wasn't very satisfactory. Finally, Little, in a fury of impatience, stripped off his clothes, plunged over the side and swam out to the rearming boat. He interrupted a tense conference between Simmons and Deir.

"How big is the hole?" he asked.

Simmons, still peeved with Little, gestured vaguely. "Oh, yay big," he said.

"*Yay big?*" shouted Little. "What's that mean? Look, buddy, you're a sheet-metal worker. Never mind 'Yaying'! Damn it, give it to me in feet, yards, inches!"

"Well," said Simmons, "there are a lot of holes, not just one. Hell, I don't know how big they are."

"Well, is it something where small patches will fix it up, or one big patch, or what?"

"Look," said Deir with asperity, "let him find out what's down there. There's no sense asking Maurice what kind of patch she needs. He's not the engineer on this job! That's for you and me to decide!"

Furious, Little glared, then wheeled and dived back into the water. When he reached the ship he grabbed a rope hanging over the side and pulled himself up hand over hand, a feat that left Simmons gaping. "Boy," he said, "I couldn't do that."

As the afternoon wore on, Simmons ventured closer and closer to the rent side of the tanker, and Deir, concerned, kept a tighter hold on the rope. "Hey," said Simmons in a provoked tone after one dive, "either you're gonna saw me in half with that rope or I'm never gonna get close enough to see anything. Cut it out, huh? Give me a little slack."

"Hell, you go ahead and pull, man. I'm not gonna give you any more line than what you have. If you go flying into that big hole down there I want to *know* it!"

And then, during one descent, Simmons inadvertently kicked the line. Suddenly it pulled tight around his waist and he shot toward the top. He grabbed the metal plate to hold himself down, but it did no good. He swept upward, plate and all. He flailed his arms and legs and reached down frantically to grab up a big piece of pipe that lay on the bottom. He gave two yanks on the line to signal Deir that everything was all right. He tried to swim against the pull of the rope. Nothing made any difference. Off balance and helpless, he flew up through the water. Finally he broke the surface and pushed up his mask, chuckling. "Something you wanted?" he asked Deir. "Or is it all right with you if I go back to work?"

Simmons made fifteen dives that day. By the middle of the afternoon they had a clear picture of the damage. It was extensive, appalling. The side of the ship was slashed and scarred almost as if by an explosion. The big funnel-shaped hole, farthest aft, was the worst. Leading into it was a great L-shaped gash that ran diagonally down from the upper right to the rim of the funnel, and then vertically toward the bottom of the sea. Above the funnel was a small ragged puncture, and forward of that, above the L, was another small hole with deep dents around it. Still farther forward was another vertical slash perhaps ten feet high, and beside it a smaller horizontal one. There were exceedingly deep dents on both sides of the damaged area, and the whole center of the area was concave, battered in. Where the diagonal slash met the big hole, one piece of metal was flapping free.

From the deck of the tanker, Little let down two weighted lines and Simmons planted them on either side of the perforated area. Then they measured the size of the damaged section from above. About thirty feet—a tremendous distance. Simmons also measured the top-to-bottom spread: twenty feet. There was one piece of good news: all the damaged plates appeared to be above the bottom curve of the hull. The damage was accessible.

Thoughtfully, the men on the rearming boat returned to the tanker. It had been the busiest and most sobering day's work of the entire operation. On the deck of the *Queen* they all gathered around for a conference, and Simmons once again drew his picture of the damaged area.

The flapping plate worried Deir. "How fast do you figure that water's moving in and out of there?" he asked. "Could you keep your hand in front of it?"

"Not a chance," Simmons said. "You put your hand in there"—he held up his hand, then whipped it back—"and, boy, it's gone!"

"Man, it can't be that bad," Deir remonstrated anxiously.

Sadler had been listening. "Well, Deir, what do you think?"

"Same as before," Deir said instantly. "We're gonna fix her and get her out of here. Don't you think different for a moment."

The discussion went on long after they had moved indoors for supper. Everyone pitched in, glad to have something to talk about at last. For the first time they could start making plans.

One plan both Deir and Little agreed on without argument. Any thought of small patches was out of the question now. It would be one big patch—one *huge* patch, a patch of such dimensions that it was staggering to think about, a patch that would create problems far beyond anything they had encountered so far.

12

SEVERAL IMPORTANT things remained to be done before the actual repair and refloating of the ship could be attempted.

In the first place it was agreed, at last, to try hard-hat diving. A new man could confirm Simmons' findings (although Deir considered this unnecessary). If he was a diver of experience, he could presumably offer some guidance on the over-all job as well. And possibly most important, as Little repeatedly pointed out, a helmeted diver would have instant communication with the deck by phone; he wouldn't have to keep bobbing up and down to report, as Simmons did.

Little himself had entertained some thought of diving and had actually tried it during Simmons' first day of underwater inspection. He had used scuba paraphernalia, which was new to him, and, much to Simmons' delight, it had given Little so much trouble that he had finally had to quit. Now he tried to get hold of a helmet and suit that he could use, but was unable to. He gave up his plans to dive and instead, in mid-June, he and Brady arranged for the employment of a professional diver, starting in July.

This would make necessary the use of a diving stage, or elevator. A hard-hat diver would have to be lowered into the water in his bulky, heavy equipment; he couldn't merely flop overboard, as Simmons did, and swim to the bottom. Deir hastened back to Suffolk and, with some assistance from Simmons, constructed a suitable elevator in just three weeks. It was a notable feat—and not least for the ingenious design of the elevator.

The principal component of this device was a steel lattice-work boom forty-seven feet long which had once been the long arm of a derrick. A thick pipe was welded to one end of it to make it a few feet longer, and it was then set on end with the pipe resting on the sandy bottom, thirty or thirty-five feet below the water. Running the full length of the boom was a double track. On this vertical track rolled a framework of steel pipes which could be moved up and down by means of an electric motor at the top of the boom. A stage for the diver to stand on was set on the framework, and this platform was so arranged that it could be tilted into a horizontal position no matter which way the boom was made to lean. Because of the way the tanker was listing, the boom would—at least part of the time—have to lean away from the ship, with its base set under her slanting side. This would enable the diver standing on the platform to work in close to the hull, regardless of the ship's list. And the tilting of the platform would always provide him with a horizontal floor. Furthermore, the platform could slide forward and back—toward the ship and away from it—thereby controlling proximity to the sloping hull. Later, iron pipes were fitted to the platform extending in both directions parallel to the hull, so that the diver could sidle along them and work on the ship's side at some distance from the boom itself.

It was essentially a simple structure, but it performed a highly complicated function. On it, a diver could rise or descend, slide in and out toward the vessel, move forward almost to the tank deck and aft almost to the stern, always with a perfectly level stage beneath him.

This masterpiece of improvisation was not the first of Deir's "inventions." He had demonstrated his ingenuity to his partners some weeks before in the process of loading the light pump-testing generator aboard the *Queen* from the re-arming boat. To accomplish this, Deir had simply run a cable between a lifeboat davit and the generator's motor, compelling the generator to hoist itself up—by its own bootstraps, so to speak. In the final analysis it was Deir's inventiveness that chiefly compensated for the project's chronic shortage of funds—that plus tireless and imaginative shopping, in which Little played a major role, plus a great deal of hard work and plain, never-look-a-fact-in-the-face stubbornness on the part of all hands, a trait which they got by infection from Deir. He never gave up. His favorite expression came to be "Don't *worry* about it"; he used it so often that it got to be a joke among the men. As the problems multiplied and were met his self-assurance increased until at last he seemed to feel that he could do anything.

At one point Brady, undergoing one of his periodic fits of uncertainty about the whole project, was driving with Deir to Suffolk when they heard a radio newscast of another ship aground, off the Carolinas. The ship's owners had pointedly announced that *this* vessel was *not* abandoned but was being manned by the company's representatives. Brady chuckled. "They're scared you're gonna go get that ship," he said to Deir.

There was a brief silence; then Deir said soberly, "I don't think we'd have time."

It had been decided, for various reasons, to use the starboard boat deck as the work area for the forthcoming repair job. That deck was directly over the damaged side; it had davit winches that might prove useful for handling heavy loads; it was right under the engine-room cargo boom, which was hinged to the base of the smokestack and might be adapted to swing the patch overboard; and, except for the flimsy sun deck, it was the highest spot on the stern of the tanker, and therefore the only starboard deck that was above water. It also had major disadvantages, but these had to be accepted since there was no other place on the tanker that didn't have the same ones. It sloped sharply. Its low side dipped close to the sea, and during some high tides it was actually swept by waves. It was narrow: a scant twenty feet wide, or about the same as the width of the patch they would soon build there. But it was the best they had.

They decided to set up the divers' elevator just off this deck; it would then be possible for the divers to step right aboard the platform from the work area. To swing the big elevator into position Deir used the cargo boom, but first the boom had to be lengthened to extend well out over the ship's side. He achieved this by simply cutting the boom in half and welding in an eight-foot section of oil pipe from the tank deck. Then he ran a cable from the boom back to a pulley already installed on the smokestack, and from there to a davit winch on the boat deck. Later the boom would have to be strengthened to handle heavier burdens, but for lifting the diving stage it was entirely adequate.

Once in position the elevator was fixed firmly in place by guy wires fastened with some difficulty to the edge of the boat deck. The men were working close to, and sometimes right in, the swells. Everybody got thoroughly soaked.

Finally Deir walled up the deck below the boat deck. Waves were rushing in and out of this space, creating such turbulence as to endanger anyone using the diving platform. Heavy planks and metal plates set up vertically along the deck's edge created a solid barrier that kept the waves out.

While Deir was working on the diving stage Little was

buying steel for the patch. For a time the partners had considered getting secondhand stuff and had even bought one big curved piece before they knew the nature and extent of the damage to the hull. But they had finally decided that old metal wouldn't do; this was one place where bargain hunting would be false economy. Little bought four new sheets of three-eighth-inch steel in Virginia, just to start with. They were twenty feet long—the height of the damaged area—and as wide as he could get them, which was five feet. They cost two hundred dollars each.

Each big sheet of steel weighed twelve hundred pounds and was terribly unwieldy, tending to flap and buckle while being moved. Hoisting them from the rearming boat to the boat deck was exceedingly difficult. Little first burned a hole through each sheet (the steel could be welded as good as new later on), then strung a cable through, and had the steel hand-cranked aboard by means of the boom-and-davit winch. It was back-breaking work, performed largely by the two strongest men, Mack Duncan and Henley Doughtie. The salvagers got it aboard, but they still didn't know just what they were going to do with it.

Not long afterward, Henley got a chance to demonstrate prowess of another kind.

One Sunday toward the end of June, Deir and Little were both on board completing preparations for the hard-hat diving, and Simmons, Tom Doughty and Henley were helping.

It had been months since anyone had tried to board the *Queen* without permission. To be sure, the salvagers were accustomed to visitors. Scarcely a day passed that the tanker wasn't called on by a Coast Guard motor vessel. Furthermore, the sides of the ship below the surface of the water were now encrusted with marine growth that attracted fish, and boatloads of fishermen often anchored close by. Other boats were beginning to appear, too. Now that warm weather had come, a few enterprising Ocean City boatmen were bringing out sightseers at so much a head to watch the salvage work. Occasionally some of these visitors asked to come aboard; they were rarely permitted to do so.

The salvagers had concluded that it was simply safer not to run risks. Gifford Warner, the Connecticut salvage man who months before had challenged their right to the tanker, had never stopped pressing his claim. He had taken over the bow, which was still drifting around the region upside down —the *Queen* salvagers had by now decided not to fool with it—and he kept speaking of the rest of the vessel as if it were legally his. The four partners could never entirely dispel the fear, however irrational, that Warner might someday try to put someone aboard the *Queen* to back up his claim. As a result, nowadays when anyone asked to come aboard the tanker the crewmen usually rejected the request politely.

On this day the visitors didn't even ask.

They were four tough-looking young men in a small plastic outboard motor boat, and—like the previous boarders—they came from the direction of Lewes. Again like the other Lewes boatmen, they obviously had nothing to do with Warner. They were simply interlopers. They calmly pulled up to the rope ladder the salvagers had placed on the port side and made ready to climb up. Deir swiftly moved to meet them.

"What can we do for you?" he asked.

"We're comin' on."

"Sorry. We can't let you do that."

"Why not?"

"Well, a lot of reasons. One of them is that this is private property. Another is that you could get hurt and we'd be liable."

The man stared at Deir insolently. "Yeah?" he said. "Well, I think we'll come on anyhow. We ain't afraid of getting hurt. We're big boys. We can take care of ourselves." His meaning was unmistakable.

Deir turned to where the other salvagers were standing on the after section. "Get the guns," he said quietly.

At that point the four toughs pulled a surprise of their own: they produced pistols.

For a moment it actually appeared that there might be a brisk gunfight, pistols against shotguns. But the interlopers weren't prepared for a showdown against those odds. They let go the rope ladder and started their engine. Then, instead of leaving, they began to circle the tanker, shouting obscenities. As they reached the stern they suddenly opened fire—not against the salvagers, but against the sides of the ship. The crack of gunfire and the clang of ricocheting bullets resounded through the tanker, while her crewmen—all except Doughtie, who had been quietly observing the incident from a passageway—stared at one another helplessly.

As the small boat emerged on the starboard side, guns still popping, Little, holding one of the shotguns, roared furiously, "You take one more shot and I'll blow that boat right out from under you!"

One of the strangers thumbed his nose.

Henley, whom the intruders had not yet seen, stepped out of the passageway, clearing his throat. Henley was a rumbler rather than a shouter, but his rumble had plenty of carry. As he now began to speak, his voice rose easily over the sound of the outboard motor, the shooting, the ricochets and the shouting. In an almost conversational tone, he said, "You goddam ugly motherloving sonsofbitches do that once more I tell you I'll goddam well burn your cowardly ass out here this day till you wish you never got born."

The four men stared up at Henley, looming over the ship's side, his granite face hard and awful. Suddenly the little outboard motor roared, the plastic boat turned sharply and the intruders fled. Later inspection showed that they had done no damage, aside from a few small dents in the tanker's hull.

The excitement may have been too much for Tom Doughty.

For weeks, Tom had been Henley's constant companion on the *Queen.* The two men had bickered constantly over everything; this experience had quickly made Tom almost Henley's equal at profanity. They fought over who was working hardest, who was eating most, and especially over who would get the last drink in the bottle. Beldon Little, who had long since overcome his original objections to their drinking, always took care to bring separate bottles aboard for the two men; they would steal secret nips, each unaware that the other had a supply of his own. This made the liquor last longer—and, most important, it reduced the squabbling.

"You two guys are like a husband and wife," Deir said. "I never heard such spatting."

Also like husband and wife, they were fiercely protective of each other. It was not safe for anyone else to criticize either of them in the other's hearing. The rest of the men on the tanker found this very funny.

"It's a damn good thing they really like each other," Little commented. "If they ever got real mad they'd spill blood all over the ship."

Tom had been aboard the *Queen* for twenty-one consecutive days, the longest stretch anyone had put in up to that time. For the last week or so he had been suffering from a cold. The day after the shooting incident, while he was cleaning some of the mess out of the food locker, he threw up. Nobody thought much of it—he was working with a nauseating stew of rotted vegetables and decayed, greenish meat that was enough to make any man ill—but after a while he approached Little, his face white.

"I'm real sick," he said. "I got a pain around my heart like to kill me."

"You go lie down," Little urged him. "No more work for you today, hear? You rest."

A moment later Deir came by and Little told him about Doughty. "He looks like hell," Little said. "I made him go rest, but we better keep watch on him. Damn, I feel bad about that. He asked me to bring him back a bottle when I went in with Kin yesterday afternoon, but I got to the store too late. Right now a drink might do him some good."

"Well, it might kill him, too," said Deir. "I'll go see him."

Tom was lying on his bunk in great pain. "It's getting worse," he said.

"We'll send you in," said Deir. "You'd better see a doctor."

Kin Reed quickly got the rearming boat ready, and they put Tom aboard. Once ashore, Reed took him to the hospital in Salisbury. There the doctors diagnosed his trouble as a heart attack, and he was put to bed.

It was some weeks before Doughty recovered. He never returned to the *Queen*.

13

DUKE MORRIS, the master diver, arrived on June 30. He inspired confidence from the moment he stepped aboard the tanker. A short, moon-faced man in his late thirties, he had an air of calm assurance that heartened the salvagers greatly. They were beginners at this game, a fact which was making some of them increasingly nervous. Here at last was a veteran, very sure of himself, very much the old hand.

Morris moved and spoke with deliberation. Puffing gravely on his pipe, he surveyed the sloping, slippery decks without surprise, taking in the surroundings with a professional eye. He examined the elevator carefully and approvingly, found a place for his equipment and supervised his tender in setting it up. Unlike Simmons, who carried his air with him in tanks when he dived, Morris, the hard-hat diver, had to have his air pumped down to him. He had brought along his own gasoline-driven compressor, a battered and rusted machine which dismayed Deir and impressed the others. It had clearly seen hard use.

Duke's tender, Woody Crisp, was a short, muscular, handsome young fellow, with a blinding grin and a soft South Carolina accent. Woody was, in the tidewater vernacular, a Christian—that is, not merely a churchgoer but a zealot. He had scarcely come aboard before he had cornered one of the crewmen and was earnestly offering to help him find salvation. They learned later that Crisp had once been a hard-drinking roisterer who had been saved for Christ by an evangelist and now spent all his spare time laboring in God's behalf. He was a lay preacher of strong fundamentalist leanings and an indefatigable proselytizer. He was also a thoroughly likable man, and a conscientious worker who was quick to lend a hand to the *Queen's* crew whenever Morris didn't need him.

Duke had been hired, with Crisp, at a hundred and fifteen dollars a day for every day he worked, which made him by far the most expensive single item in the entire salvage budget (his bill, at the end of the job, came to six thousand dollars). He was needed primarily for three reasons: to give Maurice Simmons' findings the benefit of an experienced eye, to examine the damaged area from inside the tanker and, eventually, to help put on the patch.

Brady and Sadler had come out to see the start of the hard-hat diving, and Brady watched in an agony of impatience as Morris slowly and methodically made his preparations to go down. Finally, while the *Queen's* full complement stood around and observed, Crisp helped the diver into his suit, with its weighted belt and shoes. Then Duke waddled over to the diving platform, turned and faced his assistant, and bent almost double so Woody could slip the great metal helmet over his head and tighten the bolts that held it fast. Woody cranked up the compressor—it coughed and missed and on the whole sounded no more dependable than it looked—and then checked Duke's communications. The diver's voice, metallic and imperturbable, could be heard through an intercom speaker on deck. At last Morris gave the signal, Deir started the elevator and the diver went down.

Halfway to the bottom Morris called up, "Okay, stop her here."

The silence that followed seemed interminable. Minutes passed—five, ten, fifteen. They tried to imagine what Morris was doing down there; he didn't enlighten them. Woody, quietly standing guard over the compressor, shrugged off questions. Duke, he said, knew what he was doing.

After a time some of the men drifted away; there was other work to do, and it obviously would be a while before they heard any news from Morris. Nobody wanted to hurry him. Deir moved around to the port side of the boat deck. He was standing there when the compressor stopped.

For the barest fraction of a second he stood there, shocked. Then he headed for the compressor, fast. Instead of running around by way of the stern, which was cluttered with equipment, he hurled himself up the ladder to the sun deck, leaped across the planking and flew down the other side. Simmons reached the compressor at the same instant. They shoved Crisp aside, much to his amazement, and Deir grabbed the crank. He cranked once, twice. Suddenly the engine caught, coughed, caught again. Deir sank back weakly. "Man, that was close," he said.

Crisp grinned. "Now, look, if you're gonna do like that every time that machine cuts out," he drawled, "you're gonna wear yourself out right quick. *Duke*'s all right. He's got about ten minutes of air in that little deck tank that's connected to the compressor. When he hears the pump stop he just turns the valve on his hat and waits to hear if she starts up again. If she don't, he asks up. But he's in no hurry."

They all thought about that for a moment, then Brady spoke up. "He's never in a hurry about anything, is he?"

"That's right," said Woody.

They stayed close to the compressor after that, not wanting it to stop in spite of Crisp's reassurance, and also increasingly anxious to hear from Duke. At last Brady could stand it no longer. He stepped to the intercom, pressed down the button and said, "Duke?"

"Yeah?"

"What's it look like down there, Duke?"

There was a brief pause while Morris weighed his reply. Then: "You guys better put this thing in drydock."

There was a startled silence. Surely the damage couldn't be so bad that they couldn't repair it themselves. They didn't pursue the conversation further but waited soberly for Morris to finish his inspection, so they could talk to him on the surface.

He was down for something more than an hour and a half. In that time he methodically studied the entire damaged area, foot by foot. He had the elevator lowered until he could step off onto the bottom, and he moved down almost to the oil tanks before returning to the diving stage and asking to be raised to the surface.

They all stood around and watched as Crisp helped the diver get his helmet off. As soon as his head emerged Deir asked, "How does it look? What's the damage like?"

Duke shook his head. "I'm not sure I can tell you," he said. "I've never seen anything exactly like this."

"Well, man, you've gotta tell us *something!* How big is the hole?"

Duke took his pipe from Woody, lighted up, then puffed thoughtfully. "It isn't a *hole*," he said. "It's a lot of holes, and scratches, and tears. . . . Look, get me a piece of paper and I'll show you."

Somebody handed him paper and pencil, but he disdained the pencil. He held up the paper and, as they watched in astonishment, began punching his fingers through it. Then he wrinkled it in the center, held it out at arm's length and studied it a moment, and said, "There. That's what it looks like."

They stared at the crumpled paper. Somebody whistled. Brady said in a low voice, "It really looks like *that?*"

"Look," said Deir. "I've gotta see a picture of that daggone thing. Think you could go down for another look, then come back and draw me a picture? Just go down and look and take your time. No hurry."

Morris nodded placidly. "I think I can probably do that," he said.

His second dive was shorter, and when he returned he quickly sketched the damage on a sheet of paper. His picture was precisely the same as Simmons'. They studied it, and at last Sadler spoke, his voice calm and dignified.

"There's a question we are all waiting to hear answered, and that is, what are the chances of getting this here ship repaired?"

By now they were becoming accustomed to Morris' long silences, and they waited patiently while he considered. Finally he nodded. "I'd say pretty good," he said.

The next day Morris went down inside the tanker. The fact that he was able to do so represented something of a triumph for Deir—and, in a curious way, for the manufacturers of a detergent paste that was much used aboard the *African Queen.*

From the time the salvagers had first boarded the tanker, a

heavy film of black oil had floated on the surface of the water that flooded the engine room–boiler room. The oil made diving there impossible. Deir had tried a variety of remedies, but nothing had worked very well. The surface oil could be pumped out, but it soon returned; apparently it was leaking from some piece of machinery deep within the engine room. That meant that it had to be pumped repeatedly, and this chore was rendered almost prohibitively onerous by the changing tides, which made it necessary to shift the pump's position constantly. Deir tried mounting the pump within an empty fifty-gallon drum that floated on the surface whatever the level of the tide. But even so, the pumping process was painfully slow.

Then Deir noted that there were times when the water surging rhythmically within the ship rose up above the sill of the engine-room door, across the corridor from the cabins they were using as living quarters. If the door was opened a crack at just the right moment the surface oil poured out and ran down the corridor and out to the deck, where it drained off. The trouble was that the door had to be closed between surges to keep the oil from running right back into the engine room. So with Simmons' assistance Deir worked out an automatic system. He tied open the heavy steel door and installed in its stead a lighter one removed from a hose box. An electric contact held this door closed until the weight of the water inside the room forced it open. Just enough water would pour through before the door closed again. The system worked fine, but it had one major drawback. It worked only at high tide; the rest of the time the water level in the engine room was far below the door sill.

Now somebody suggested a new method: build a wooden well that could be placed on the surface of the engine-room flood, with sides deep enough so that the lowest tide would not drop below the well, nor the highest tide rise above it. This would, at least, keep a small patch of water clear for the diver's use after the surface had been pumped clean. Construction was begun on the well.

By now Deir and his chief assistant, Simmons, were black with oil and tense with frustration as a result of their exertions. One day Deir was standing on the balcony that encircled the engine room, trying to get some of the grease off his hands with the paste detergent. A glob of the stuff dropped off his hands into the oily water. Magically, a clear spot appeared. Deir, growing excited, flicked in a bit more. Within a few moments, the entire surface was free of oil. He ran from the engine room, shouting and laughing. By the time the others got there the water was so clear that it was possible to see all the way to the bottom of the room, more than thirty feet below them.

A few hours later the oil skim had returned, but nobody minded any longer. It was a simple matter to toss in a handful of the detergent paste; within minutes the oil was gone.

Although the detergent solved the oil problem once and for all, diving within the engine room–boiler room presented certain other difficulties that were not so easily dealt with. A wilderness of machinery, pipes, ladders and catwalks crisscrossed the two rooms, making progress extremely hazardous. As a further complication, the same pushing-pulling action of the water that made it so dangerous to approach the damage from the outside was also present inside, but it was sure to be much more intense because of the limited cubic area into which the water was pounding and sucking. The experienced, steady Morris was the obvious candidate to investigate the inside of the ship, but his air hose made just one more encumbrance to get caught in the snarl of metal down there. So Deir worried as Morris prepared to enter the big, deep room. As for Duke, he made his preparations phlegmatically as usual, and when they were finished he calmly stepped into the room and walked along the steel balcony to the nearest ladder, then without hesitation started down into the water. He disappeared from sight behind some machinery.

The engine room was of particular interest to Duke. He had done engine-room duty in the Navy during the war, and later held an engineer's license in the Merchant Marine. He looked about him curiously. Entering the engine room was like stepping into a huge, dark, spooky, but half-familiar house. Various unrecognizable objects were wiggling and flapping in the turbulent water, and numerous surprises greeted him as he picked his way down the ladders and along the steel decks—a great deal of small equipment had been dislodged and shifted about by the action of the sea. Like any good ship's engineer, he checked the engine-room telegraph as he walked by. It was on STOP.

He moved along slowly, painstakingly, unhooking his air hose when it snagged on a pipe, finding safe pathways through the tangle. The great engine room was murky rather than pitch dark, and as he neared the damaged area it grew perceptibly brighter: daylight was seeping through the rips in the ship's side after filtering down through five fathoms of water. He reported his first sight of the holes to Deir over the intercom.

On deck, Deir had been following Morris' passage closely, checking with the diver frequently and fretting over the ragged sound of the compressor, chugging away on the other side of the ship.

When the compressor stopped, Deir was ready for it. Once again, he raced over the top of the tanker rather than around the stern—except that this time he began from a deck lower. Gasping, he arrived beside the compressor and immediately began to crank. But it wouldn't catch. It wouldn't catch at all. He cranked furiously, frantically, perspiration standing out on his face. Nothing happened. Several minutes went by. It would take Morris at least a quarter of an hour to climb up out of the engine room, Deir figured. His face contorted, he cranked and cranked.

It caught just when he was giving up hope, when he was wondering whether it would help at all to rip the air hose off the machine and try to blow air into it with his mouth. The engine *putt-putted* and grunted and started up sluggishly. He played the choke and throttle until the beat of the engine smoothed out, and he stayed there until a shout from the engine-room entrance told him that Morris was out.

Limp and exhausted, Deir walked slowly around to the port side and down one deck to where Duke and Woody were standing at the center of a small crowd of crew members. As Woody took off the diver's helmet, Deir said, "You okay?"

Morris nodded calmly. "Sure," he said. "You shouldn't worry about that compressor. I never go anyplace I can't get out of with just the air in my tank."

"Naw," said Deir wearily. "That isn't enough for me. We gotta make another arrangement here, I tell you. I can't stand any more of this sort of thing. I got enough to think of without this."

"Don't let it bother you," Morris said easily. "Anyhow, it waited until I was finished. I was about ready to come up when it quit."

His report on the state of the engine room was even more disquieting than his description of the damage from outside the hull. A maze of tubing was crowded against the inside wall of the ship. "It's mighty near impossible to get anywhere near the damaged plates from down there," Duke said. "There are all kinds of pipes in the way. I don't know how you're gonna put on a patch. If you had any idea of putting bolts through the side and screwing on the nuts from in there . . ." He gestured, then shook his head. "Not a chance."

Deir listened in silence. Then he said, "Don't worry about it. We'll figure out something."

The next day Morris went down on the outside again, primarily to measure the dimensions of the damaged area. His measurements fell considerably short of those reported earlier by Simmons. Deir, by now fully sold on Simmons' accuracy, was troubled by Morris' report. He knew that because of the battered condition of the tanker's side it was extremely difficult to tell where the damage began and where it ended. But Simmons had spent a great deal of time down there; he had measured against cables lowered from the deck; he simply couldn't be wrong. The other partners were not that sure. The patch was going to run into a good deal of money, a large patch more than a small one, and that made Brady and Sadler yearn desperately for a small one.

"Paul," Deir said, "there's just no sense building a patch too small. Too big may cost more, but it'll cover the hole. Too small would be a *real* waste of money: it won't cover a thing."

The solution to this uncertainty had already been suggested, in part, at least, by Little, but it was at this time being stubbornly resisted by Deir. Little's idea was to construct a template—a rectangular gridwork of pipe—that could be lowered over the damaged area and pinned firmly against the ship's hull. It would then serve both as a means of measuring the damage and as a standard from which to determine how much of a curve would have to be built into the patch to make it fit snugly against the tanker's twisted side. Template-to-hull measurements could be taken at specified intervals along the grid; each such measurement would show how much bend would have to be made in the patch at that point.

Deir felt that the template was unnecessary, time-consuming and—at least in the form in which it was being considered—impractical. Little and Morris talked of making the framework of half-inch iron pipe. They acknowledged that it would be flimsy, but it would be easier to handle than a template made of heavier stuff. Deir was convinced that the surging of the water would twist the frame all out of alignment and cast doubt on any measurement obtained from it. He felt certain that Simmons' dimensions were the right ones anyhow. As for obtaining the curvature of the hull, he could do that largely from blueprints found on board.

"Damn it all," said Little, reddening, "the original contour of this ship is *gone*. We've gotta figure what the new shape is, all beat in the way it is!"

In the end Little prevailed. But both men were annoyed.

The dispute over the template pointed up a growing split between Deir and Little. This particular disagreement was just one of many; it was noteworthy mainly for the fact that Deir eventually had to give way before the unified opinions of his three partners, plus Duke Morris and Maurice Simmons.

At the start Deir and Little had shared responsibilities and authority. As time went on Deir had made more and more of the decisions. When no one else seemed able to find a solution he could usually be depended on to supply one, and the crewmen turned to him increasingly with their problems. As this situation developed, Deir came to have less and less respect for Little's suggestions. Little, for his part, felt that his counsel was being pointedly ignored and that Deir had seized the leadership of what had started out as a joint venture—to the detriment of Little's standing with the crew. Sensitive and eager for the respect of others, Little was hurt and angry. Deir, now attacking the salvage problems with single-minded fervor, had no time to worry about Little's sensitivity; it merely irritated him. Bit by bit, they were rubbing each other raw.

14

AND NOW EVERYTHING hinged on the patch. Deir went home to figure out how to pin it to the ship; Duke Morris and Woody Crisp left to await word from Deir; Beldon Little stayed aboard with Henley Doughtie to start welding sheets of steel together and to finish work on the template. The *African Queen,* crowded on Friday, was almost empty by Saturday night. The date was July 4. It was virtually the last quiet weekend the tanker would have that summer.

The usually effervescent Deir was silent and thoughtful as he rode back to Virginia with Brady and Simmons. He was suddenly alone with the critical dilemma of the entire venture, and he had to find a way to solve it. For weeks he had been pumping confidence into everyone else ("Don't *worry* about it"), assuring them that no problem would arise that couldn't be overcome. Now the knottiest puzzle of all had arisen, and he didn't have an answer ready.

As the car sped through the dark Maryland countryside, he sat hunched in a corner, staring out the window. His brain was processing ideas like a business machine, rejecting the impractical, putting some by for further study, focusing his attention on a few glimmerings that seemed really promising.

The task was staggering. It was not simply a question of how to attach a piece of steel to the side of a ship. This piece would weigh at least—he did a hasty calculation—ten tons, probably more. It would measure something over thirty feet by twenty, roughly the dimensions of the side of a barn. How could they mold a great sheet like that to fit a surface that was crumpled like Duke Morris' sheet of paper? Having molded it, how would they make it keep its shape? Having shaped it, how to strengthen it against the battering of the sea? And once it was built, how would they scoop it up off the deck, swing it into thirty feet of roaring water and then set it into precise position over the damage? Once they had it there, how would they hold it in place so men could work on it?

And then the big question, which would arise last but must be solved first because everything else depended on it: how in God's name were they going to attach that huge, heavy, unwieldy patch to the side of the tanker if they couldn't use bolts?

Or *could* bolts be used? From the start Deir and Little had assumed that all necessary patching would be done with nuts and bolts: shove a bolt through patch and plate and dog it down with a nut screwed on from inside. Morris had killed that plan with his report that the inside of the ship was so lined with pipes that nobody in the engine room could get close enough to the bolts to thread the nuts on.

At the time Deir had suggested an alternative. Why not burn a series of fairly large holes, one to each bolt hole, all around the damaged area? The holes would be large enough for a man to slip his arm through. Couldn't a diver then reach in and run the bolt through the hull from inside? The bolt could later be passed through the patch and held with a nut applied from *outside* the ship. The arm holes could eventually be covered over easily with small plates held down by toggle bolts.

That suggestion hadn't gone over very well. Deir had had trouble explaining it; everybody had had trouble understanding it. "We don't need *more* holes in the ship!" Little kept protesting, and after a time it had begun to seem a little impractical even to Deir. Suppose, for one thing, that the diver shoved his arm into the hole—and found his hand, absurdly, groping around the inside of one of the pipes Duke had seen there? Nevertheless, the idea had stuck in Deir's mind, and now he was beginning to see a way of using it to solve one of the many lesser puzzles with which he was grappling. But it didn't help with the main problem.

Actually, the bolts weren't the real headache; they could be put in all right. It was the nuts. What kind of bolt might work without nuts?

He straightened in his seat. Tap bolts. They were threaded and could be screwed into threaded holes in the ship's side. Suppose a hole was made in the patch, and through it another slightly smaller hole was drilled in the hull. Suppose, then, this second hole was tapped, or threaded. A tap bolt passed through the first piece of steel and screwed into the second would hold every bit as well as a bolt-and-nut combination. It was like dispensing with nuts and, instead, using the whole side of the ship to hold the bolts fast.

That raised new problems, of course. He settled back into the seat, his brain churning. The holes in the hull would have to be made with absolute accuracy—a bolt held on by a nut could rattle around, but a tap bolt would have to fit within a fraction of an inch or it wouldn't screw in. That meant the holes would have to be drilled, not burned, and the drilling of the hull would have to be done underwater while the patch was lashed against the ship's side. Duke Morris had said that underwater drilling was tough because of torque: that is, a drill that spun to the right had a tendency to twirl the diver to the left. A drill with a tap attached to it, biting into the side of the hole, probably would flip a man over completely. Duke had also warned that just the simple matter of exerting enough pressure on a drill to force it into steel was almost beyond a diver's capacity, since he had almost no leverage underwater.

All during the five-and-a-half-hour drive from Ocean City Deir sat in his corner, thinking hard, weighing alternatives, discarding them, mentally circling around the difficulties as they arose, solving them, going on to the next problem, keeping track of his moves like a chess player. By the time he reached home he had a plan he was sure would work, and it covered everything from the molding of the patch to the insertion of the final bolt. He said a hasty good night to Brady and Simmons and hurried inside. In a few minutes he was out again and on his way to his workshop in back. He could hardly wait to get his hands on the metalworking equipment.

For most of the week that followed, Deir worked in the shop, growing more and more elated. He had worried about whether he could drill through the *Queen*'s plates. He had a small piece of tanker steel left over from the piece he had removed at the request of Commander Young of the Coast Guard. He tried it; it cut like butter, the mark of high-quality metal. Next he had to thread the sides of the hole, then screw in a tap bolt. For this job he had another idea: if a drill wouldn't work, why not an impact wrench—the air-driven device used by garages to remove the wheel lugs when changing an auto tire? It had no torque but imparted a turning motion by the hammering of compressed air. He thought before he tried it that it might break the bolt—but no, it worked like a dream!

Finally it was time to try his key plan—the single idea that promised to solve most of the remaining problems. It couldn't have been simpler. He would use guide rods—first to be sure the drill was positioned accurately, then to force the drill into the steel, and finally to guide the impact wrench in threading the hole and driving in the bolt.

He took two nuts and welded them, eight inches apart, to a piece of steel. Then he took two threaded rods and fitted them into the nuts, so that they stood out from the steel like parallel fingers. For drilling he had decided on a pneumatic drill—a T-shaped air-driven device. At either end of the handle, the crossbar of the T, he made two holes, eight inches apart. He positioned the tip of the drill so that it was pointed at the sheet of steel, and lined up the holes in the handle so that the drill slid smoothly down the threaded guide rods and touched the metal plate. He slid it up and down. It touched in the same place every time. Here was the accuracy he needed. The two rods would guide both the drill and later the impact wrench to precisely the same spot, so the two holes—one in the ship's side, the other in the patch—could be drilled exactly in line, and the tap would follow right behind.

Now on to the next problem: forcing the drill into the steel despite the diver's lack of leverage underwater.

He took a metal plate, cut holes in it eight inches apart and threaded a set screw into its center. He slipped this plate over the two guide rods, behind the drill, and fastened it to the rods. Then he started up the drill and began to turn the set screw with his hand. As the screw descended through the plate it exerted pressure on the back of the drill. The drill was forced against the steel, and the bit ground slowly into the metal. In a short time the bit had gone completely through. Deir turned off the drill and straightened up, delighted. There was no reason why a diver couldn't do the same thing underwater. Instead of trying to press the drill against the ship's side by sheer physical force, all he would have to do was fasten the plate behind the drill and turn the set screw.

The nuts to hold the threaded guide rods could be welded all around the edge of the patch at eight-inch intervals *before* it was lowered into the water. Only a few of the guide rods would be needed; as each hole was drilled and threaded, and each bolt was driven in, the rods could be threaded into the nuts at the next position.

There was just one thing. The patch would be curved, rounded; in some places a pair of nuts fastened to its surface eight inches apart would be facing a few degrees away from each other. Rods screwed into these nuts would diverge sharply. They wouldn't be parallel at all, and unless they were they could not be used as guides.

The solution was simplicity itself. Deir would thread a couple of rods off-center, so they would screw in at an angle, erratically. At each turn the top of the rod would then describe a large circle, and at one point in this circle the rod *would* be parallel with its mate. It could be stopped there and used just like the others.

Deir felt good. The plan was now complete. It provided at least an operating outline—a step-by-step pattern that embraced everything from the bending of the steel to the eventual placement of the patch. For as he had worked on the major problems he also had cleared up some of the minor points troubling him.

The patch, the first sheets of which were now being welded together by Little on the *Queen,* would be molded to the shape of the hull by attaching cables to its surface at selected points as it lay on the deck, then plucking the steel upward. It could be pulled up more at some points than at others, and pinned down at the edges wherever a sharper curve seemed called for. Then, once the curve was formed, it could be fixed in shape by a series of strong steel girders welded across it. The girders, of course, would have to be shaped to fit the curvature of the patch; this could be done by cutting small pie-shaped pieces out of them, bending them until the lips of the pie cut met, then welding the cut to-gether. Before returning to the tanker Deir planned to pick up some ten-inch steel I-beams at Sadler's place that ought to be just right for the job.

Once shaped, the patch would be hoisted over the side. It would have to be pinned fast against the side of the *Queen* while the divers did all their drilling, tapping and bolting. It could be held by cables—if the cables could somehow be fastened to the ship.

It was here that Deir revived his arm-hole idea. Divers would reach in through the arm holes and push the cables back out through smaller holes in the ship's side. Shackles to be attached to the cable ends would keep the cables from slipping back out, in the same way that a knot on the end of a thread keeps it from passing through a needle.

There were two reasons why the arm holes made better sense used this way than they might have if used to put on nut-and-bolt combinations: fewer holes would be needed, which lessened the chances of meeting a pipe inside the ship; and the arm holes would have served their purpose by the time the patch was lowered, so they could be burned in a part of the hull that later would be covered by the patch. The holes would be sealed up at the same time as the damage in the ship's side.

There would be two horizontal rows of cable holes, one row high on the hull, the other about twenty feet lower down. The cables in the uppermost row would be looped through matching holes in the top of the patch, and then fastened to shackles on the deck above, so that the patch would hang from them. The other cables, attached nearer the bottom of the ship, would simply pass over the patch and strap it against the side; these cables, too, would be fastened on the deck.

With the patch lashed firmly in place, the divers could drill their holes, tap them, put in the bolts . . . and the salvagers could pump out the ship and go home.

There was one more thing Deir had to do before returning to the *Queen* on Saturday. He built a gear box about the size of a large book, and in it he assembled a forty-to-one reduction gear that fit on the end of a one-and-a-quarter-inch drill. Now every time the drill spun forty times the chuck on the other side of the gear box revolved just once. With that gear ratio, the drill had enough power to move pretty near anything—ten tons of steel, for example.

On the *African Queen,* Beldon Little and Henley Doughtie were having their troubles.

Being on the ship by themselves had been pleasant for the first few days. There was a lot to do, the weather was good, there was plenty of food aboard and there had been enough visitors to keep the salvagers from being lonely. Fishing parties and sight-seers had come out daily from Ocean City, and although they had not been allowed on board they had been able to come up close enough to chat with the men on the tanker. In addition, the Coast Guard had paid its daily visit, the long boat purring up close and then quietly moving off with a wave from the crew. Little enjoyed those days, not least because he found Doughtie a good companion and fellow worker—strong, willing, amusing and easy to get along with. Even better, he was an excellent cook; the eating was always good when he was around.

Little had gone right to work on the template, welding together lengths of half-inch pipe until he had a gridwork: two rows of four rectangular sections, braced at the corners, the entire framework thirty feet long by twenty feet high.

When it was completed he stood it against a bulkhead to await the return of the divers and got to work on the patch.

He lapped the sheets of steel by several inches to make a strong bond, then welded along the edges. The patch could be welded only on one side at this stage; later it would have to be turned over and welded on the other. In this good weather the sea, even at high tide, was several feet below the boat deck on which Little was working, but still an occasional burst of spray would drench him. The welding process makes an electrical field of the metal being worked, and Little several times received shocks that stood his hair on end. But he kept at it.

On Tuesday afternoon Paul Russell came by in his boat and waved a paper. "Says here there's a bad storm coming up the coast, maybe a hurricane," he called. "You better take care. If it gets real bad I'll come out and maybe take you off."

His was the only boat that came near that afternoon. All next day there was nobody. The skies were gray but not threatening, the seas a little rougher than usual. "I tell you," said Little to Doughtie, "if the fishing draggers aren't working there's bad weather close by for sure."

All that day and the next they went about making things fast. They welded the patch to the steel deck and welded down everything else of value that was metal and could not be moved indoors. They cleared away all the lighter valuables and made sure the ports and hatches were closed. After that they dragged the life raft to the sun deck at the top of the after deckhouse, where it was thirty feet above normal high tide. They provisioned it and equipped it with a few essentials like battery lights and life jackets. They then tied it down firmly and left it for possible future use.

All this time the seas had been growing angrier. The skies were still a flat gray, but the atmosphere was oppressive. Most worrisome of all, even the Coast Guard failed to show up, apparently being busy elsewhere.

"What do you think?" Doughtie asked, with no particular concern. "Figure this sonofabitch can ride out a hurricane? Gonna get wet as a bastard out here."

"I don't like hurricanes," Little said. "I've been in seven of them on the high seas and three typhoons besides. But I tell you, if she don't go much worse than maybe forty-five, fifty-

142

mile-an-hour winds, like if we just get sideswiped by the storm, then we got nothing to fear. But if she hits full force"—he shook his head—"then watch out. I've seen what these storms can do. A hundred-mile wind could break up this ship, helpless the way she is."

Doughtie went back to work making things secure, but he was irritated now. Little heard him muttering in annoyance. "Goddam if Miz Doughtie's boy is gonna get drownded in no bastardly hurricane," he said once. It was said not in fear but in defiance.

On Thursday it began to rain, and by afternoon the seas were furious. The worst of the swells were washing clear over the ship, soaking the life raft on the top deck. The wind was a constant threat on the rain-swept, oil-soaked decks. Spume was blowing clear over the smokestack, sixty feet above the normal high-water level, and the pounding of the waves was slamming the tanker up and down in her sand bed for the first time since the storm of March 21 that had so worried Little and Deir.

By late afternoon the wind was almost too strong to stand against, and it was blowing up towering seas. The rain, falling almost horizontally, had so cut the visiblity that it seemed unlikely a boat could find the *Queen* even if one came looking.

This thought had barely passed through Little's mind when Henley suddenly let out a bellow from indoors, where he had gone to tighten a porthole. "Hell, Little, the damn *Coast Guard's* out here!"

Little ran to the port rail. There was the forty-foot motor lifeboat from Ocean City, bobbing violently in the waves, daylight clearly visible from time to time under her bow. There were four men in her, three of them thoroughly occupied being sick over the side. A seamy-faced coxswain sat impassively at the tiller. "We've come to take you off of there," he shouted across.

"What's the weather?" Little yelled back. It was not so ridiculous a question as it sounded; he hadn't heard a forecast since Russell's visit, and if this was the worst of the storm he saw no point in leaving.

"Hurricane is off the Virginia Capes and coming this way. It'll be worse before it's better. Fifth Coast Guard District sent us out to get you."

Doughtie and Little consulted briefly. "I'll do whatever you say," Henley said, shrugging. "One goddam way or the other it don't make no difference to me."

"Well, Henley, if it's as bad as he says, it's no use risking our lives out here. It isn't as if there was something we could do, more than what we've done already. There won't anybody come out to jump our claim in *this* weather, that's for sure. When the blow's over we'll come back." The tanker lurched under a wave that sailed right over them, as if they were standing inside a waterfall, and Little added, "That is, if she's still here."

Henley went inside and a few minutes later emerged carrying his suitcase.

"Great God, Henley," cried Little, "what have you got there?"

"All my stuff is in here, my fry pan and all," rumbled Henley, aggrieved. "You sure don't expect me to *leave* it!"

"Well, you're damn right I expect you to leave it. We'll be lucky as hell to get on that little boat ourselves, much less get that suitcase on there. You'll be doing well to save your own hide."

Muttering, Henley returned the bag to the cabin, and the two men stepped to the rail. Slowly the lifeboat moved in to the tanker's side. She had fenders over her gunwales to provide some protection from collision, but they wouldn't be much help if the two craft hit in these seas. Normally the deck Doughtie and Little were on was fifteen feet above high tide; now the Coast Guard boat was rising above it at the crest of each swell.

"Don't throw a line," Little called. "Just come up close."

The two men stepped over the rail and waited. As the lifeboat rose beside them they stepped quickly aboard; the coxswain shoved the throttle forward and they moved off.

As they lurched through the swells, headed toward Ocean City, Little looked back at the *Queen*. She was all but lost in the sea. Thousands of gallons of water were pouring over her, and spray completely hid the two deck houses. In a moment she was out of sight in the rain. The coxswain looked at Little. "Came mighty near not finding you," he said. "We spent two hours trying and then just happened to catch a look as we passed by."

That night Little and Doughtie stayed at Kin Reed's. The wind screamed and the rain pelted down and the radio reported substantial damage along the coast, although the hurricane's center was well offshore. At last, after some hours, it died away.

The next morning, early, they were back on board. The storm had left its mark on the tanker. The breakwater Deir had built of steel plate and three-by-ten-inch oak timbers below the starboard deck, as protection for divers, had all but disappeared; only three of the original twenty planks remained. All the decks had been swept clear of light objects. And a crate containing six hundred pounds of ball bearings, part of the *Queen*'s original stores which someone had dredged up from below, had traveled fifty feet from the point at which it had been left on deck. Otherwise, everything appeared to be as it had been left.

Little spent the rest of the day cleaning salt water out of electric engines and wiping off other equipment that might have been damaged by it.

On the next day, Saturday, Deir arrived in his cab-over-engine truck with so much in it that he ruefully reported he had been fined thirty-five dollars at a Maryland state truck station for being overweight. The total was close to twenty-five thousand pounds, and it included some steel, Sadler's heavy I-beams, a heavy-duty jack and a big borrowed air compressor which Deir intended to use to blow out the tanks, operate the impact wrench and save Duke Morris' life. The load also included Mack Duncan and Maurice Simmons. Simmons had been the last of the cargo to board the truck, and since the overweight had amounted to less than two hundred pounds Deir had kept telling him all the way out that if he had been a sensible man instead of a kindhearted one he would have left Simmons at the weighing station and saved thirty-five dollars.

When Deir learned that Little and Doughtie had left the tanker during the storm his brow darkened. He said nothing then, but later he told Brady grimly, "We can't leave Little aboard the ship alone again. He shouldn't have left it—not for anything."

15

DEIR'S PLAN received a merciless going-over from the other men as soon as he explained it. Brady heard its complicated details with growing consternation. He had hoped for a quick windup to the project now that they knew the scope of the problem; Deir's plan struck him as needlessly difficult. "Golly, there *must* be an easier way," he said. Everyone else seemed to agree, and a number of alternatives were suggested. Deir listened to all of them politely.

Someone urged applying the patch with toggle bolts, which have swivel bars that would open up after insertion and hold fast inside the ship—a suggestion originally put forward by Duke Morris. But then someone else pointed out that toggle bolts of adequate size would require impossibly large holes, and probably would have to be hand-made at a high price.

Brady held out for a velocity gun, which fires a stud into steel by means of an explosive cartridge. After a great deal of searching, he even got one—it had to be a very large one to suit their purposes—and tried it out. "You see, the stud builds up heat in the steel as it goes in," he explained to a small group of fascinated onlookers, "and then the steel cools, contracts and grips it. This ought to be perfect for us. Now watch." He fired the gun and everyone jumped. The stud went in beautifully and Brady looked pleased—until he discovered that a few turns with a wrench would pull it right back out again.

The most vociferous objection to Deir's proposal came from Little. He felt that it was too difficult and too time-consum-

146

ing, and he contended that Deir was underestimating the problems it would raise.

"By God, if you can get to where you can really make speed with those bolts like you say you can, I'll eat them," he told Deir. "Tapping and drilling takes time. Putting in rods takes time. Screwing in bolts takes time. It'll take forever. We'll be out here all year."

When it became apparent that no one had a practical alternative to the tap bolts, Little insisted that at least they should use the conventional nut-and-bolt combination whenever they could. "Through bolts are twice as fast . . . ten times as fast," he said. "And they're twice as good. Those tap bolts will be trouble, sure as sure. All right, now, some places you can't push a bolt through. I understand that. Then you use tap bolts. But, damn it, from what Duke says, seventy per cent of the time you could use regular bolts, and no trouble— no trouble at all!"

Although Little was overruled, he never stopped believing that the job could be done faster and more efficiently his way. "You can't tell Deir anything," he protested to Brady.

With the dispute over the bolts settled, at least for the moment, all attention turned to the patch. Although at that point it was much less than its ultimate size, it already was huge. It now consisted of four five-by-twenty-foot plates lapped together side by side into a single sheet almost twenty feet square. It still hadn't been reinforced or shaped, and only one surface had been welded. Just how much larger it would have to be they did not know. That must await the lowering of the template against the damaged side of the ship; they could obtain precise measurements then. In any case, they would need more steel, and Little went off to get some.

Meanwhile, before they could do any work on the patch, they had to shift its position on the deck. The work space there was only twenty feet wide, and the big sheet of metal had to be fitted into that space with great care—particularly now that the patch was to be made longer. (Deir had even removed the deck rail so the steel could extend out over the water.) So moving the patch was the first order of business.

Deir eyed the engine-room cargo boom doubtfully. With

the addition he had made to it, it was now long enough to reach all the way across the deck, and a little beyond. But it was pretty weak to heft a load like the patch. Even half finished, the patch weighed well over three tons. Furthermore, the cable on the boom was a rusty makeshift they had found aboard the *Queen*. It should work out all right, but they would have to be careful not to put too much strain on the boom. He shrugged. A salvage job like this was bound to involve some risks. If they were careful everything would be safe enough. But before lifting anything heavier—the finished patch, for example—he would have to strengthen that boom and replace the cable. He already had some new cable just for that purpose.

He burned two holes in the top of the patch, threaded a cable through them, then looped through the cable from the boom. It was late afternoon before they were ready to start hoisting. Mack Duncan stood by the davit winch; hand-cranking that weight would not be easy, but Mack was a powerful man. Brady, who had brought out some equipment that day and was staying the night, stood on one side of the patch with Deir; Simmons stood on the other. Duncan began cranking, and slowly the patch slid erect, scraping along the deck. Then, as Duncan labored at the winch, the big sheet rose a few inches into the air.

"Okay, hold her there," Deir called. Then he said to Brady and Simmons, "Watch it, now. Turn her, but stay out from under that boom. If that thing falls on you it'll mash you to nothing."

The patch was halfway around when the cable snapped.

Several things happened in rapid succession. The patch dropped to the deck with a thunderous crash and began sliding down the sloping surface toward the water. The boom followed hard behind it, flattened the patch with a second ear-splitting slam, halting its course toward the ocean, and broke in two.

The three men stood there, shocked into immobility, half deafened by the noise and, as soon as they could think about it, amazed at their luck. Both patch and boom had fallen among them with practically nothing to spare on any side; a few inches one way or the other and one or all of them could have been crushed. Furthermore, if the boom had not fallen precisely as it did, the patch would certainly have gone overboard and straight to the bottom. It had been headed that way. That might have meant the end of all their hopes. As it was, they were alive, and so was the project.

"My gosh," said Brady finally, "even without being hit by the patch we might have been scared to death by the noise!"

By now it was getting dark. Deir looked about him at the cluttered deck and frowned. "Well," he said. "We'd better get going. We can't leave this stuff here. Let's start fixing the boom and then we'll move the patch back into place. Only this time let's get that daggone boom up there right!"

Brady stared. "You don't mean you're gonna repair all this damage right now? After dark? What on earth for?"

"Well, we can't leave that patch hanging half off the deck the way it is. One good wave would sweep it away. That's point one. Point two: I don't want to leave the broken boom lying here either. Come morning there'll be boats around, and we don't want anyone carrying word to the Coast Guard that we're in trouble. We're supposed to be showing *progress* here. This sure as hell doesn't look much like progress!"

"Yeah," said Brady slowly, "I guess you're right." Just that day he had brought word of a newspaper story in which the Coast Guard was quoted as saying that no visible progress had been made toward salvaging the *Queen*. They had all been troubled by the story. There seemed to be an implied threat to their possession of the ship, since Commander Young had told Kin Reed nobody could dispute their right to claim her *so long as they showed progress*. Well, it was true enough that no progress could be seen by the Coast Guard motor boat that came by daily; all the progress was out of the government boat's sight high up on the *Queen*'s deck. Until the newspaper story had come out they had been lulled by the ritualistic nature of the Coast Guard visits. The Guardsmen would call out to the tanker, "How you doing?" And the men on the *Queen* would shout back that they were doing fine, and think no more about it. Now it appeared the Coast Guard hadn't believed a word of it.

So the men aboard the tanker rigged spotlights above the boat deck that night—"We'll be needing them later anyhow," Deir said—and got to work on the boom. As the night wore on Duncan and Brady gave up, exhausted, but Deir and Simmons kept at it. At 4:00 A.M. they called a halt. The boom was welded back together and restored to its position at the base of the smokestack, ready for the new cable and a general reinforcing. That could be done by daylight. The patch was secured; they had inched it back up the slanted deck with crowbars and chainfalls and tied it down with cable. Wearily, Deir and Simmons put down their tools and went to bed.

The next day Deir reeved in the new cable and strengthened the boom by encasing it in a bridgework frame improvised from some two-inch pipe he found lying around on the tanker. He felt that the boom was now ready for anything.

Three days later, on July 18, Duke Morris returned with Woody Crisp to make the cable holes and arm holes in the hull that would be needed to strap the patch down before the bolting could begin. While they were there, the template was lowered and Maurice Simmons went over the side to check the exact size of the damaged area and the contours of the hull.

The template, with its ironwork grid, provided a frame for the damage and gave the divers their first real perspective about the dimensions of the patch that would be required to seal off the holes. For one thing, the template was exactly thirty feet long, and when the damaged area was viewed against it, it became apparent immediately that the patch would have to be somewhat longer than that, to cover the dents that led into the gashes in the tanker's side. Full-size steel sheets would not be required for the extensions; smaller flaps tailored to cover the dents would suffice. It was also decided to add an additional small tab at the top of the patch, to seal off a dimple that could be seen above the template, high on the ship's side. They now knew, for the first time, how long their patch would have to be: forty feet.

Establishing the existing shape of the hull was a simple

matter. The template's vertical bars hung down straight, so Simmons merely measured at regular intervals the distances from these bars to the hull; a plot of these figures showed precisely how much curvature there was along the ship's side. They had earlier found an old blueprint among the stacks of papers in the pilothouse, so Deir knew the vessel's original contours. Working with both the old and the new information, Deir was now able to sketch out a fairly exact contour for the patch. Among other things, Simmons discovered that part of the *Queen*'s internal bracing had been bent outward, creating a knee that the patch would have to fit around.

While this work was going on, they were joined by a new crew member—the last permanent addition to the *Queen*'s complement. His name was Pearly Strait, and he had been hired by Little during his most recent shopping expedition. Both Deir and Little had worked with Strait in the past. He was a fine crane operator, welder and general workman—a deliberate, ruddy-faced, handsome Coloradan with powerful shoulders and a pleasant disposition. Little had stopped by Portsmouth Salvage in his search for steel and had encountered Strait there looking for work. The *Queen* needed a man to replace Tom Doughty, and Little had promptly signed on Pearly. He was a real find, and Deir was delighted to have him. Pearly was put to work immediately, helping to weld new sheets to the patch.

Steel was proving hard to find. The steel strike of 1959 was threatening, and this had caused a general drying up of supplies as steel users hurried to put away stockpiles. Portsmouth Salvage, the partners' principal source of plates up to then, was all out of them. Little finally turned up a couple of sheets elsewhere at a somewhat higher price than they had paid in the past, and he had rushed them out to the waiting welders on the tanker.

No welders ever worked under more trying conditions. The seas, which had relented a little during the early summer, at least in good weather, began to build up again toward the end of July. At high tide the waves washed up on the boat deck, eddying around the men crouched on the patch with electric welding rods in their hands, shocking them violently and threatening to sweep them overboard. They finally posted a guard to warn of the worst waves; every few minutes the guard would shout, "*Watch it!*" and the welders (two usually worked at a time) would leap up and run for safety. To avoid shocks they tried to keep from touching bare metal with their hands. At the start of each day they would hold the welding rod in a shirt tail, and then, as the shirt tail got wet, in another, dryer part of the shirt. After a short time they always found themselves twisting around to use the shirt areas under their armpits—the only bit of dry cloth left. And all the while they would be clutching frantically at tools to keep them from being carried away by the waves, and trying unsteadily to keep their balance on the patch, as it rocked and shook in the grip of the swells and their backwash.

But at last this stage of the work was finished. By the end of July one side of the patch was completely welded, and the tricky job of contouring lay before them.

The shape of the finished patch would be roughly that of a half cylinder—something like a rain gutter turned up on one edge, although much more gently curved. To bend the great sheet of steel into approximately this shape, they would proceed as planned: pluck it up in the center, then shape the twenty I-beams by cutting those pie-shaped pieces out of them and welding the cuts back together so that each beam would assume precisely the bend called for by Simmons' contour measurements. Each of the beams would have a curvature all its own, and when all of them were welded to the patch, side by side, the great sheet would be rounded into the exact form required to fit the battered hull. The beams would remain on the outside, vertical, parallel and facing the sea.

The beams were the key to the whole plan: if they were curved properly, the patch would fit. To assure the accuracy of their curvature, Deir first sketched the contour line for each beam on the deck. Then, instead of merely trying to match the big girders to the lines he had drawn, he threw in an intermediate step. He took some flat steel bars which could be bent with relative ease and welded them to the deck, narrow edge down, along the contour lines. Now he had not only a curved *line* to fit the beams to but a sort of curved *wall*. When the beams nestled snugly against this wall they would be shaped just right.

He and Maurice Simmons went to work on the beams, aided briefly by Paul Brady, who was on another of his periodic visits. They cut the wedges in the girders at intervals of approximately thirty inches, bent the beams to conform to the curve of the flat bars, then welded the cuts closed.

Midway in this process the weekend loomed, and Deir sent everyone but Simmons home. "It's just a two-man job," he said. "No need for everyone to hang around."

The next step was to pull up the center of the patch into roughly the rounded shape it would finally take. Each beam would then be set on top of the patch, the patch itself would be pulled tight against the curve of the beam, and the two would then be welded together.

To raise up the center of the patch, Deir burned two holes roughly along the center line, threaded a cable through one with a shackle to hold it, and fixed a big hook in the other. Then with the cargo boom he hoisted the center of the patch off the deck; the top and bottom of the patch drooped down and touched. This was the basic shape. It was essential to keep those two edges pinned down if the patch was to hold this curve. Deir and Simmons jammed the top edge under some big pipes that ran the length of the boat deck on which they were working, right up against the deckhouse bulkhead. That edge was now held fast. Since there was nothing to shove the bottom edge under, it was fixed firmly to the deck with three bolts. Then, so that the patch would not belly up too far at certain key points, it was held down by lashing a chain and a cable across it. And finally, at one corner where less curvature was required, the steel was pulled off the deck a few inches with a chainfall attached to a davit winch.

They stood back and looked it over. The patch was now twisted in several directions at once, under severe strain. As they prepared to crawl on top of it with the first girder, Deir warned Simmons to be careful. "You better be ready to jump fast," he said. "If anything gives that thing'll snap you into the ocean like a tiddlywink."

Well into Saturday night, Deir and Simmons welded beams to the patch, varying the stresses on the great steel sheet wherever necessary to fit it to the girders. By 11:00 p.m. they had affixed four beams and were able to remove the cable-and-shackle, leaving the patch pulled up only by the big hook, which was attached to the reinforced cargo boom.

The waves had spared them all day, but as it grew dark the seas worsened. When they knocked off work Deir lingered on deck for a while with Simmons, staring out uneasily at the ocean. He couldn't see much, but it sounded bad.

"Boy, if the seas start coming over this daggone thing now, we'll be in bad trouble," he told Simmons. "A couple of real good waves will straighten that hook right out."

Simmons stared at the hook, which was made of one-and-a-half-inch steel and was supposed to be able to support up to ten tons. The strain on it now couldn't be much over a ton.

"You're kidding," he said. "You've never *seen* a wave that'd bend that steel."

"I just don't want to see one until we get all those beams on," Deir said. For safety's sake he eased off the cable slightly to relieve the strain on the hook. At last they went to bed.

Deir was awakened at daybreak by the sound of very heavy seas, accompanied by an ominous racket from the boat deck. He sprang out of bed, shouted for Simmons, and ran out. They stood in a sheltered place and watched grimly as a great parade of towering waves came in off the Atlantic and swept onto the boat deck. As each swell came aboard it slammed the patch down against the deck; as the water rolled back it lifted the steel into the air, where the next sea caught it and slammed it down again. While they watched, the three bolts holding the bottom edge of the patch to the deck sheared off, one after another. At one side of the deck the sixteen unattached I-beams, which weighed six hundred pounds each, began to shift with the swells.

"Let's go," shouted Deir. "Damn if we can afford to lose those!"

They hurried onto the windswept, spray-soaked deck and, one by one, burned holes in the beams, then tied them down with cables.

"Look at that hook!" Deir called. As Simmons watched, a sea swept across the patch, and the big hook gave visibly. Simmons looked again. "The hell with the hook!" he cried. "Take a look at those beams on the patch. They're being pounded straight!"

The patch was taking a ferocious beating. The seas were hammering it against the deck repeatedly. The lower edge, which had been held by the bolts, was being twisted and dented. The curve had almost disappeared from its center. The entire patch was shifting and sliding. The hook was no longer helping to hold it; the big sheet of steel, now lashed to the deck only by a single chain and a light cable, was in danger of being swept into the sea.

Deir raced down the deck and snatched up a loose cable lying there. "If we can lace this through one of those holes in the patch and tie it down we may be able to hold her," he said. "You grab hold of this end and I'll run onto the patch and try to slip the cable through."

"For God's sake, be careful. You go overboard and you're gone, and nothing I can do will make a damn bit of difference."

"Man," said Deir earnestly, "I'm not *going* overboard!"

There was no denying the danger. To tie in the cable he would have to race halfway across the patch, which sloped toward the sea, run the cable through the hole and tighten a shackle, and he was going to have to do it without being swept off the deck by those huge breakers.

He watched for his chance, yelled, "Here goes!" and sped toward the center of the patch. He threaded the cable through and was beginning to put on the shackle when he heard Simmons' shout of warning. He dropped the cable, wheeled and sped for shelter. He made it—wet but safe. Simmons was not so lucky. Deir saw him scrambling to his feet, dripping. He had been caught by the wave and knocked over—and he had lost the cable.

Frantically they ran around the ship trying to find another cable. At last they located one and tried again. This time when the wave came they were ready for it. They ran back up the deck and stood against the wall, where they had found shelter before. But now it wasn't enough. This breaker was enormous; it was obviously going to sweep clear over the ship. "Jump!" roared Deir, and he pointed over his head.

Above the starboard boat deck on which they stood was a framework of two-inch pipes. On the port side it supported the wood-and-canvas sun deck. On the starboard side the boards had been stripped away by previous storms, and nothing was left but the bare pipes. As the great wave approached, Deir and Simmons leaped for these pipes and pulled themselves up as far as possible. Deir, wiry and acrobatic, heaved his torso up past the pipe, stiffened his arms in front of him, and rested erect with the pipe across his thighs, like a man leaning on a porch railing. Simmons chinned himself and then swung his legs up in front of him until they were high above his head.

Almost immediately they were inundated. Long seconds passed. The water still churned around them, and Deir thought, My God, I can't hold my breath much longer. He was struck by the absurdity of his position; here he was with his head three feet above the highest deck on the ship, and he was entirely under water and in danger of drowning. The wave seemed to stay forever.

At last it was gone. Deir and Simmons emerged, coughing and gasping. Almost immediately another wave swept over them, worse than the first. When the water subsided again the two men dropped off the pipes and sped around the deckhouse to the shelter of the port side.

They stood there, soaked and panting; minutes passed before they could speak. Then Simmons said, "Look at my shoes." Deir looked.

"What about them?"

"They're dry," Simmons said in wonder. "I stuck my feet up so high my shoes were clear above the water. How about that? They didn't even get wet."

"The rest of you didn't do so good," Deir said.

They discussed their situation briefly, but there was nothing much to discuss. Waves or no waves, they simply had to return to the starboard deck and lash down that patch. As they came around the deckhouse they could see that the div-

156

ing platform also was in danger. It was guyed to the deck with two cables, which were now loose and shaking. The vertical boom supporting the platform was swaying unsteadily.

"The patch first," said Deir. "Same thing. You hang on to one end of the cable and I'll run the other end through the hole in the patch."

He waited for a break in the waves, and then sped out to the patch again. He passed the cable through the hole, then raced back to safety ahead of the next wave. Then he ran back and put in the shackle. Dashing back and forth between waves, he finally managed to get the cable on and tie the patch down. It now was fairly secure. Next he and Simmons raised up the patch with the heavy-duty jack and shoved some strong timbers under the steel to preserve whatever curvature remained. They accomplished all this too while running up and down the slanted deck to avoid being washed away by the waves.

Fixing the diving elevator was far more dangerous. Since the patch extended out beyond the edge of the deck, it hid the bases of the two cables supporting the elevator. One of the cables was completely out of reach anyway; the only possible way to secure the diving boom, therefore, was to get to the other cable, hitch a new cable to it, and draw it tight. And the only way to hitch on a new cable was to fasten it to a shackle that was located just under the edge of the patch! To do the job, Deir would have to dash headlong down the sloping patch toward the sea with the cable in his hand, skid to a stop as close to the edge as possible, reach under the patch to the shackle and try to attach a new cable before a wave could sweep him away.

Simmons shook his head. The sea just off the edge of the boat deck was a churning caldron; if Deir ever went in at that spot he would be beyond help. "You be careful," he said. "If you go in there I gotta go after you and I'm too young to die."

"Boy, don't you *worry*," Deir said. "I don't *want* to go in there."

His years as a steeplejack had given Deir a co-ordination and sense of timing far beyond that of most men. Simmons watched him in admiration as he went about rescuing the diving elevator. He ran down the patch so fast Simmons thought he must certainly plunge overboard before he could stop. Then, at the last possible moment, he came to a dead halt, dropped to his knees, reached under the patch for the shackle, threaded the new cable through with steady fingers, and raced back before the next wave could sweep him away. As it was, he was knocked off his feet and drenched once again.

With both the patch and the diving elevator secured, the worst of the crisis was over. They spent the rest of the day keeping things safe, moving about from patch to beams to diving platform, tightening cables and chains and bolts. They worked at such chores until long after dark. At last the swells seemed to die down somewhat, and they went wearily to bed.

The next day the water was still so rough that they knew the rest of the crew would never be able to get out to the tanker. It was now clear that the patch would have to be raised out of the sea's reach once and for all. They spent the whole day doing that. The top edge, which had been stuck under the deck pipes, they now lifted until it rested on top of the pipes, roughly thirty inches off the deck. The lower edge, which had been bolted to the deck, they raised onto steel sawhorses which Deir welded to the deck plates. Now the seaward side of the patch was several feet off the deck, and the patch itself was roughly level. Resting high in the air, the patch was safe from all but the heaviest seas—and it could never again be slammed up and down by backwash.

A great deal of work had to be done just to catch up. The patch was almost flat. The beams which had been welded to it had been pulled virtually straight; they had to be removed and recut. They went right at it. By the time the others came back on board Tuesday, two days after the great seas had half drowned Deir and Simmons, the four beams were re-curved and set back in place. With more help the work went even faster. By Wednesday all twenty beams were on, in orderly parallel rows, and the molding of the patch was finished. The previous week Little had brought out a couple of light railroad tracks; these were now welded to the top and

bottom edges of the patch to provide stiffening and to rein-
force the edges against the cutting action of the cables that
would soon be strapped across them.

The patch was a trim, handsome piece of work. It had a
gentle, graceful curve, yet it looked sturdy, professional and
businesslike. It was also enormous—half the size of a tennis
court, almost as long as a five-story building is high. It
seemed beyond belief that they could hoist this huge thing off
its supports and over the side into that boiling sea and then
pin it firmly to the ship's side.

They had only one more day to get ready for the divers,
who were due out Thursday, and there was still a great deal
to do. The schedule had been thrown off by the wave damage
and by the bad weather that had prevented the crew members from getting back on board. Now, with Duke and
Woody on the way, they had to catch up, fast: before the
patch could go overboard it had to be flipped over and
welded on the reverse side—all in just a few hours.

There were now plenty of hands available for the work.
Little, Duncan and Doughtie were back, and so was Paul
Brady.

Brady had decided to stay a while. He had been running a
regular shuttle service between Suffolk and Ocean City;
there were times when he would drive out one day, return to
Virginia that night, work in his store all the following day,
and be back on the road to Maryland by nightfall. The *Queen*
was beginning to occupy his thoughts even more than his
beloved business. Finally he made his decision. He would go
out to the tanker and remain a few days—at least until the
patch went overboard. He had found that he could safely
leave his store in his wife's care; he wasn't nearly so confident
about the *African Queen*. He was worried about the progress
of the work, and by the amount of time it was taking. What
had originally been described to him as a project that would
take only a few weeks was now ending its fifth month. He
decided he had better be on hand to urge the work forward.
Besides, Deir always seemed glad to see him and reluctant to
have him leave. Maybe he would welcome the help.

There was considerable uneasiness as they prepared to turn

the patch over. It now weighed about thirteen tons; could the reconstructed boom handle all that weight? This also was to be the first test of Deir's ingenious electric drill–reduction gear combination; more than one crew member had quiet doubts about the ability of the one-and-a-quarter-inch drill to hoist that great mass of steel, reduction gear or no reduction gear.

Everyone was on hand that morning to watch as Deir fitted the gear box to the winch on the boat davit, and then the drill to the gear box. The cable ran from the davit to the smokestack and from there to the boom. The patch would be lifted, seaward edge first, until it stood vertically against the deckhouse. Then the bottom would be swung out, and it would be lowered again, other side up.

Deir pulled the trigger, the drill hummed, the cable ran through the boom, and slowly and steadily the huge patch rose off its supports until it was standing against the bulkhead. The cargo boom was as steady as a rock. The men swung out the bottom of the patch and, with Deir at the winch, let it down gently so that the side that had been hidden was now exposed. They carefully set one edge on the pipes, the other on the steel horses. There was a sudden relaxation of tension. Somebody whooped. It had all been so easy.

They gathered around the patch and studied it. It was now bowl-shaped, and the inside of the bowl was flaked with rust.

"Can't weld with that rust in there," Deir said. "Pearly and I'll do the welding, but somebody's got to go ahead of us, chipping off the rust. We got a lot of welding to do today if we want to have everything ready for Duke tomorrow."

"I'll chip," Brady said promptly. "Damn if I'm going to have Morris out here at a hundred and fifteen dollars a day and nothing for him to do."

All the rest of that day Deir and Strait welded, with Brady and Mack Duncan tirelesssly cleaning away the rust ahead of them. They worked virtually without a break from 9:00 A.M. until 4:00 P.M., and when they quit, the patch was finished.

"I'm close to finished myself," Deir said, stretching. "I

swear, I've never been so tired of looking at a welding rod in my life." The standard rate of speed for a welder is considered to be about eight feet an hour. For seven hours Deir and Strait had averaged better than ten feet an hour each.

But there was no rest yet. That evening they rerigged the patch, raised it up again, the outside curve facing the sea, and got everything ready for the next day's work. When dark came Deir turned on the lights he had set up after the boom broke, and they worked away far into the night, tying down cables, positioning the patch, cleaning up details.

Before they went to bed Deir confronted Brady. "Well?" he said. "We making progress enough for you?"

Brady grinned. "Boy, I don't mind telling you, there have been times when I thought the great day would never come. When I see that patch go over the side I'm gonna draw the first untroubled breath I've had in five months."

"Well, don't get too untroubled. We still got an awful long way to go."

The day dawned mild and sunny. Morris and Crisp arrived with Kin Reed. Alvah Sadler was along, too. No one wanted to miss the big effort.

Morris went down and threaded the cables through the ship's side, using the arm holes he had burned earlier. The cables were carried to the deck and tied down there. Then, as everybody watched, Deir manned his drill again, and the patch was slowly raised into the air. Because of the way the ship sloped, the patch tended to swing toward the stern, but they got a line on it and held it steady. Then, as it hung there over the deck, they arranged the cables through and around it.

Four cables had been threaded into holes far down on the hull, under the damaged area, and these now had to be pulled up vertically and strapped across the patch as it hung from the boom over the side of the ship. The task proved unexpectedly tricky, because it was necessary to determine exactly where each of the four cables went in relation to the twenty vertical beams welded to the outside of the patch. Only after that had been done could the cables be flipped out from the deck and swung over the patch. That, too, was exceedingly difficult. At last Little solved the problem in the only way possible: he coolly climbed to the top of the patch as it dangled out over the sea, and from this precarious position he took the cables as Deir passed them up from the deck.

Once the cables were properly arranged the patch was carefully lowered until it was just above the water. Seven more cables had been strung through holes burned in the hull *above* the damage, and these were now threaded through matching holes just below the top edge of the patch.

The diving elevator had been unhooked and allowed to lean out away from the tanker's side, and its supporting cables were spread wide so the patch would go down between them.

Then the patch was lowered into the heaving seas alongside the ship. They had to work fast; the swells were beating the patch against the ship's side, setting up a fearful racket and doing the patch no good. As the patch descended, a shackle got snagged somehow on the hull below; they struggled for a while to free it and finally had to jack the patch away from the ship against the force of the seas before they could get the shackle past the obstruction.

Hastily they lowered the patch under the surface, where the waves could no longer batter it. As soon as it was in position over the damaged hull area, the cables were pulled up snug and fastened to the deck. The patch was now hanging from seven cables and lashed to the hull by four more. At last the sunken interior of the *African Queen* was no longer open to the sea. When they looked in the engine-room doorway they found that the swinging and splashing of water had died down to little more than a soft ripple.

16

Now, WITH the coming of summer, as many as nine men often slept aboard the damaged tanker at a time, and after early July—with the single exception of the weekend Deir and

Simmons spent there alone—there were never fewer than four or five. For these men life aboard the *African Queen* had a quality all its own, a little like army barracks life, a little like living on a desert isle, but in most ways like nothing else in the world.

From the start the salvagers were confronted by unique problems of environment. As time passed, the men adapted to some of these conditions and changed others to make them more acceptable. By the time the patch went over, the adjustment was complete. The crewmen were never really comfortable aboard the tanker, yet they got along remarkably well, worked hard, and even came to enjoy themselves. This called for a triumph over some very strange circumstances.

The twelve-degree list was always with them. Depending on the direction, any short stroll along one of the decks was an exercise either in climbing, descending or scuttling along "one foot short and one foot long," and often all three. The men slept in individual bunks now, so they did not have the unpleasant close-quarters difficulties that had afflicted Little and Deir that first week, but they had difficulties enough. Some bunks ran along the ship's longitudinal axis, others ran athwartships; either way no one ever slept in complete comfort. Some men lay in a trough between the cabin bulkhead and the bottom of the bunk. Such men customarily got up in the morning with one arm and leg tingling from poor circulation. Others, sleeping head-down along the direction of the slope, greeted each day with a stiff neck and faces diffused with blood. If they swung around and slept with their feet toward the low starboard side they often woke up in the middle of the night sprawled half out of their bunks. Maurice Simmons, assigned to such a bunk, found that on stormy nights water frequently collected in a sizable pool in the low corner of his room, with the result that he sometimes awakened with one foot ankle-deep in water. When he managed to stay dry he usually discovered that his shoes had slid into the puddle anyhow.

It made little difference. Nobody stayed dry for long aboard the *Queen*. The tank deck was normally ten feet below water on the starboard side, with roughly a three-foot dry strip along the port side at high tide—roughly because the ship, besides being canted to starboard, was also slightly stern-low, so the strip narrowed down to nothing near the aft superstructure. This meant that for most of the months the tanker was inhabited, the crew had to wade a short distance to go forward, and since it was simply too much bother to remove their shoes, they were constantly sloshing around with wet feet. Later, Deir strung a cable over the tank deck as a support for the pumps with which he expected to drain the tanks. Someone promptly suspended another cable from it, right over the wet spot; thereafter it was possible to clear the wading area by swinging down from the aft superstructure like Tarzan. But this offered scant comfort; it was almost impossible to stay dry anyhow, because the work area was frequently swept by waves, and practically no part of the ship was really protected from the sea. Furthermore, clothes that had become wet refused to dry; after a week they were still damp to the touch. Simmons was not the only one, therefore, who had to put on wet shoes in the morning. Everyone had to do it, constantly.

Insects were another source of discomfort. For some weeks the *Queen* was infested with mosquitoes and beach flies. No one ever figured out how they had made the ten-mile sea trip, but they were all over the tanker. The mosquitoes seemed to lurk in special hiding places; a man might walk fifty feet along a deck unmolested and then suddenly find himself under heavy attack. And late workers soon gave up any hope of grabbing a daylight nap; during the day the flies would swarm all over them as they lay on their bunks.

Finally there was the grime, probably the most irksome problem of all. Everything on the deck seemed coated with oil. Over the months, dust blown out of various crannies of the ship or carried from shore by the wind had settled on the sticky black surfaces. In addition, paint had begun to flake everywhere. The result was that no one stayed clean for more than a few minutes after donning fresh clothes. Personal cleanliness was a never-ending challenge. There was no way to bathe; the sea water was too hard to wash in and fresh water had to be carried ten miles from the mainland.

There were never more than fifty gallons of it aboard the *Queen* at any one time, and that quantity would last only a few days. The men "bathed" with the paste detergent that Deir had used to clear the oil from the water in the engine room; they would spread it on their bodies, then wipe it off with a clean rag. Fresh water was so closely rationed that each man had to wash his face, brush his teeth and shave every day from a single cupful. (Though shaving was a problem, getting a haircut was not. Woody Crisp was an accomplished barber, and he cut everyone's hair while he was aboard.)

As time passed the ship became dirtier. Rust began to appear on the whiteness of the two superstructures, and the decks were scored with it. The inexorable decline of the *Queen* was clearly perceptible to the men, especially after they had been away a few days, and it bothered them all—Deir in particular. It was shocking to see a beautiful ship waste away, and it was going to be costly, too, when the time came to sell her. Deir made bad jokes about the flaking bulkheads; from time to time when everyone was working at some back-breaking project, Deir would gaze around him at the rusting steel and say, "I guess we'll have to knock off pretty quick and paint this ship." It always got a laugh, but Deir himself didn't really find it that funny. "God *knows,* I hate to see this thing go to pieces like this," he told Brady. "It just doesn't seem right."

The living quarters suffered to some extent from the all-pervasive oiliness, but they were far cleaner than the rest of the ship. During the early weeks of the operation, when there were seldom more than two people on the tanker at a time, everybody slept in the room originally selected by Little and Deir (it still had Deir's penciled diagram of the *Queen* in cross section on one wall as a reminder of that first furious storm). Later Deir and Little moved to another room, and their original cabin for a time became a galley (or kitchen, as they always referred to it)—simply because it still contained the stove on its slanted shelf, as well as the equally tipsy table, which was used for meals. But by now, after five months, a fairly permanent arrangement of rooms had been worked out which provided each crew member with a bunk of his own. All the living quarters were still located, of necessity, along the same corridor (the matching corridor on the starboard side was under water). The kitchen was moved to a new room farther aft, with a pantry next door. The next cabin was used for Simmons' diving equipment, and the one forward of that as a storage room for tools. Next came the original kitchen, where Henley now slept. Bounding this cabin was the passageway to the port deck which Deir and Little had raced through to save the life raft. On the other side of it was the cabin of Maurice Simmons and Mack Duncan, and beyond that the new living quarters of Deir and Little, with one more room still farther forward. Each of the four sleeping cabins contained two double bunks, so as new crew members arrived they found sleeping space ready for them. All of these cabins were on the same side of the corridor. On the other, inboard, side were lockers and the entrance to the engine room.

The toilets used by the *Queen*'s original crew were in small rooms along a transverse passageway near the engine-room door. They were still in use. To flush them, the men carried pails of water from the flooded engine room. No one ever quite figured out where the waste went, but it apparently went away, so no one worried much about it.

If Deir was work boss aboard the *African Queen*, Henley Doughtie was the central figure in most other respects. Early in the game, the men sharing guard watches with Henley discovered that they ate better when he was preparing the food; he was a superb cook. The rest of the time they didn't fare so well. As more and more men stayed aboard the ship, mealtimes became a mad scramble. The men would drift away from work when they got hungry and go to the kitchen. Each would prepare his own meal. Since there were few good housekeepers among them, and no good cooks aside from Doughtie, this got to be a pretty messy practice, and the food was always terrible. Usually it consisted of the inevitable canned beans and Vienna sausage. The room became dirtier and dirtier, the food less and less palatable, the men more and more dissatisfied. At last Deir asked Henley to become full-time cook; he hated to lose a strong and willing worker, but the advantages clearly outweighed the disadvantages. Henley was delighted.

"The main thing," said Deir, who had been most repelled by the messiness, "is to keep the place clean. I know that won't be easy"—he glanced around at the oil-blackened deck—"but it sure will be great if you can do it. I know you don't like this dirt any more than anyone else."

"You ain't gonna be able to find a speck of dirt nowhere around that goddam food," said Doughtie, immensely pleased with his new responsibilities. "You gonna be able to eat off of the motherlovin' floor. But I tell you one damn thing right now—all them sonofabitches better clean theirself off before they set foot in my kitchen. Or they goddam well don't eat."

"Fair enough," said Deir, grinning. "I'll tell 'em. You make 'em do it."

"They'll do it," growled Henley.

The change was spectacular. Henley took to wearing white clothes. He kept his kitchen swept and washed. After a short time he moved it to a better place, urged on by Alvah Sadler. "This old room is really bad," Sadler told Doughtie during one of his weekend visits. "There's no air. It's all dirty now. It's full of flies. We'll just move it down the hall to that big empty cabin and we can make a larder out of that room next door." There already was a galley on the *Queen,* of course— the big gleaming stainless-steel room on the deck above. But it was inconvenient, it was much too large, and it was taking seas in one corner. Nobody ever considered using it. The room they did pick was just fine. They removed the bunks and put in a larger dining table and benches, all properly leveled; the plumb bob was moved to the new location as an aid in determining the angle of pitch and also so it could be checked regularly for signs of instability in the tanker. Sadler and Doughtie took off the door to the new kitchen and re-placed it with a screen door to keep out flies. They put in new shelves.

The improvement in the environment was nothing compared with the improvement in the food. Pork and beans disappeared from the menu. When Brady sent out a big bag of beans one day (you could feed a lot of men a lot of meals on a bag of beans) Henley peered at the instructions and grunted. "Says they gotta soak twenty-four hours," he said. "I'll soak them good." And he threw them into the sea. "We already *got* one bag of the bastards," he muttered.

Doughtie began to make out shopping lists for Kin Reed. Fried chicken appeared on the table. Corn bread was served for breakfast. There was green salad, and pan-fried potatoes, and hamburgers served with a delicious onion gravy. Although pork and beans were out, there were bean dishes of other kinds, the most popular of which was chili con carne. Beldon Little, who disliked boiled potatoes, found himself eating Henley's. "I don't know what you're putting in them," he mumbled around a mouthful, "and maybe I don't want to know, but they're sure good." Sometimes there were surprise dishes. Sadler frequently sent out treats—soft drinks, pastries, fruit. In addition a wide variety of canned goods had been recovered intact from the ship's original larder: among them fruits, soups and all kinds of sauces. Some of these items were *real* surprises: the labels had been washed off and there was no way to tell what was in the cans until they were open. Some of the contents proved completely unidentifiable; the crew members, gastronomic conservatives, took no chances on these. They threw them overboard.

Fish was served often. Henley would catch bass off the starboard side, up forward near the pilothouse, where they were occasionally so thick that he could fill a bushel basket in half an hour. Sometimes Duke Morris, working down below, would call up over the interphone, "Tell Henley to move aft about twenty feet. That's where the fish are." Henley often caught so many he couldn't serve them all at one meal. He took to keeping the leftovers, alive, in the pool of water that formed in the old galley, where the seas swept in through the messhall doorway and were trapped by the raised threshold. Fish, in fact, got to be too much of a good thing for Henley. He had to catch them, clean them and cook them, and he hated the cleaning. Periodically he refused to serve them, but anyone who wanted fish badly enough could talk him into changing his mind. Henley would grumble, stomping about the kitchen and complaining profanely. "Next sonofabitch wants fish gonna clean them hisself. Gonna be a new rule around this goddam kitchen. Miz Doughtie's boy got a damn sight more important things goin' on than messin' around with no stinkin' fish." But he would clean and cook them painstakingly; the one thing he could never resist was a satisfied customer.

No one escaped Henley's good-humored grousing. He was after Little constantly; Little liked to poke around the stove, and whenever Doughtie caught him at it he unceremoniously threw him out of the kitchen. Little would flee, chuckling. He was a finicky eater and that, too, annoyed Doughtie. One night Little said he didn't want onions in his pan-fried potatoes.

Henley frowned. "Look, dammit, everybody else here wants 'em with onions. What you want me to do?"

"Make two batches."

"In what?" snarled Henley. "My goddam pocket?"

Deir also had dietary crotchets—notably a dislike for fried fish and corn bread, two of Doughtie's greatest culinary triumphs—and though Henley greatly admired Deir he had no compunctions about cussing him out ferociously. "Gotta keep the little sonofabitch in his place," he once confided to Brady, gazing after Deir fondly. "Gotta tighten up on him once in a while. Ain't he a goddam wonder, though? That motherlovin' figurehead."

"Figurehead?" asked Brady, puzzled.

Henley glared. "Goddam it, you know anyone *else* can do figures in his damn head the way that man can?"

With the peppery Kin Reed, Doughtie carried on an endless feud. All the men made it a practice to check with Doughtie whenever they couldn't find a tool, and at last he pre-empted a room near the kitchen as a tool shed, muttering sourly about people who couldn't keep track of their things. But Reed never *could* find his tools, and his constant requests annoyed Henley—especially when Reed irritably accused the cook of hiding things from him. The day Kin borrowed Henley's own personal hammer and then forgot where he left *that* was one the crew members long remembered. Henley treated them to a display of profanity that left them slack-jawed in admiration. He finally found the hammer himself, but he stayed angry about it for weeks afterward, rumbling fiercely at the mere mention of Reed's name.

Another of Henley's butts was Mack Duncan, whose sheepish grin when Doughtie swore at him merely encouraged the cook to greater efforts. Over a period of months Henley cussed at Duncan enough, as he said later, "to send any man in the world to hell." Duncan survived, grinning.

But of all Henley's targets, the clean-cut, cheerful Maurice Simmons was easily his favorite. "That bastard is so goddam good," he would protest to the others. "He just makes me mad. He's gotta have his ass eaten out once in a while. It's good for him." Doughtie didn't usually offer a reason for attacking his victims, but in Simmons' case he made an exception. Simmons was the crew's champion long-distance eater. He ate prodigious meals, and he ate endlessly between meals. At night he could drink half a dozen after-supper cups of coffee. Doughtie, secretly pleased at Simmons' enjoyment of the food, professed to be furious.

"Goddam you triflin' no-account," he would snarl at Simmons. "Make your own coffee. Wasn't for you, I'd be in the sack an hour ago."

Like everyone else, Simmons was amused by Henley, and fond of him. Nevertheless, he frankly found Doughtie's profanity a little hard to take. He was not a prude; he occasionally used mild profanity himself, and in the Navy he had heard it employed by masters. But never had he encountered anyone like Henley. Simmons was a devout Catholic, and much of Doughtie's language was blasphemous. Simmons was willing to make reasonable allowances, but one night the cook somehow managed to combine in one sentence the name of the Deity and a particularly atrocious sexual reference, and Simmons abruptly stood up and walked out of the kitchen.

Woody Crisp, also a devout man, was the only one aboard who flatly refused to let Henley swear at him "You can cuss all you want to and I can't stop you," Woody said levelly at the supper table one night, "but you keep your mouth off me, or I'm going to crawl all over you."

Henley, towering over the diver's tender, looked perplexed. "Well, Woody," he said, "damn if I know what I said to rile you, but whatever it was I didn't mean you no harm."

"Okay, then; that's fine," said Crisp, and returned to his supper.

One day, to everyone's surprise, Kin Reed brought out Simmons' wife and mother, who had come up from Norfolk unannounced to visit him. Dorothy Simmons was attractive, blonde and pregnant. Mrs. Floyd Arner, Simmons' mother, was a pleasant, gray-haired, bright-eyed woman. Both women clambered up the swaying rope ladder and were taken on a brief tour of the tanker. Then, while Maurice and Dorothy went off to a quiet corner to talk, Mrs. Arner was entertained in the kitchen by Henley.

For a while Doughtie kept his vocabulary under tight rein, his face showing the effort. Then the talk turned to Simmons' appetite, and he could control himself no longer. "Why, goddam, Ma'am," he rumbled enthusiastically, "that boy of yours is the eatingest sonofabitch I ever saw in my life!"

Mrs. Arner responded like a Virginia lady. "I know he is, Mr. Doughtie," she said gravely. "I raised him that way."

"Now that's a nice woman," Doughtie said afterward. "She told me she used to send that goddam Maurice off to school with four, five sandwiches to eat. I told her, 'Well, hell, that ain't got a chance with him now; he'll eat that between breakfast and lunch.'"

Although it was a Friday, Henley had to serve the women meat; for two days he had been unable to catch a single fish over the side. He apologized—all summer long he had managed to have fish for the Catholic crewmen on Friday—but the women said graciously that they understood and were sure it would be all right. Simmons fussed about it later, glad for a chance to ride Doughtie. "A *good* cook would have had fish, one way or another!" he stormed.

Henley was delighted, "It ain't no damn fault of mine if the fish wasn't biting," he growled, stomping around the kitchen. "I didn't have no bait worth the name. Maybe the next time I'll cut *you* up, you ugly cross-eyed bastard. You keep track of your own goddam religion."

Life aboard the *Queen* was not easy for Doughtie. For one thing, he was virtually indispensable, so he could not be spared ashore for long. Although Mack Duncan did fill in for him for a couple of weeks, everybody was glad to see Henley return, and he ultimately remained on the tanker for fifty-eight consecutive days, a record no one else even approached. All during this time his principal difficulty was maintaining a stock of alcohol; on a good day he managed to put away four quarts, and he could scarcely get by on less than one. His chief supplier was Kin Reed, who understood Doughtie's need and regularly declared a truce in their feud to keep Henley in liquor. Henley paid him for the stuff in advance, but on more than one occasion Kin quietly added money of his own, knowing that the cook would run dry otherwise. Nevertheless, Henley continued to have problems. One day Lloyd Deir was helping Reed unload kitchen supplies when he came across a shapeless parcel and tossed it from the boat to the deck of the *Queen*, where Doughtie had been signaling frantically to Kin for his special package. There was a splintering crash, and the tangy aroma of distilled spirits filled the air. Swearing viciously, Henley grabbed up the broken package and hurled it into the sea.

Drunk or sober, Henley kept turning out hearty meals, and he did so under the worst possible circumstances. His equipment was primitive; he fed as many as a dozen people (including visitors) on a temperamental two-burner kerosene stove, using only the few skillets and pots he had brought with him and serving everybody out of eight plates and five coffee cups. Nobody ever thought to buy more—mainly because there usually were not more than half a dozen people aboard at a time, and one or two of these often could be counted on to skip coffee.

No cook ever got along with less water. Instead of salting cooked vegetables, Henley would throw in a cup of salt water, thereby saving a cup of fresh water. For dishwashing he used two basins, one for soaping, one for rinsing, and tonight's rinse water became tomorrow's soap water. If the dishwater stayed reasonably clean he might use it once again to scrub up the kitchen, which—especially by late summer— began to show the effects of months of use by oil-impregnated crewmen. In addition, he surreptitiously took more than his allotment of water to wash himself: he just couldn't stand to handle food when he wasn't clean. He never told the others because he wasn't sure they would understand—particularly since he frequently heckled Simmons for being wastefully sanitary. "Goddam if I don't think you been sneaking a bath," he once said balefully. "You just remember one thing, boy— out here you don't stay no cleaner than no other sonofabitch."

Henley put in a long day. He didn't get up any earlier than anyone else, but he managed to get breakfast ready on time anyhow. On most days the men would rise when they felt like it, but usually they were up by eight o'clock. While Brady was on the ship he took charge of routing everyone out ("Time is money"). He'd get up at about seven and start hollering down the corridor, "*All right! Hit the deck! Everybody up!*" The men would complain bitterly, but he'd get them up. He had the most trouble with Duncan, who often had to be threatened by Henley with the loss of his breakfast before he could be lured out of bed.

Breakfast was well worth getting up for. Henley would have the coffee going, but everything else was cooked to order. The men could have any kind of eggs they liked, or pancakes if they preferred, and there was usually bacon and corn bread for those who wanted it.

Lunch was a problem. Usually the work couldn't be interrupted arbitrarily—a piece of heavy steel can't be left dangling on a cable just because it's time to eat—so the lunch breaks varied widely, tending to get later and later as the summer wore on. Henley railed. He kept getting the food on the table at a later hour, until at last he was serving lunch at 2:30. At that point he called a halt. "Anybody comes to eat later than what I get it on the table is just gonna be one hungry sonofabitch," he said. "This is what time Miz Doughtie's boy serves lunch and this is what time you bastards gonna eat it." And that's what time they ate it thereafter.

For a few weeks that summer, late afternoon was Henley's time with his birds. One day a whole flock of small yellow-and-brown birds appeared out of nowhere, presumably blown out to sea by the offshore wind. Nobody knew what kind they were, but they remained aboard, and every day Henley put out food for them. One or two became so tame that they would alight on the cook's shoulder. After a couple of weeks one was found dead on the tank deck, then two more the next day. Day by day more of them sickened and died. At last the entire flock was gone, and with it a source of deep enjoyment for Henley.

Supper was even more uncertain than lunch aboard the *African Queen.* Henley never did get it nailed down fast. Deir hated to knock off work for the day, and Doughtie eventually learned to wait him out. As a result supper was usually eaten very late—at around 8:00 or 9:00 P.M.—because Henley wouldn't even start cooking it until he got the word that work was finished.

For most of the men, the period after supper was the most pleasant of the day. The *Queen's* crewmen were, in Duncan's phrase, a happy family, and the late evening gave them their best opportunity to enjoy one another's company. They would sit around the table for hours, talking about their past lives ("Telling lies," Henley called it), discussing women and philosophizing generally. One day Pearly told Brady about a loud-speaker system he had at home that wasn't working properly. Brady promptly diagnosed the trouble from Pearly's description, and Pearly went home the next weekend and fixed it. Brady enjoyed these sessions when they occurred at night, but when they came after lunch—as they sometimes did—he found they were traps. He would be chattering away with the rest when he would realize suddenly that an hour or more had passed without profit. He would leap to his feet and cry, "Let's get out of here to where the work is!" The other men amiably referred to him as "the pusher."

While the talk went on, Henley would be doing the dishes, occasionally tossing in a few lies of his own and griping steadily. All night long—and sometimes the bull sessions lasted until long past midnight—he would be badgered for fresh cups of coffee, especially by Simmons, and he would have to get his dishes dirty again. He complained fiercely, but he always had hot coffee on. These talkfests, which he professed to hate because he had to stay awake cleaning up after everybody, were really the best part of his day—the one time when he had plenty of people to talk to, swear at and cater to.

One frequent subject of discussion was what they would do with their accumulated salaries, plus the thousand-dollar bonus they had all been promised. Duncan talked longingly of the beer joint he dreamed of buying, others of new cars, new houses, clothes for their wives. Little reported that one of his little girls had placed a firm order for a new pony.

"What are you going to do with your money, Henley?" someone asked one night. "You haven't got family to spend it on."

Henley paused, dishcloth in hand, and said gravely, "I'm gonna invest in houses and lots." There was a moment of surprise at this sensible answer, and Henley let it last a while. Then he explained. "Whorehouses and lots of liquor."

Not all the daylight hours were spent at work. Occasionally there would be a pause while Deir figured something out or waited for new equipment or supplies, and then the men would stretch out on the port sun deck, which was still relatively clean, and catch the sun, or they would use the diving platform for swimming (but not Deir; all that summer he swam for pleasure just once).

As among any sizable group of men, there was a great deal of horseplay, much of it fairly crude. The most memorable practical joke was set off by some watermelon Sadler sent out as a surprise for the men. While Deir and Simmons were diving voraciously into a couple of large slices, Woody Crisp slipped up quietly behind them and gave each man a great push that sent him into the melon up to his ears. Duke Morris, who usually stayed in Ocean City but was eating aboard the *Queen* that night, gasped at this rough treatment of Deir, but when Deir emerged from the melon dripping from brow to chin and grinning widely, Morris roared with all the rest. Simmons, wiping watermelon from his face, said solemnly to

175

the chuckling Crisp, "Your time will come." It came at midnight, when Crisp was awakened from a sound sleep and, as he sat up blinking, was shoved head first into a piece of melon that Simmons had saved for the purpose.

Crisp, ruefully scrubbing the sticky juice from his face, glanced at Deir, who was enjoying the spectacle, and said, "I guess that's all the sleep for me tonight, huh?"

"Naw," said Deir. "You go on back to sleep. I won't bother you." Then he grinned and added, "I'll save it for later."

In the days that followed, Crisp never stopped expecting retribution from Deir. It didn't come, partly because Deir had more important things to concern him and partly because it was more fun keeping Woody worried.

Simmons was irrepressible. Besides being one of the hardest workers on the tanker, he was the crew's most incorrigible teaser. He hid his colleagues' tools, splashed them with water when he came up from a dive, told them outrageous stories so solemnly that they never knew when to believe him and, in general, kept them off balance constantly. He particularly enjoyed surprising Deir; any unconventional behavior seemed to do it. Deir always wore a hat while working—in the early days a high-peaked cap, then an old felt, for a while a construction worker's helmet and finally an incongruous narrow-brim dark straw that looked as if it had come fresh from a Madison Avenue haberdasher's, with a stop in a grease pit on the way. One day, as he and Simmons were climbing the rope ladder on the tanker's port side, Deir tipped his head back too far and the construction helmet dropped overboard. Instantly, as Deir gaped, Simmons flipped off the ladder and into the sea, fully clad. A moment later he popped up, the helmet in his hand. He grinned and held it out. "Your hat, sir?" he said.

On another day Paul Russell brought out his boat with a load of sight-seers and—as was his practice—threw a tightly rolled newspaper to the crewmen gathered on the tanker. It was a rough day and a long throw, and the paper struck the ship's side and fell into the sea. Simmons, standing at the deck's edge, promptly grabbed his nose, took a great step forward and, to the immense delight of the tourists, dropped twenty feet into the water. As he climbed back up with the paper, the people on the boat gave him a great round of applause. Simmons, equal to the occasion, turned and swept a magnificent bow to his audience.

Word of Simmons' feat apparently spread all over Ocean City. After that every boatload of sight-seers would cry, "Jump in! Jump in!"

Simmons would grin at whatever crewman was nearest him and say, "Your turn, pal."

The sight-seers were now a regular feature of life aboard the *Queen*. Ocean City was jammed with summer visitors, and every pleasant day hundreds of them paid two dollars each to ride out to the grounded tanker. There were several sight-seeing boats; Paul Russell's alone held close to a hundred passengers. Russell, who had been friendly with the salvagers since his first meeting with Little and Deir, would usually circle the tanker twice, while his passengers would take pictures and shout questions ("Do you guys really live on there?" "Aren't you scared of storms?" "How long you gonna stay out here?"). On his second swing Russell would try to deliver the paper, and, encouraged by him, his passengers would often pepper the ship with gifts: cans of food and beer, bars of candy, sometimes even their own waxpaper-wrapped lunches. The tanker crewmen always knocked off work when the sight-seers arrived and answered their questions until they were out of hailing distance. "Be polite," Deir advised. "We can use all the friends we can get."

Many of the Ocean City boatmen were still outspokenly antagonistic, as the salvagers knew from Kin Reed's reports. Recently, moreover, Paul Brady had brought a radio out to the tanker, and they could hear the radio-equipped fishing boats commenting acidly on the salvage crew's lack of progress.

But there were other boatmen who followed the lead of Reed and Russell and were both encouraging and helpful. They would come up close, shout greetings, exchange news, perform small errands and even served occasionally as a free taxi service to Ocean City when Kin wasn't around.

Woody Crisp, in particular, made use of this service. During August, Woody received Duke Morris' permission to join the tanker crew as a regular member while things were slack in the divers' trade. One of Crisp's reasons for wanting to be aboard was that he had met an evangelist who was running weekly tent meetings just outside Ocean City. Woody, being a lay preacher himself, would meet him on weekends whenever possible, help pass out pamphlets and assist in the Saturday meeting. Getting in to Ocean City was easy in calm weather, but when the seas were rough, passing boats couldn't come in close. More than once, Woody, anxious to do God's work, plunged over the side and swam to the nearest friendly boat to hitch a ride into town.

All of the *Queen's* crew managed to get into town once in a while. The resort was a crowded, busy, exciting place in the summertime, with a bustling boardwalk, bright lights, bars, movie theaters and numerous other attractions that were very appealing to men leading as relatively bleak a life as that aboard the *Queen*.

Their headquarters in Ocean City was Kin Reed's house. Mrs. Reed was a slender, vivacious, articulate and long-suffering woman who soon found her home virtually taken over by the *Queen's* men and their affairs. She took phone calls for them, gave them sleeping room (even though it meant that she and her daughter Jan, a girl of about twenty, often wound up in a corner of their small apartment), did their laundry, helped them shop and generally made them at home. That summer the parade of visitors seemed endless—not only crew members but assorted relatives and friends and once in a while other people with business aboard the tanker. Ethel Reed once counted twenty-four people who had spent the night at her house during those weeks.

Almost every night there was someone in off the ship. Invariably the crewman, whoever it was, would shuck off his grimy clothes and head gratefully for the shower before putting on clean clothing and heading for the boardwalk. Mrs. Reed would patiently gather up the dirty laundry and wash and iron it, sending it out to the tanker with Kin as soon as it was ready. She never got entirely caught up with her own laundry that summer; one shower couldn't possibly get all the oil out of the men's hair, and when they slept they deposited black smears on her pillowcases. Months later she was still trying to scrub out the stains.

For a long time Mrs. Reed didn't charge the salvagers for any of this, and she might never have done so if the four partners hadn't finally insisted on it. She never did charge for doing the laundry. Deir and Little felt that she was not paid enough for all she did (Little became quite severe with her for not keeping careful track of the men who stayed over) and they tried hard to make it up personally. They gave her a check for twenty dollars, and when she tried to give it back they insisted that it was meant in part as a birthday present and could not be returned. When Deir got himself a new watch he gave the old one to Kin, and he bought a large piece of white coral at a local shop that sold sea shells and presented it to Mrs. Reed. On June 18, Little said to Jan Reed, "Isn't this your birthday?" When she nodded, he said, "Well, Deir and I want you to have this." He handed her a small box and fled. When she opened the box she found an expensive new wristwatch inside.

Since Mrs. Reed refused to take money for doing the men's laundry, Deir refused to let her touch his. He sent his soiled clothes in with Kin, but with strict instructions each week to take them to a commercial laundry.

One day in mid-August Ethel Reed rebelled. Kin had brought a bundle of Deir's laundry to the house, and she decided on her own hook to do it herself. It was ridiculous, she thought, to have Deir, who had done so much for them, pay for his laundry while the other men got theirs done free. She washed and ironed the clothes, folded them up in a box, and sent them back to the ship with Kin. "Just don't you say a thing about it," she said. "I'm just glad I had a chance to do them for him."

So Kin took the laundry out to the *Queen* and set it down on the port deck, where he always left the men's washing. Then he went off to find a tool he had mislaid. The laundry lay there, Mrs. Reed's good deed, ready to go off like a box full of dynamite.

17

IT HAD BEEN apparent to everyone for weeks that the two working partners were not getting along; indeed, by midsummer they were not taking very great pains to hide it. Little was openly critical of much that Deir was doing; Deir was openly contemptuous of practically everything Little said. Several times they had exchanged heated words in the presence of the other members of the crew, and there was quiet speculation among the men: how long could things go on without an open break?

The salvage operation was now definitely Deir's responsibility; Little had been relegated to a subordinate position, and he resented this intensely. He fought against it with vigor, offering suggestions of his own, making new rules for the men, protesting plans and techniques that he didn't like and criticizing Deir's loose way of running the crew. Deir and Little were still rooming together, and when they were alone the disagreement between them frequently grew bitter.

"It's just no damn use," Little said angrily one night. "There's just no getting along with you. Anyone can see you don't want to work *with* anybody; you want to be Mister It. Well, I'm damned if it's going to work with me. Every time I say something you try to make me look like a fool—flaring up in front of the men just like you took pleasure in it. Well, I tell you, it can't go on like this!"

Deir replied coldly, "There's no question out here of who's doing what, as long as it gets done. I'll guarantee you, any time you come up with anything that's worth doing, it'll be done that way. Meantime, don't act like a fool and you won't be treated like one."

The fact was, as the more perceptive crewmen understood, both partners were enmeshed in an emotional situation that had long since passed beyond their control. "I don't think they can stop themselves," Maurice Simmons said at the supper table one night when neither Deir nor Little was present. "Those two guys are just bound to argue, like a dog and a cat. Deir has to do things his own way or there's trouble. Little wants to be important and make decisions and have everybody think he's worth something, and he just can't stand to have Deir take over and make him look like nothing. No matter what Deir does it gets Little madder and madder, and the madder he gets the madder he makes Deir. Maybe you can't blame either one, but, boy, you watch, there's gonna be a hell of a blowup here someday."

Little took many of his grievances to Brady. "We've been out here all the damn summer," he said earnestly, "and where are we? We could have been finished weeks ago if things had been done right. It took from March to June to get a hard-hat diver out here, and all that time we didn't even know how bad the damage was. When we found out, we should have gone right ahead and ordered enough steel for the patch. Instead we did it piecemeal, where it was bound to be more expensive and take up more time. There's just too damn much back and forth around here, and not enough real planning where a man can see twenty-four hours ahead!"

Deir's handling of the men drove Little to distraction. "Great Lord," he said, exasperated, "one man'll mislay a tool and four others will stand around waiting for him to pick it up. They're always pranking and wasting time, jawing away when they should be working. Then before they know it it's dark and they're working under the lights where they can get things ready for the diver the next day. You can't tell me a man can get good work done at night the way he can in the day when he's had plenty of sleep. The men aren't getting the rest they should, and then they sleep all day and waste the best daylight hours. It's a damn disgrace the way things are run out here."

Brady privately agreed with some of this. From the start he had been troubled by the tendency of every worker on the ship to stand by while Deir solved some vexing problem, when they might just as well have been working on something else. He felt that Deir was a poor administrator, wasteful of manpower and with little conception of time and expense. One weekend not long before, Brady had taken his family to Ocean City, both to give them a holiday and to show them the tanker that was taking up so much of his time. They had taken a ride on one of the sight-seeing boats, and he had been appalled upon reaching the *Queen* to see every man aboard her quit work and stroll up to chat with the tourists over the side.

"It really is a shame," he reported to Sadler. "There sure is a lot of time lost out there. But I tell you one thing: Deir is our only hope. Maybe some other boss would get more work out of the men, but I don't see how anybody else could do as well all around as Deir. Some of the things that guy has thought up are just hard to believe. He's a smart man, and I don't think we have any choice. We have to let him do things his own way."

"That may be," said Sadler slowly. "But I'd like to see someone out there getting things done while Deir is busy thinking. I'd like to see *you* go out there for a while."

"Maybe I will," said Brady thoughtfully.

Meanwhile, Little tried one remedy of his own. He called a halt to the practice of knocking off work to get a cup of coffee whenever a man felt like it. "From now on," he decreed, "there's gonna be two coffee breaks a day. We've got to have a daily routine and stick by it. We have a job to do out here and everybody's got to work at it. We've got to be organized like on any other job. We'll organize in sections, and when one section stops for coffee the other one will keep on the job."

The men were irritated and resentful over the new rules, but they felt better when they saw that Deir was simply ignoring them.

Of all the sources of discord between Little and Deir, perhaps the most curious was the issue of nautical terminology. "That man doesn't know a damn *thing* about the sea," Little exploded one day. "He keeps calling the stack a chimney, and talking about left and right instead of port and starboard, and stairs instead of ladders, and he doesn't know bow from stern. He keeps talking about the *back* and the *front* of the ship, for the Lord's sweet sake!" Little claimed that he had given Deir a timetable of the tides but that Deir couldn't understand it, and that he had once caught Deir instructing Kin Reed in the operation of his boat. "He thinks he knows everything," said Little, "but he doesn't know damn-all."

Both men were working hard, and the bickering was a strain on both of them. But, as Simmons said, they simply couldn't help themselves. On August 14 Duke Morris and Simmons started the bolting of the patch. Only two bolts were put in that day, far fewer than Deir had hoped for. Little immediately resumed the debate over bolts. "With through bolts we'd have a dozen in by now," he urged. "I told you these would be slow. We have a hundred, a hundred fifty bolts to put in this patch. You tell *me* how long it's gonna take at the rate of two a day!"

"Man," said Deir, "give them a chance! This is just one day. They'll get the hang of it. And when they do you'll see lots of bolts going in. Let's not have *that* argument again. We're not gonna change now, and that's all there is to it."

Little reddened. "Nobody can tell you a thing!" he said, and walked away.

"I wonder," said Deir the next morning, "where my laundry is. I gave it to Kin days ago. It surely ought to be back by now."

They were standing on the port deck before breakfast, hanging over the rail, chatting and watching a school of large fish that had appeared in the water below them. Deir and Little were there, and Henley Doughtie and Pearly Strait, brushing their teeth and washing up and enjoying a moment of relaxation before the day's work.

"I don't even have anything clean to change into," said Deir. "Shouldn't be taking all this time."

Henley gestured toward a box lying on the deck. "Lloyd, I believe that there box is your clothes," he said. "Been there since yesterday."

"Naw," said Deir. "That's divers' stuff that Duke Morris brought out. Some rags, I think."

"Sure they're yours!" said Little impatiently. "Kin brought

them out. If you leave them there they're gonna get washed away." Little went to the box and tore open a corner. "There!" he snorted. "There's your goddam clothes right there, just like everybody's been trying to tell you!"

Deir started for the box, and Little stood up. "Boy," Deir said disgustedly, "you sure shouldn't talk like that first thing in the morning. Nobody here wants to listen to that kind of talk. These boys don't and I don't either."

At that moment all of Little's pent-up fury and frustration burst loose. He took a step forward, swung with all his strength, and knocked Deir sprawling on the deck, dazed, one eye bleeding. "Get up!" shouted Little in a strangled voice. "Get on your damn feet now and let's finish this!" Pearly hurriedly stepped between them, and Little yelled, "You get away, Pearly. This has nothing to do with you! This is between Deir and me!"

Deir lay there for a moment, trying to figure out what had hit him. A large cable with a heavy shackle on the end had been lashed to the rail close by and for a moment he was sure it had come loose and struck him on the head. Then he heard Little shouting and saw Pearly pushing him away, and he realized what had happened.

"Boy," he said to Little, "you shouldn't have done that."

He got up and went into the kitchen, followed by most of the crew. Simmons put a plaster on a three-quarter-inch cut under Deir's eye. The incident had shocked everybody, and there was not much conversation. Not the least shocked was Beldon Little. It had been an act prompted by the sheerest impulse, and although he was still angry, he was also shaken and miserable. While Simmons was fixing Deir's eye, Little entered the kitchen. "I'll put my hands behind my back and let you hit me right here!" he blurted out.

Deir didn't bother to respond. "One thing's sure," he said after a moment. "One or the other of us is leaving this ship."

Little flared up again. "Well, goddam if it's gonna be me!" he said, and left.

A few minutes later Duke Morris arrived to begin the day's diving and with him came Alvah Sadler. Sitting in the kitchen, Deir and the others told Sadler what had happened.

Sadler shook his head slowly. "That sure was an awful thing to do," he said. "I'm sorry as can be to hear it."

"One of us has got to go," Deir said. "This place won't hold both of us; I don't want to have anything to do with him again. Either he leaves or I do."

"He'll leave," said Sadler. "I'll talk to him."

Duncan spoke up. "It's gotta be Little that goes," he said. "We've all talked this over, and nobody wants to work for anyone but Deir. If he leaves, everybody is gonna leave, too."

"There's no question about it," said Sadler. "Deir stays and finishes the job. Leave Little to me."

He found Little on deck, working uneasily. "Beldon," he said, "I hate that this thing happened, and I want you to understand one thing: I'm not siding with anybody. But I know you're run-down and need a rest. This shows you've been working too hard. I'm asking you to go ashore for a while. Maybe after a few days, after I've talked to Lloyd and Brady has talked to him, we can fix things so you can come back. But right now Deir's mad and the men are upset— they're afraid someone's going to be hurt if you both stay. It would be better for everyone if you left."

"No, sir," said Little. "Let *him* go. He needs a rest as bad as anybody."

"Beldon," said Sadler quietly, "I just don't think that'll work. The men want you to go. I think you should."

"I'm not going," said Little. But he knew as he said it that it was a losing fight.

Twice that day he stopped Deir and tried to apologize. Deir, not so much angry as determined, brushed past him.

That night Deir moved his stuff into the cabin occupied by Simmons and Duncan, and Duncan moved in with Little.

The next day, a Sunday, Sadler approached Little again.

"Beldon," he said, "I'm driving back to Suffolk today and I want you to come with me. There's a lot more equipment that's needed and you can be real helpful in getting it. But you just have to leave the tanker, and there's no two ways about it. The way things are, this job can't be done without Deir. You know that. I know you won't stand in the way of getting the job done, even if you have to make a sacrifice.

You come along ashore for a while, and let's see if Paul and I can't get all this straightened out."

So on August 16, Beldon Little packed a bag and left the *Queen* with Alvah Sadler. "I just want one thing clear," he told Sadler before they left. "I'm coming back. If you and Paul can get things cleared up, God knows I'll be tickled to death. But, either way, I'm coming back to the ship."

18

THE CRITICAL WORK now lay in the hands of Duke Morris and Maurice Simmons. Every day the two divers would ride down on the diving elevator, their tools protected from the ocean currents in an iron-pipe-and-canvas basket Deir had designed. Standing on the bottom, or on the diving platform and its pipe-bar extensions, they would work for hours putting in the bolts. As Deir had predicted, the pace picked up after the first day. Not only did the two men quickly get the hang of the drilling-and-tapping process, but they soon discovered that they made a wonderfully effective team.

The great handicap of the unhelmeted diver is his inability to communicate with the surface. If Simmons wanted a tool he had to come out of the water and ask for it. Working with Morris, he was able to signal his needs and have them passed on to the deck by phone. Duke had certain limitations of his own, the chief of which was his lack of mobility. He could move only with great deliberation, and then not very far, and he could scarcely bend over at all. On this job Simmons did all the moving, all the picking up, all the difficult turning underwater. He would drill a hole in the hull, then step aside, hand Duke a tap and watch his companion thread the hole. Whenever Morris needed something down below, Simmons would get it. Whenever Simmons needed something up above, Morris would call for it. In the evenings after work the two men—and their respective supporters—carried on an amiable feud over the relative merits of helmeted and unhelmeted diving ("Aw, the only thing you can do that we

can't," Woody Crisp said to Simmons, "is turn a somersault").
Underwater, they worked together smoothly, swiftly, efficiently. After a while Simmons increased his effectiveness
further by putting aside his air tanks in favor of a hose that
was connected to the same compressor Morris used. He
could now stay down as long as his colleague, with only a
minor loss in mobility.

Inevitably, Simmons tended to work a good deal faster
than Morris. This was due in part to the difference in their
equipment, in part to the difference in their temperament.
Simmons was fast thinking, fast moving, impatient. Morris
was methodical, steady and imperturbable. He carried a
hammer with him, and from time to time he would rap the
hull—or the patch—and then stand and listen; to an experienced man the sound told a great deal about what lay
under the metal plates. To Simmons the whole procedure was
amusing—and exasperating. Once when he heard Brady commenting dolefully on Duke's slowness, Simmons grinned and
said, "Hide that peapicker's hammer and we'll be out of here
in a week."

Morris hurried things just once—for a good reason—and
then it led to trouble.

At the time they started the bolting they had found that
the patch was not held completely motionless against the
ship's side by the cables but was shifting slightly with the
seas. Since the patch still had a certain degree of flexibility,
this was somewhat dangerous.

"She keeps banging against the hull, rubbing and bending,
and it worries me some," Duke Morris said. "I think we better
tack her down quick here and there, so she'll be firm and stop
beating against the ship."

Within a few days they had a couple of dozen bolts in,
concentrated at the lower left-hand and upper right-hand
corners, but spaced at fairly wide intervals to hold the patch
as steady as possible. A spell of bad weather interrupted the
work, and then there was a day when they could go down,
and they got in six more bolts. Most of the bolts were now
along the bottom edge of the patch. Then the bad weather
returned, and almost a week passed before the divers could

go down again. It was a long, anxious week, and when Morris and Simmons were finally able to dive again they found that it had been an expensive one. When they came up and reported to Deir their faces were dark.

"Every damn one of those bolts along the top of the patch has been sheared off like it was done by a bolt-cutter," said Duke, disgusted and chagrined. "The top of the patch is flapping loose, as if it never had a bolt in it at all. I'm sorry, Lloyd. I should never have hurried. I should have known better, but I was afraid the patch would bend out of shape and maybe break. Now look at it. It was a mistake to skip around the way we did. She held along the bottom, but the top kept flexing, rubbing up and down. She cut off every damn bolt."

They stood on the deck in a little cluster and talked it over.

"There's only one thing to do," Deir said at last. "Finish bolting the bottom edge so it'll stay firm, then do the top afterward. The top should hold pretty fair anyhow, with the cables threaded through the way they are. It's the bottom that worries me. Get that fixed and we'll come back to the top later. And don't blame yourself for it. It was the weather that made the trouble."

When they finally got around to doing the top, later, they found that the holes in the patch no longer matched the holes in the hull but were now off roughly half a bolt's width—which meant that new holes had to be drilled and tapped, half in the ship's steel, half in the stubs of the broken bolts. They eventually managed the job, but only after the greatest difficulty.

Various other problems dogged them, none serious but all annoying. First the beams had to be cut underwater to improve the fit of the patch, especially around the projecting knee where the ship's internal bracing had been bent out beyond the hull's normal contours.

Then the small flap of steel forward, which had been added to cover the dents in the hull, almost got ripped away by the sea. Deir had anticipated this and had urged the divers to get a cable over it.

"Gee, we don't have to bother with that," Simmons said. "It's holding fine."

Then one day Morris suddenly called up. "Hey, send down a cable, quick!"

"Damn!" said Deir. He found a cable and hurriedly lowered it to the divers. A little while later they came up. The patch had a fourteen-inch crack at the point where the flap joined it, but they had caught it before any real harm had been done.

Deir looked at them balefully. "All right, all right," said Simmons hastily. "Next time we'll do what Poppa says."

"I guess," said Paul Brady with a thoughtful expression, "there's probably such a thing as hurrying *too* much."

Brady was now on board on a permanent basis. Shortly after the bolting started he had arrived at the ship, his suitcase full of clothes, his face full of determination.

"Well, you've been asking me to stay," he told Deir, "and now I'm gonna do it. I tell you, I just can't keep away any longer. Lib's taking care of the store." He shifted impatiently. "The way my mind has been lately, always on what's happening out here, she can probably do better than I can anyway."

Brady had spent the previous weeks working hard on the problem of finding the tap bolts they needed for the patch. He had discovered that no one manufactured bolts which precisely suited their purpose and had finally had to order some custom-made ones from a company in Boston. The bolts varied in length from three to five and a half inches, and they had to be threaded almost all the way to the head. The ones from Boston came threaded to within only two inches of the head, and for some reason the company could do no better, so Brady had them threaded the rest of the way by a machine shop in Suffolk. By the time they got out to the *Queen* they cost five dollars each, and they were hoarded like gold coins. "Hell," said Brady, "you lose a handful of these, and it isn't so much the expense; it's where are you gonna get some more?"

Once he was out on the *Queen* his interest in the bolting led him to pay particular attention to the divers, and soon he had taken charge of the whole diving operation, freeing Deir to prepare the pumps for the vast water-removal project that lay ahead. The diving fascinated Brady. For one thing, it was where the work was—as long as he could keep things moving there, he felt that progress was being made toward an early finish. For another, the bottom of the sea was a place of mystery, even when it was only thirty or forty feet away, and Simmons and Morris were constantly getting involved in intriguing adventures, including some that Brady comprehended only vaguely.

One thing he never did figure out was what Duke Morris found so funny down there. Usually when he worked, Duke sang to himself, like a man in the world's biggest bathtub. His voice would come crackling over the intercom, softly crooning the popular songs of ten years earlier. But then suddenly he would stop and chuckle. And sometimes the chuckle would turn into a delighted laugh, followed by much exclaiming and giggling. It would frequently be some minutes before he would get back to his singing.

"Duke," said Brady one day, "what's so damn side-splitting down there? Boy, you laugh and laugh like something was just tickling you."

Morris looked uncomfortable. He puffed on his pipe uneasily, then said, "Heck, there's nothing funny down there." He eyed Brady sidelong. "I just get lonesome, see, so I sing or talk to keep myself company." Brady reluctantly dropped the subject.

The fact is, Morris was playing with fish. Great schools of bass hovered around him constantly. As the drill chewed into the barnacle- and mussel-encrusted hull of the tanker bits of shellfish floated away. The bass would gather around for the free meal, meticulously spitting out the shells and steel shavings that found their way into the food. The fish enchanted Duke. Sometimes he would break off some of the marine growth and crumble it in his fingers; his friends would come hustling over like chickens at feeding time, gobbling the delicacy out of his hand and pulling and tugging at the pieces he wouldn't let go. When he grabbed playfully at the fish they would scoot contemptuously away, only to return quickly for more food. When it was all gone they would crowd around, waiting for the next serving. Occasionally a few would drift up and stare anxiously into his mask. He was never able to contain his laughter at their behavior, but how on earth could he ever explain it to Brady?

Simmons, too, found the fish comical, but he was able to keep his laughter a secret, since it couldn't be heard on deck. Once a drill bit slipped away from him and got lost under-foot. Simmons hunted everywhere for it. Finally he got down on his hands and knees in the soft sand and began pawing under the surface to see if the bit had been covered up by the swirling bottom currents. Some sea robins—a kind of fish that crawl around the bottom on leglike gills—promptly came over to see what strange work he was up to. He would lift a stone to see what was under it, and the sea robins would slip swiftly in, nosing about curiously and hiding the hole before he could see into it. They got in front of his face, under his hands, between his fingers—everywhere. Simmons found himself in a cloud of sea robins so thick that he had to keep sweeping them away from the bottom to continue his search. He enjoyed it all hugely.

Sometimes the people on deck did a little laughing of their own, at the divers' expense.

One day Duke Morris was finishing up some work toward the end of the day when he called up to Woody, "Hey, I've gotta come up."

"What for?"

"Gotta go to the bathroom."

"Aw, come on," remonstrated Woody. "Stay down a while longer, Duke. The day's 'most done and it takes hours to get you in and out of that rig. It'll be suppertime soon. Can't you finish up?"

"Well, I can't stay down long."

"Just a little while longer," promised Crisp. "Then we'll bring up the elevator."

A little while later Morris said, "Boy, listen, you better get me up soon."

"We will, we will. Just you say the word."

Soon afterward the word came. "Let's go! I've gotta get up there and I've gotta get up there now!"

"All right," Woody said, grumbling. "Seems to me you could've finished the work first."

He got everything ready to bring the diver to the top and was just about to signal Deir, who was operating the platform, when Duke's voice came over the intercom, heavy with disgust.

"Never mind."

He stayed down an hour longer. After that Crisp watched Morris carefully at mealtimes to make sure he drank no more than one cup of coffee. "Heck," Woody said, *"I'm* the one has to clean his suit."

Inevitably, there was danger as well as fun under water, and Simmons seemed to run into more than his share. One reason was that he was doing the moving around for both of them and was thus subject to a difficulty that rarely affected Morris: his air hose occasionally got a kink in it that cut off his air. If he could spot the trouble, which was usually caused by his having turned twice in the same direction, he could fix it by quickly rotating his body until the hose straightened out. But if he couldn't spot it (and often he wasn't even aware of his danger until he found himself suffocating) there was nothing to do but head for the surface, fast. He tried to remember to counter every turn to the right with a corresponding turn to the left, but it wasn't always easy to keep his mind on it.

One day, while he was working with Morris about halfway up the side of the ship, one of them dropped the socket from the impact wrench. The platform was out six feet from the boom, and Simmons had increased his distance from the boom even farther by sidling out along one of the pipes which served as extensions to the platform. So instead of going all the way back to the boom and climbing down to the bottom, Simmons took a short cut: he clambered down the I-beams on the patch. Hanging from the patch at full length, he had only about a one-foot drop to the sand. He touched bottom, took one step and suddenly was without air.

Simmons' dilemma was grave. He had been without air before but never in a situation remotely like this. He was forty feet from the surface, a long way from the boom—his only way up—and completely out of communication with everybody. Morris couldn't even see him. He was unable to move fast because he was weighted only lightly and he had nothing to hang onto and pull himself along by. He looked up. The kink, wherever it was, was too high to see. There was nothing to do but go back the way he had come and find the bend in the hose. The question was, how long would it take to find it?

Holding his breath, he turned slowly back to the ship, leaped up and grabbed the patch, pulled himself all the way onto it, then went up a beam, hand over hand, until he was back at the platform extension. It was a long journey, and his heart, starved for oxygen, was beginning to pound.

He crawled along the pipes on all fours (it was much faster than shuffling along them erect) and got back to the main part of the platform. His lungs aching, he leaped across the six-foot gap between platform and boom, and started upward as fast as he could go. He had roughly a three-story ascent ahead of him.

On the deck the intercom crackled. "Watch out for Simmons," said Duke Morris. "His air must be off. He just came through here like a streak!"

To Simmons, the climb seemed endless. He scrambled frantically up the latticework of the boom, racing against the moment when he would have to open his mouth and suck in a lungful of water. The sea around him grew lighter as he neared the surface. Suddenly he broke through, and the air returned to his hose. He drew a tremendous breath, then another. He took a moment to make sure the kink was straightened out, then turned and started down again without even raising his mask. He worked the rest of that trick with no trouble. In fact, he scarcely gave the incident another thought until the end of the day, when it suddenly occurred to him that while his air had been off he had traveled a truly incredible distance underwater, holding his breath all the way. He began adding it up. It came to seventy feet, half of it vertical.

"My lord," he told the others. "I'm not even sure that's *possible*."

He continued to run the risk, never knowing from which direction the danger would come next. One day Morris and Simmons were getting their air temporarily from Duke's beat-up, wheezy compressor (Deir needed the new one on the tank deck) when it played its old trick and unexpectedly stopped running. Although this was not serious for Morris, as he and Crisp kept telling Deir, it was potentially very serious for Simmons, who did not have a reserve tank. Simmons, however, didn't even know anything was wrong. Morris, who had the word from Crisp, tried to gesture Simmons back toward the boom and up to the surface. He waved Simmons away more and more violently, as Simmons watched, bewildered. *"Back, back!"* Duke gestured. Simmons backed off a. few feet and stared. Morris, sweating inside his suit, waved wildly. Simmons moved away a few feet farther, convinced by now that the more distance he put between the apparently beserk Morris and himself the safer he would be. In desperation, Duke pointed vigorously upward, and the men on deck heard him shout, "Damn it, go up! *Up!* up!" Simmons gazed upward, twisting and turning to see what Morris was pointing at.

"Okay, Duke," Crisp suddenly called down. "She's working again."

"Well, thank the lord," said Morris. "This guy was just gonna stay down here and dance all night!"

He beckoned Simmons back to work, gesturing toward himself with both arms. Simmons stared warily. He moved back part of the way and stopped. Morris waved him closer. Simmons sidled a few feet. The grinning Morris finally got his companion back on the job, but Simmons kept staring at him uneasily. After a while he went up to have a smoke.

"My gosh," he said, "that peapicker down there has lost his mind! What are you putting in his air?"

The men on deck explained, laughing. A short time later

Morris came up on the platform, finished for the day. Simmons watched Crisp remove Duke's helmet. Then the two divers grinned at each other. Simmons imitated Morris' beckoning motion with both arms. "I thought you were asking for a kiss," he said.

In addition to the scores of small fish that thronged the shoal, the divers occasionally encountered much larger fish. There was one stretch in mid-summer when the water was so clear that it seemed to Simmons that he could see at least two hundred feet, and fish of all kinds showed up in the tanker's vicinity. Simmons was working alone for a brief period during this time, and one day he glanced up and saw three great fish bearing down on him—two of them eight or nine feet long, the other about six. He was startled only briefly; for one thing he recognized them as tuna, and for another there was something so playful and friendly about them that it was simply impossible to suspect any of them of any harm. They came from the direction of the bow, swimming in a kind of formation, with the smallest in the middle, and maneuvering in a gentle swinging motion that resembled a three-dimensional snake dance: both side to side and up and down. They were upon him before they saw him, and they paused and then swung around and stopped to look at him with intense interest. He was delighted with them, and they with him. They went back to their game, but they never left the ship. All that day, as Simmons worked, the three tuna frisked around him, swimming in formation and occasionally stopping to peer at him amiably. When he finished up for the day, shortly before sunset, he went up with great reluctance.

On deck, Mack Duncan was waiting to speak to him. For weeks Mack had been begging for a chance to try Simmons' diving gear. The water had always been too rough, or too cold, or too murky. This time it was perfect.

"Sure enough, now's your chance," Simmons said. "It'll never be clearer or quieter down there, and the water's as warm as a bath."

It wasn't until Duncan was climbing down the boom that Simmons remembered the tuna. "Oh, brother," he said to

Deir, chuckling in anticipation. "He'll see the quarter-moon tails on those tuna and he'll think they're sharks."

The whole crew stood at the edge of the deck and watched Duncan descend. He went down about ten feet and stopped and looked at him. Then he carefully climbed down ten more. At last he got down thirty feet, not far from the bottom, and stopped, apparently enjoying himself greatly. Suddenly he froze. Then he started back up the boom, moving fast. It had taken him five minutes to get down. It seemed to take him no more than five seconds to get back up, legs pumping. He emerged in a spray of water and leaped across to the deck. "My God," he panted, "down there is the biggest goddam bunch of sharks I ever saw in my life!"

They roared. At last someone let the puzzled Duncan in on the secret. He grinned and looked a little foolish. "Well, boy, they sure *looked* like sharks.

Henley Doughtie shook his head in wonder. "Goddam your hide if you didn't come up that goddam ladder like a man in a movie cartoon," he said. "You kept climbin' *long* after you got past where the boom was!"

The next morning, right after breakfast, Simmons went down to move the basket of tools from the bottom, where he had been working the day before, to the elevator, where he and Morris would be working next. Pearly Strait acted as his tender. Simmons rode down on the platform, which stopped about six feet off the bottom. He jumped off and got the basket, then started back.

Just as he put his hand up on the platform he glimpsed the crescent tail of a huge fish not far away. Boy, he thought, this must be the *grandfather* of the ones I saw yesterday. He swung himself up on the platform and stiffened in horror. This was no tuna. This *was* a shark—and a shark at least fifteen feet long! It slowly glided toward him.

Simmons was terrified. As the fish came closer he could see the great ugly slash of its mouth, held open several inches so that the rows of terrible teeth were visible. The shark stopped barely six feet away and stayed there, almost within reach, staring at Simmons with one hard, cold eye. It was a simply tremendous specimen, with a vast barrel of a body. Simmons was transfixed. He had no life line to signal by, only his air hose, and he was afraid to reach for it. He just stayed perfectly still, certain that the shark would whisk across that last six feet at his first move. Out of the corner of his eye he could see the bubbles rising from the exhaust valve at the side of his mask, and he wished desperately there were some way to stop them. He didn't know what to do. He was beyond any coherent planning. He just wanted that terrible creature to go away. Somewhere he had read that if you charge straight for a shark he will turn tail. The idea of charging straight for this shark was absolutely absurd. Simmons prayed helplessly. For long minutes they remained there. My God, my God, Simmons kept thinking as he stared at that sharp nose and the awful undershot mouth, he is so ugly, so terribly, terribly ugly; I never saw anything so ugly.

In the contest to see which would outwait the other, Simmons gave way first. He knew the shark could stay where he was forever, while he, Simmons, was a surface creature, out of his element and never more poignantly aware of it. Slowly he began to raise his hand toward the air hose on the right side of his head. He watched for any response from the shark. In the basket at Simmons' feet was a hammer. It was a ridiculous weapon against a shark, but if the monster moved Simmons intended to grab the hammer and make the best fight he could. His hand slid up past his chest. The shark stayed where it was, that one hypnotic eye fixed on the diver. At last Simmons' hand reached the hose. The emergency signal was four pulls and a pause, then four more, repeated over and over. Simmons began to tug on the hose for dear life, counting as he did: "One-two-three-four-pause-one-two-three-four-pause . . ."

It wasn't until he was two thirds of the way up that he realized that he was pulling on the pauses as well as on the numbers. But it made no difference. Strait was getting the elevator up fast: there was no mistaking the urgency of those tugs, however many of them there were. To Simmons' unspeakable relief, the shark watched him leave without making a move. Just before Simmons broke the surface, he saw the monster glide smoothly away.

He ripped off his mask. "Boy," he cried, "you have just seen me make my last dive!"

"What on earth happened?" asked Pearly. "You mighty near pulled me into the water."

Simmons told him. For the rest of that morning he stayed above water, shaken and exhausted. That afternoon he went down again and returned to work.

He never again saw another shark.

With only two dozen bolts to go, trouble struck. The drill housing broke.

"Oh, man," Brady moaned. "Now what?"

"Well," Deir said slowly, "we could get a new drill, all right. But it would take a lot of time. Let's see the broken one."

It had a bullet-shaped snout, like most drills, with a flange several inches back through which went the bolts that held the drill housing to the handle. The bulletlike nose was badly cracked.

Deir got a piece of steel and busied himself for a time with torch and welding tools. When he was finished he had a collar which slipped neatly over the cracked nose and held it firm. He ran long bolts through the flange and then through the new collar, and he tightened them up so that the collar was pulled up tight on the housing. He surveyed the job. "She'll do," he said.

In a few minutes the divers were on their way back over the side. The mended drill lasted almost to the very end—when there were only two bolts to go. Then it broke again, and the last couple of bolts were put in—clumsily and not very well, but well enough—with the impact wrench. But by then Deir wasn't on hand to help.

19

ALL DURING the weeks when Brady was overseeing the diving and bolting, Deir had been looking ahead to the time when the patch was on and the pumping of the *Queen* must start. A tremendous amount of preparation was necessary.

To begin with, there were certain small flooded areas that had to be dried out immediately. This task could not be delayed because all the available pumps would soon be needed for more important work. A rope locker in the after-section, brimful of water ever since scavengers had removed the hatch months before, was quickly pumped dry. Plans were made to do the same for the two tank deck cofferdams, small dead spaces just forward of the aft superstructure, built into the ship to provide a barrier between the cargo tanks and the ship's own fuel tanks (not to mention the living quarters) in case of fire. The cofferdams were supposed to be kept empty, but, like the rope locker, they had filled with sea water after their hatches were opened.

Besides these small jobs—it took only one pump to get the water out of the rope locker, and two more were considered adequate for the cofferdams—electric lines and hoses had to be rigged for the really big pumping job that lay ahead. The fourteen great petroleum tanks, their Butterworth covers gone, were full of water. The tanks and the engine room to-gether contained no less than 13,000,000 gallons, most of which would have to be removed as soon as the patch was on tight. For this job they had bought twenty-two pumps in all —none too many. In addition, the tank deck had to be rigged for a second operation: besides pumping water out of the tanks, Deir planned to pump air in. That is, he still intended to "blow" the intact tanks—fill them with air under pressure— to increase the buoyancy of the ship. A second air compressor was brought aboard for this purpose.

Finally, there were many openings around the tanker that still needed to be sealed up—hatches, ventilators, portholes, even doors that might swing open and let in the sea. Most of these were on the high port side, so far above water, as the ship was now tipped, that for all these months no one had worried about them. But once the ship righted herself, some of these openings might be lowered into the sea again. A few starboard openings also remained, including certain deck hatches that had been left uncovered simply because no one could figure out an easy way to get at them: the starboard side of the tank deck was never completely out of water. All these submerged holes now would have to be taken care of.

The way to fix most of these openings, of course, was to seal them. Where doors were missing new ones were installed from other parts of the *Queen*. Portholes were covered over, ingeniously, with the circular blades from disk harrows—steel saucers about two feet in diameter with holes in the center through which bolts were passed, so the blades could be dogged down tight or pulled fast with cables from the inside. Elsewhere metal covers were cut to fit the openings and welded fast.

But some openings were not sealed at all. Tank hatches, for example, had to be left open so the tanks could be pumped out. The same was true of the cofferdams. So instead of making covers for these hatches Deir suggested the fabrication of long metal cylinders which could be fitted over the hatches as standpipes—in effect raising the mouth of each hatch high enough so that no water could get in no matter what happened.

The unpleasant task of working on the starboard side was assigned mainly to Simmons: it was clearly a job for a diver who could move fast. He started late one afternoon, with Paul Brady as his tender; he had already put in eleven hours on the bolting that day, but there was still some light left and the salvagers wanted to take advantage of the low tide. The surf was breaking on the tank deck, but Simmons pulled down his mask and ventured into the turbulent water. The attempt was a fiasco. He could work only between waves; while the swells swept the deck all he could do was hang on to the nearest pipe and try not to be swept overboard. One breaker almost tore the mask off his head, despite the eight strong straps that held it there. Another ripped off a boot. Finally one great sea yanked him loose from the pipe he was holding and tumbled him along the deck, dragging him into pipes, hatches and valves. Bruised and aching, he stumbled to safety on the high side of the deck and pulled off his mask. "Boy, I don't want any more of that," he gasped. "Let's come back and try again at *high* tide. Maybe I'll be under all the rough stuff then." And that's the way he finally did it, although not without great difficulty.

The cofferdams proved to be a problem—or at least one of them did. Deir had started work on them weeks before, when Little was still aboard. The one on the port side gave no difficulty. But the starboard cofferdam hatch was underwater. Worse, although it was flooded it still had a cover on it, and this lid had to be removed before a standpipe could be mounted there. Several attempts failed. At last Pearly Strait splashed into the surf, ducked under, and with a great deal of trouble got the cover off. Then Little put on the standpipe, again with much hard work.

That had been weeks before. And now, after all that, it was apparent that the standpipe was going to be too short, that even with the starboard side raised, in the early stages of the pumping the tank deck probably would still be taking breakers high enough to enter the pipe.

While Deir was trying to decide what to do about that (it looked as if the standpipe would have to be removed and a taller one put on in its place, a job nobody relished), Pearly made a discovery that solved the whole problem. He began to pump out the port cofferdam and was surprised to find that the water level was going down much more slowly than he had expected. Then, peering into the standpipe Little had installed, he saw that the water on *that* side was going down. It was obvious that the two cofferdams were connected, and both were being drained through the same hatch.

"Well, then," said Deir to Brady, relieved. "All I have to do now is weld a cap on the starboard standpipe and close it up for good, and we're in business."

"Weld?" said Brady. "Lloyd, honest, I wouldn't want to go anywhere near those tanks with welding equipment. That's dangerous. There's apt to be fumes down there, or oil, or the Lord knows what."

"Well, there shouldn't be, though I guess it's possible. But that place was supposed to be kept empty, and then all it had in it after that was water. Should be perfectly safe."

"Look, Lloyd. Why not just take a piece of wood, cut it to the right shape and size, and pound it right into the top of that pipe?"

"Naw. We don't have the right wood. Nothing big enough."

"Well, hell, then take a smaller piece and put packing around it."

"Well. Yeah. I suppose."

But Deir was sure that welding was best. Packing probably wouldn't stay, and he hated to think what might happen if those two cofferdams became half filled with sloshing water while the ship was precariously afloat during the pumping-out process. It was going to be hell keeping her balanced as it was, even with everything under control—just the right amount of water out of her tanks on port and starboard, just the right amount of air added under pressure, everything mixed just right to counteract all the forces that might try to capsize the ship once her broad bottom got up off the sand. There was one holed tank that he knew about, on the starboard side, and it was sure to make trouble, one way or another. The thought of those two cofferdams suddenly getting water in them too, just because the standpipe was inadequately sealed, was simply too much. He'd seal it good.

Although the standpipe was surrounded by frothing water, its mouth was, by fortuitous circumstance, easily accessible. The cofferdam was located at the part of the tank deck that was farthest aft—that is, right in front of the big bulkhead that was the forward wall of the aft superstructure. Just above it was the deck where Deir and Little had stood the day they had been threatened by that first party of Lewes boatmen, and where Doughtie had stood when he scared off the second party weeks later. Off to one side was the passage-way along which all the living quarters were located. At the forward edge of this deck, on both sides of the ladder to the tank deck, was a deck rail—and by sitting on this rail and facing forward Deir found himself with the top of the stand-pipe practically in his lap. So he could weld the metal lid to it without getting anywhere near the water.

The standpipe cap had to be a tight fit; it could be welded only on top, of course, so it would have to be wedged in firmly to keep it from ever breaking loose. Deir cut a disk just the right size from a sheet of steel, then tamped it into the pipe a couple of inches. And, just in case Brady was right about oil fumes, he decided to play safe and start welding the side of the lid farthest from him, so that if there *was* an explosion the cap would flip back and fly away from him instead of toward his head.

It was a blistering hot day, and before starting to weld he stripped off his shirt. As he prepared to work, a number of crewmen were lounging around the deck. The divers had knocked off for lunch. Duke and Woody had headed straight for the kitchen. Simmons, still in his diving suit, was sitting on a rail about fifteen feet from Deir, smoking a cigarette. Strait, who had finished pumping the cofferdams dry a short time before, was chatting with Simmons. Kin Reed was up forward. Mack Duncan was on his way out to the deck, walking along the passageway that led from the cabins and the kitchen.

Brady watched Deir get ready to weld, and thought, Well, there he goes, doing it his own way as usual. He shook his head, torn between exasperation and admiration, then walked over and handed Deir his electric welding rod. Brady stood a few minutes, watching Deir's preparations, and then ambled away before the glare hit his unprotected eyes. He sure doesn't need help, he thought. He had just started for the passageway when he heard a noise.

They all heard the noise, and no two heard it the same. To Brady it was a muffled rumble, followed by a hissing (Compressed air, he thought immediately). To Simmons, sitting on the other side of the deck, it came as a tremendous, ear-splitting bang. Deir heard a sharp crack, and then nothing. Kin Reed heard "S-s-s-s-s-s-POW-ow-ow-ow-ow." Duncan, just stepping out of the corridor, was greeted by a shattering roar and ducked back as fragments of something flew past him.

Simmons, looking up, startled, saw three objects in the air, one flying toward the smokestack, another toward the tank deck, the third into the sea. They were, respectively, Lloyd Deir's welding mask, his hat and the steel lid.

Brady was the first to see Deir. He was lying crumpled on his side, limp and torn, on the narrow deck behind the rail. There was blood on him, and some sort of blackness, and he lay perfectly still—terribly still. Brady was stunned and un-comprehending; there was something incongruous, incredible, about the sight of the vital Deir sprawled so helplessly on the deck. Brady thought, My God, my God, he's dead! Abruptly, he turned away, unable to look. Duncan, sticking his head cautiously out the doorway to the passage, heard Brady saying, "My God, my God, it's Deir. It's Deir." Duncan whirled and looked, then gasped. There Deir lay, his head a mass of blood. Strait, on the other side of the deck, yelled, "*Damn, Deir's hurt!*" Simmons saw him then, looking as if his head had been blown off, and, like Brady, he turned away, sick.

Just for that instant they froze, while the debris still pattered to the deck around them. Then the tableau broke. Everybody moved at once. Stumbling in their haste, Brady, Simmons, Duncan and Strait converged on the fallen Deir. At the same moment, to their great shock, Deir himself began to get up. Badly hurt, he still acted with characteristic vigor. He tried to scramble to his feet. He brushed one bloody arm against the oil-smeared bulkhead beside him and cried out with the pain. He lurched unsteadily erect, his face blackened and pitted with spots, his head and chest brilliant with blood, his arm torn. As the others stood watching with horror, he reeled across the deck and began to shout hoarsely. "Where's some water? Where's some water?" He raised his tortured arm and said, "Get some water. My *God,* it hurts." A drop of blood fell past his face to the deck and he raised an oil-smeared hand wonderingly to his head. He brought it down red and stared at it. "Better stop the bleeding," he said.

He turned and stumbled down the ladder to the tank deck, picking his way weakly over the pipes toward the surf. Simmons leaped after him. "Where's some water? Get some water," said Deir. Simmons, afraid to touch his wounds, got him turned around and led him back up to the deck. Duncan by then had rushed to the kitchen and returned with a full tub of fresh water. Deir, still looking dazed, hurried to it and plunged in his arm. He began to splash the water up onto his head, and as some of the grime washed away the men clustered about him could see his injuries.

He had received the full force of the explosion on his forehead and chest and on his right arm; his face had been protected by the welding mask. Since Deir always held his mask in his hand instead of strapping it to his head, his arm had caught much of the blast that might otherwise have battered his head. The mask had stayed in place just long enough, perhaps, to save his life before it sailed to the upper deck, thirty feet away. The metal lid to the standpipe, welded on the side farthest from Deir, seemed to have flipped back away from him, just as he had planned. But in doing so, it had directed the full force of the explosion right at him. A thousand tiny flakes of oil-blackened rust had poured out of the standpipe like grapeshot fired out of a cannon and had embedded themselves in Deir's head, chest and arm. As the men washed away some of the oil and gore with paste detergent, they saw that the blood on his chest and forehead came from a multitude of little holes, while that on the back of his head came from a single deep cut, apparently suffered when he fell back against the bulkhead before tumbling to the deck. The worst damage had been done to his arm, which had been badly burned, peppered with rust, scraped against the bulkhead and smeared with oil. The new wristwatch he had bought in Ocean City had disappeared completely; fragments of it were later found all over the aft part of the ship.

By now the tanker was in turmoil. Henley, Woody and Duke had rushed out of the kitchen. Kin Reed had run up from the forward part of the ship. Someone yelled, "Start the scow!" Woody leaped into the rearming boat, which Kin had brought out that morning, started up the engine with a roar and shot forward along the side of the ship toward the port-side ladder. But he had forgotten to untie the painter; the seven-inch line snapped just in time to keep the boat's bow from ripping off. They all shouted at Woody.

There was some earnest, noisy discussion about what should be done next. Deir kept saying, "God *knows*, it hurts!" Brady ran in and got a towel, soaked it with water and carefully tried to remove some of the oil that was irritating Deir's cuts. Henley started out of the passageway with more water, and Duncan ran in front of him. Henley roared at Duncan, and Duncan, stung and upset, roared back. Brady and Reed began to lead Deir toward the rearming boat. Just then a party boat from Ocean City came roaring over, engine wide open, to find out what all the fuss was about.

By now, Deir was emerging from the shock. The bleeding had stopped, and though his face was gray and drawn, he kept denying vigorously that there was anything seriously wrong, insisting that except for his arm he was fine. "I'm all *right*," he said. "I'm all *right*. Don't *worry* about it."

Brady ran to the side of the deck and called to the Ocean City boatman. He explained the situation, and said, "Your boat is a lot faster than ours. Can you take us in?"

"You bet," said the boatman. "Get him over here."

"I've gotta have clothes," said Deir. "I can't go anyplace like this!"

"Forget about clothes," said Brady. "I'll take care of that. You get into the boat."

So Deir stepped into the party boat, and Brady, grabbing up Deir's shirt, leaped in after him. The boatman turned toward Ocean City and sped for shore.

The day was still extremely hot, although a summer storm was threatening. There were three passengers on the boat, and they hovered over Deir solicitously, much to his embarrassment. "Naw, I'm all right," he kept saying. "Don't go to any trouble." As a matter of fact, he did not feel a bit weak. His arm still pained greatly, and he had a ringing in his ears that was not to leave him for months, but otherwise he felt reasonably well. He saw Brady looking at him and shook his head. "All this oil smeared on me makes me look bad," Deir said. "I feel okay. Honest."

"You may *feel* okay," Brady said firmly, "but you don't *look* okay, and I'm not talking about oil. You just sit down and stay there."

The boatman had a two-way radio and he had sent in a call to have a doctor waiting on their arrival. But it was a one-hour trip, and in the meantime he offered Deir a shot of whisky. Deir declined politely. But he was now beginning to suffer a raging thirst, and when the boatman offered him a can of cold beer Deir was surprised to find that he really wanted it. He hadn't even tasted beer in fifteen years. He accepted it gratefully and drained the can before tossing it overboard.

It began to rain; by the time they reached Ocean City it was pouring. They jumped out of the boat and hurried up the pier to a little restaurant. Deir was still bare to the waist, but he turned down Brady's offer of the shirt. The doctor had not yet arrived. They waited for him on a protected bench outside the restaurant.

In a few minutes Deir jumped up, and nothing Brady said would make him sit down again. He was not going to be treated like a sick man, and that's all there was to it. He was on his feet when the doctor arrived, much to that man's astonishment.

"Sit down, sit down," the doctor ordered.

"I'm all *right*."

The doctor looked at him sharply. "No, you're not all right. You're in shock. Now, sit down!"

"Lloyd," said Brady. "You heard what the doctor said. Sit down!"

He sat down, and the doctor gave him a shot of morphine. Then he hastily examined Deir's head and chest, seemed satisfied that there was little that could be done for those injuries at the moment, and gave his full attention to the arm. He winced when he looked at it closely. After he had studied it at some length he straightened and said, "Nothing much I can do with this. It has to be cleaned and tended to properly.

The hospital at Salisbury will take care of all that, certainly better than I can here. I'll put in a call for the ambulance."

"Hospital?" cried Deir. "Ambulance? Man, I don't *need* a hospital!" He wheeled on Brady. "Look, I've got to get back out there. *You* know how much needs to be done! I'll rest up overnight here, and then we'll go back out to the tanker tomorrow. Okay?"

"Not a chance," said Brady. "You listen to the doctor, Lloyd. If he says hospital, that's where you're going."

Deir protested further, but Brady and the doctor were adamant. They waited together for the ambulance. Deir shivered, and Brady draped the shirt over his shoulders. Deir left it there. Suddenly he jumped up. "Say," he told Brady, "I could sure use a cup of coffee. Let's go inside and get one."

After a brief argument they got him back down ("Man, I *know* it won't hurt me to get *up*. I've been sitting around enough already!") and Brady brought out some coffee.

At last the ambulance arrived, and the doctor left his unruly patient with considerable relief. "Don't let him jump up any more," he told Brady with the dubious air of a man who has just assigned someone an impossible task.

Deir climbed reluctantly into the ambulance and sat down on the seat beside the cot. "Hey, you're supposed to lie down there," said the driver.

"Man, look at those clean sheets, and look at me. You'll never get 'em clean again. I have my *shoes* on. I'm filthy!"

"Never mind all that," said the driver, surprised. "You lie down like I say, huh?"

"I'm the one who's got to sit in that seat," said Brady firmly. So Deir stretched out on the cot. But when they reached the hospital he brushed aside all help and walked to the emergency room himself. Brady stayed long enough to make sure Deir was all right, then prepared to leave.

"I'll get back, Lloyd," said Brady. "You take care, now. Don't worry about a thing. You want me to call Mrs. Deir?"

"No, no. Man, if she finds out I'm in the hospital she'll be scared to death."

"She has to know, Lloyd."

"I'll call her myself tonight."

"Okay, whatever you say. We'll be back to see you."

Despite all his earlier protestations, Deir found it good to relax and let the hospital people take care of him. Half a dozen doctors, nurses and orderlies clustered around and began to clean off the oil, using ether ("Before they could fix me," he reported later, "they had to *find* me") and then mineral oil. They shaved his head, wiped away the oil from around his eyes and picked a few of the rust flakes out of his skin (the rest were left to work their way out by themselves, a process that was still going on more than a year later). They injected antibiotics, took fourteen stitches in his scalp and treated and dressed his arm. Finally they sent him off to bed.

"How long am I going to be here?" he asked.

"It's much too soon to tell," the doctor said. "We'll have to wait and see."

"I'll talk to you about it tomorrow," Deir replied.

He didn't stay in bed for long.

"Where's a phone?" he asked his nurse.

"You're not supposed to use a phone. You're supposed to lie down."

"Daggone, my *legs* are all right. I've gotta be able to get up and walk around."

When she was gone, he slipped out of bed, found a phone and put in a long-distance call to his wife. His daughter Lorraine, eleven, answered. She was delighted to hear his voice.

"How are you, Daddy?"

"I'm fine, honey, just fine. Is Momma there?"

"She's gone out. Daddy, when are you coming home?"

"Pretty soon, soon as we get the ship in. Lorraine, you tell Momma I called. I'll call again at four-thirty."

Doris Deir walked in just as her daughter was hanging up the phone. She was troubled at this unexpected call from her husband; he was not one to use the telephone for social chit-chat. She had Lorraine repeat the conversation verbatim. It was innocuous enough, certainly, but she was still dissatisfied. She had some shopping to do for supper, and she hurried out to get it done before he called back. But she missed him again. Suffolk was on Standard Time, Salisbury on Daylight Saving. Deir's four-thirty was her three-thirty, and he had already phoned by the time she returned.

Now a sense of frustration was added to her feeling of anxiety. The more she thought about it the more worried she became. It must be something important for him to call long distance twice. But what should she do? Where had he called from? Should she call the Reeds?

Upset and uncertain, she began making supper while the children hung around the kitchen, helping and chattering. That's where the newsboy, bursting with importance, found them.

"Mrs. Deir," he said eagerly, "did you know your husband was hurt?"

"No," said Doris Deir in a steady voice. "Now, all you kids get out of the kitchen so I can finish supper."

When they were gone she grabbed the paper and sat down, her knees suddenly weak. The story was brief, and it contained little information. There had been an explosion on the *Queen;* Deir was in the hospital in Salisbury; his condition was "fair."

Only fair? She sat there a few moments, trying to fight back the rising panic. For months she had been afraid of something like this, and now it had come, with the force of a blow. The period since Deir had left on the salvage project had been the loneliest and unhappiest of her life. He had never been away from her this long before; all the household duties that he had once taken care of had fallen upon her—making out the bills, answering business calls, doing all the heavy chores around the house. She had handled it all faultlessly, hoping he would approve of her decisions, sure he would understand her mistakes. But she had missed him dreadfully. Many nights she had cried herself to sleep (he would have been astonished if he had known). As his stays on the tanker grew longer and longer, her fears had increased in proportion. Now apparently the worst had happened, and she was almost afraid to call and learn the details. Only the thought that he *had* spoken to Lorraine, and that he apparently had sounded all right, sustained her.

At last, when she had herself under control and felt she could trust herself to talk to Deir, she went to the phone and put in a call to the hospital.

The nurse who answered was brisk. "No, Mrs. Deir, you can't talk to your husband. He has been put to bed and isn't being allowed to go to the phone."

Her fear mounting, and her anger with it, Mrs. Deir spoke back sharply. "What do you mean, 'Isn't allowed'? He's already called me twice today. Now, I want to speak to him, and right now!"

There was a long wait, and much discussion in the background. And then Deir's voice, bouncy as ever: "Naw, now everything's all right, don't you worry. Just a little accident, a little combustion in a cofferdam. I'll be out of here in a day or two, good as new. I don't know what everyone's so daggone excited about. There isn't a thing wrong with me that won't be right in a couple of days, and I'll be right back on the ship working."

But he was uncommunicative about the details of his injuries, and when the phone call was finished she knew as little about his condition as she had in the first place. As for his air of unconcern, it was obviously sincere, but she was too familiar with her husband to be fooled by it. She called her father. "I want you to drive me to Maryland tomorrow," she said.

Doris spent the whole of the next day at the hospital, and it did them both good. Deir was surprised to see her; he had felt certain after finishing the phone conversation the day before that he had removed all her doubts about the state of his health. As for her, she was both shocked and reassured by his appearance. He was all bandaged and pepper-marked, but he was clearly in high spirits and anxious to get out. They had a pleasant day together—the longest uninterrupted visit they had had with each other in months. Doris left feeling a great deal better, almost ready to accept her husband's view that he would be out of the hospital by the next day.

He actually spent a week there. By the middle of it, the doctor was avoiding him; the doctor was a good-humored man, but he was tired of arguing with Deir about when he could leave. Deir's elbow developed a slight infection, and the doctor checked it from time to time to make sure it was getting along all right. But for the rest he counted on the ward nurse to keep him informed. She endured Deir's harassment stoically.

Every day he was visited by someone from the tanker, and he used these occasions to keep his finger on developments there. The last bolts were just going in; it was while he was in the hospital that the drill broke again, this time beyond repair, and they had to finish up the drilling and the tapping for the last two bolts using the impact wrench.

Brady had taken charge of the work while Deir was gone. Steady and competent and well liked by everybody, he was getting a lot done. He reported that he and Simmons had built a salt-water tank on the deck near the big generator. The marine engine that ran the generator was cooled in part with salt water (as on other engines of its kind, fresh water was used inside the radiator, but salt water was pumped into the coils around the radiator to cool the fresh water). It had been the practice on the *Queen* to use the generator sparingly because the engine gobbled down diesel fuel in great quantities, but when it did run the salt water it used was pumped in from the sea, which was within easy reach only a few feet off the port side. But it had suddenly occurred to Brady that once the ship started to come up the engine was going to be a long way from the surface of the ocean—too far for a pump to operate with complete effectiveness. Where would they get salt water then? Well, why not from the engine room, which they would be pumping out anyhow? So he and Simmons had put up a big tank to serve as a reservoir for the engine-room water.

Brady had also officiated over an ingenious leak-patching project. The men had discovered while Deir was in the hospital that the seas had ripped away some of the disk harrow blades from certain starboard portholes that were right at the water level where they were almost impossible to reach, either from inside or outside the hull. The blades had been installed originally during a period of abnormally low tides, but the tides just weren't going that low any more. Although the men could not get at the portholes from the inside, they could get within a few feet of them. So someone devised a solution: a man standing inside the hull shoved through a long board to which a cable had been attached. Once the board had been pushed through the porthole, it bobbed to the surface, where it was snatched up by another man. The cable end was then detached from the board and bolted to the center of a new disk. After that the inside man hauled away at his end of the cable—quickly, so the disk would not snag on obstructions outside—and pinned the dish-shaped blade against the porthole. Then he tied down the cable, and the hole was sealed.

One more job was accomplished during this period: they finished hooking up the pumps in the engine room. Deir hoped for a while that pumping could actually be started while he was gone, but that proved impossible. There was simply too much work to do first.

On the sixth day of his stay in the hospital Deir told Strait, Reed and Crisp, the day's visitors from the *Queen,* that he would be leaving the following morning. "Kin, do you think maybe Mrs. Reed could drive over and pick me up?"

"Sure, Lloyd. But I thought the doctors said you'd have to stay a while longer."

"They don't know about it yet," said Deir.

That same day he broke the news to the nurse. "Now, look, I'm going to have to leave here," he said. "I've stayed a fair length of time; I've met you halfway. Now I'm leaving. I've told them to come get me tomorrow."

She looked at him helplessly. "I'll send the doctor to talk to you in the morning," she said.

The doctor grinned when he saw him. "I hear you consider yourself recovered," he said. He unwrapped the bandages on Deir's arm and examined the infection carefully. Then he bandaged it up again and leaned back. "Okay," he said. "I guess you can go. It's getting along well; just don't get it wet. But I want you to come back on Wednesday so I can change the dressing. Promise?"

"I'll be back," said Deir.

As it turned out, he lost almost another week before he could really buckle down to work on the *Queen.* It was a Friday when Mrs. Reed picked him up at the hospital, but for two days the weather was so bad he couldn't get out to the tanker. He spent the time making some necessary repairs on the rearming boat, tied up at Kin's dock. It was Sunday before he boarded the *Queen* again. After a couple of days he went back ashore for the trip to the hospital—and lost another day returning because of bad weather, to his extreme annoyance.

But at last everything was ready for the climactic episode in the great salvage enterprise. The *Queen* could now be pumped out. Once that was done she would rise off the shoal and could be towed into Norfolk. The big payoff was drawing near.

THREE

20

TOWARD THE END of the third week of September, just after Deir's return, Kin brought out the aircraft rearming boat laden with a great anchor. They hoisted it up at the stern and let it hang from a boat davit. It was a happy sight. Anchors are only for vessels that float.

On September 18 Deir started the pumps in the engine room.

"It's just a test," he said. But everybody felt sure that if the test went well it would never stop. Hoses had been run through the passageways, through empty rooms, out portholes, across the decks—two thousand feet of hose in all. Of the original twenty-two pumps, four had conked out, one was keeping the aft rope locker dry and one was still assigned to the cofferdams. The remaining sixteen were installed in the engine room, under the charge of Maurice Simmons. Two more developed trouble soon after they started and were taken out of action. But the remainder continued hard at work, and the water began to pour over the side in great freshets.

As time passed, the level of the water in the engine room began to lower perceptibly, and men assigned to various duties around the tanker made it a point to stop by whenever they could to check its height. The water's recession could be measured by the emergence of the steel steps that ran down some thirty feet to the engine room's lowest deck. For months they had been out of sight under the water. Now they slowly began to come into view. Excitement and tension began to build up all over the vessel.

As the water level descended, the fumes in the engine room grew noticeably stronger, and the oil slick on the water became heavier. Pockets of oil that had been trapped under the surface were being released as the water went down.

"Watch those pumps," Deir told Simmons. "Make sure they stay underwater. They're not new, and if they start arcing with all these fumes around they'll blow us *all* up." He ordered all smoking limited to the fantail, and to Brady he said, "Well, this"—he gestured with his bandaged arm—"might have been a godsend after all. Maybe we were getting a mite careless. Now we'll watch out for sure."

Kin Reed, jubilant over the progress, poked his head in and sniffed the fumes. "Hey, Lloyd, if you'd open up that skylight a bit more all that smell'd go."

"Well, yeah. We don't want to open it too much in case of fire."

"Aw, that won't make no difference."

"Well," Deir said mildly. "I guess it'll be okay like it is."

As the water went down, it uncovered a multitude of leaks in the side of the hull, and Pearly Strait and Woody Crisp tried their hand at a little diving. They put on masks, went down a short distance on the diving platform and began patching. They pounded wood shingles, brought aboard for that purpose, into the space between the patch and the hull. Where other cracks were evident they simply stuffed them with rags.

Deir left the engine room to Simmons after a while and turned his attention to other matters: the hoses had to be checked for leaks, and the air compressors on the tank deck had to be leveled before they would work properly.

By 9:00 A.M. ten feet of dripping wall were exposed in the engine room, and excitement was running high. Leaks were now cropping up everywhere, and the men were trotting around happily sealing them up. Duke Morris, an old hand at this sort of thing, had warned them before ending his last stay that leaks would occur as soon as the internal water level went down. "You've got all that pressure outside the hull and it gets empty inside, and, boy, she starts spouting in like a watering can," he said. "Don't let that scare you. And maybe the water level will rise a little again on account of the leaks. It's natural for it to do that; don't get worried about it."

And indeed the leaks developed. Porthole covers had warped. Bolts had been sprung. Plates had separated. There were hair cracks between patch and hull. Toilets were inexplicably backing up. But the water level in the engine room continued to drop, much to everybody's joy. And the leaks were taken not as evidence of danger but rather as a sign of progress, so that a kind of carnival atmosphere prevailed as the men went around stuffing them with rags. Woody in particular made a game of this calking process. When a leak appeared that couldn't be fixed from within, he would snatch up a diving mask, shove a handful of rags or a bundle of shingles into his belt, and plunge over the side, to Brady's increasing consternation. "Be *careful*," Brady pleaded. "We don't want anything to happen *now*, for the Lord's sake."

The toilets were plugged by shoving rags into them with poles. At one point Simmons left the pumps in someone else's care for a while and helped Strait with this work. For poles the two men used hollow metal tubes that apparently had been used as closet rods; there were little holes at each end for wall hooks. The poles worked fine, but on one occasion the pressure in a toilet pushed aside the rag and sent a column of water rising in the rod itself. When the water reached the top, it spurted out of the little hole in a slender stream.

Pearly and Simmons watched silently, both struck by the same thought. "Seems only fair," Simmons commented at last.

When he returned to work in the engine room, Simmons was visited more and more often by Deir. There was a lot of work to be done now. As the water went down, the pumps had to be lowered further; they must be kept submerged at all costs, both because they wouldn't work out of the water and because of the fire hazard. Every time the pumps were moved the hoses had to be shifted, a difficult and annoying task. Deir watched the pumps narrowly and cautioned Simmons again and again to cut the switches if anything went wrong. ("Boy, that explosion of his sure made an extra-careful man of him," Brady confided to Simmons.)

But switching off the pumps had to be done with care, and Deir knew it better than anybody. While he was in the hospital, Pearly Strait had hooked up the pumps to the engine room's own switchboard. Eight of the pumps now in use had separate switches, but for the sake of convenience Pearly had hooked the other six to a single switch—"You can turn 'em all off at once," he said. There was just one trouble: if that much power was cut at once, the switch probably would burn out. Deir gave strict instructions that under no circumstance was the six-pump switch to be flipped off unless the generator was first throttled back.

And then, as Deir made one of his periodic visits to the scene of the pumping, the thing he had feared most suddenly occurred before his eyes: a pump began to arc. Worse, it was behaving in a way he hadn't even anticipated—it was arcing *under* the water. For an instant he stared. Then he roared at Simmons, *"Cut those six pumps!"*

"Hell, no!" Simmons shot back.

Deir made it across to the switchboard in three jumps and threw the switch. This was no time to worry about minor burn-outs. The switch, to his relief, did not burn out anyhow. Outside, the generator engine, roaring away since early morning, surged briefly and went back to its steady putting.

Deir turned off all the pumps while he took the faulty one out of operation. Then he hooked up the others again and started them going. Immediately, Simmons looked puzzled. "Something's wrong," he said. "Only some of the pumps are working." They quickly shut everything off and checked.

Eight pumps—those on the separate switches—had burned out. It was a calamity. The pumps were completely ruined, fried black inside their casings. That brief surge of the generator when Deir hit the switch must have sent enough current through the eight pumps to wreck them. Either that, or all eight had been faulty, just waiting for one flick of the switch to burn out. Silently the men gathered in the engine room and watched Deir open them, one after another, his face grim.

The water began to rise again in the engine room.

Brady hurried in, wearing a worried expression. "What happened, Lloyd? Why'd we stop? What's wrong with the pumps?"

Deir looked around uneasily. "They went bad," he said. "Look, Paul, we've got to get more pumps. Maybe Portsmouth Salvage will have some. But we better move fast. And, look, we ought to get new ones this time."

"Yeah, but what's bad about the old ones? How many went bad, Lloyd?" Brady asked insistently.

"Eight."

"*Eight! At one time?* Now, wait a minute, you don't just lose eight pumps at a time because they went *bad!* What *made* them go bad? What on earth happened?"

"Well, I guess they burned out. We're gonna have to get new ones, Paul."

To everyone's utter astonishment, Brady exploded. Those pumps had been hard to get, and they had cost a good deal of money.

"Damn it, what's wrong with them? We *have* these pumps! They're bought and paid for, and there were no complaints about them up to today! We're supposed to have everything we need—pumps, hoses, generator, all we need to run the pumps we've got, and, damn it all, that's what we're gonna run!"

Deir looked abashed, and everyone else stood around uncomfortably. Brady was usually so easygoing that it was a little appalling to see him angry. By now it was apparent to all that the pumps had burned out when Deir threw the switch. This was equally unsettling—and not the least thrown off by it, obviously, was Deir himself. He listened to Brady's outburst in silence, not sure what to say. It was as much a shock to him as to anyone else to see the water coming up again in the engine room. It was a terrible setback, no two ways about it. If he hadn't thrown the switch so hastily it might have been prevented. But he had *said* the pumping was only a test. And, daggone it, if he hadn't moved in haste he might never have had a chance to move at all. The salvage operation might have come to a gruesome end in an explosion that disintegrated ship and men alike.

Still, Deir didn't know quite how to answer Brady. Whether he had erred or not, he could not admit to a mistake —not for what it would do to the others (all of them, including Brady, would have quickly forgotten about it), but for what it would do to him, Deir. For it was an integral part of Deir's credo that he did not make mistakes, that anyone with sufficient foresight and ability should be able to avoid them, all of them. As unlikely as this might have seemed to anyone else, he firmly believed in it—and therefore in himself. It was this strong sense of his virtual infallibility, part of the psychological equipment that he had carried over from his steeplejack days, that gave him the steady courage to tackle jobs that would have unnerved anyone else. With this, he was indomitable. Without it, he was just another uncertain, if highly talented, workman. He *couldn't* admit that throwing that switch had been a mistake.

At this point, with Brady still furious and Deir strangely silent, and the atmosphere growing more and more tense, Kin Reed entered and saved the situation.

Ever since the salvage operation had started Kin had been having a hard time. Around Ocean City his association with the salvagers was widely viewed as a major lapse of judgment, since it was perfectly apparent that they were engaged in a hopeless, and possibly lunatic, task. Kin, far from sure himself that the *Queen* would ever be raised, had required constant reassurance from Deir. At least once a week he would ask, "You fellers really think you're gonna get this thing up?" Or, as a variation, he would state it himself, confidently, "Boy, you really *are* gonna get her up!" And then he would peer sharply at Deir and add, "Aren't you?"

When the pumps had actually started to bring down the engine room water level, Kin had been transported. He kept popping into the engine room, so excited he couldn't stand still. "You're gaining on it," he would cry. He made suggestions, tugged at hoses, got underfoot, tried repeatedly to get Deir to open the skylight, and busily shooed cigarette smokers to the stern. All morning he had been full of praise for everyone as he watched the process that would soon vindicate him in Ocean City. "You're really doing it!" he had shouted. "Boy, you're *doing* it!"

Now, bursting into the engine room, he stared for a moment at the blackened pumps and uttered an anguished wail.

"For Pete's sake!" he yelled. "Doesn't *anyone* know what he's doing out here? Can't anybody do anything *right? Look* at those pumps. *Look* at them!" He hopped up and down in the intensity of his feeling. "You fellers ain't *ever* gonna get this thing up, I *know* it!" He wheeled, raging, on the startled Brady. "Stop this fool talk," he shouted. "There's the boat." He made a furious gesture. "Get in, and go get some pumps!"

It was the only thing to do. Brady grinned faintly at the red-faced Kin, and turned back to Deir.

"How many pumps do you think we need?" he asked. "You think ten?"

"Ten would be fine," Deir said, much subdued.

"Okay, Kin, let's go." He couldn't resist one more dig at Deir. "Well, here goes another ten thousand dollars."

"Oh, naw," said Deir hastily. "They won't cost that much."

That was true, of course. Brady knew exactly how much they would cost. Back in the spring when they had been shopping for pumps he had priced some new ones at a hundred and fifty dollars each—an unusually low price. As he headed for the boat with Kin he decided to buy not ten but fifteen, just in case. Brady knew the value of money, but he also knew the danger of skimping. And at this crucial point another two thousand dollars or so did not loom so large. There were just a couple of questions now: Where would they get the pumps? And how many precious days would they lose?

In Ocean City, Brady put in a call to Alvah Sadler in Suffolk.

"Sadler, we're in trouble," he said. "We've burned out eight pumps, and we don't have but a few left. I'll tell you all about it later, but right now we have to do something fast. It's another expense we didn't figure on, but we've just got to get some more pumps—and they'll probably have to be new ones, because we don't have time to shop around. You think you could get started looking? Everything's at a complete stop here now."

"I'll get right on it," said Sadler without hesitation. "How many?"

"Fifteen, and I think they'll cost a hundred and fifty dollars apiece."

"Okay. Are you coming to Suffolk?"

"I'm leaving right now. I just thought maybe you could get moving on this. It'll probably take a couple of days or more to find pumps."

"I'll get on the phone right now. Call me when you get in."

When Brady did get in, more than five hours later, there was a surprise waiting for him. Sadler had spoken to Lib Brady. He had located some pumps in Baltimore and had asked for the loan of the Brady pickup truck to drive after them. Lib had had the truck oiled and filled with gasoline, and Sadler was ready to leave. He was only waiting for the follow-up call from Brady.

"Fellow up in Baltimore said he'd meet me at his place early tomorrow morning," Sadler said when Brady phoned him. "I'll drive up. You rest; you've had a long day. As soon as I hit Ocean City I'll give you a call and you can start back up there."

Late on the afternoon of the next day, Saturday, the call came. Sadler was in Ocean City with the fifteen pumps.

"My gosh," said Brady, "I don't see how you did it! We'll be back in operation by tomorrow night."

"Mighty near didn't do it," said Sadler, chuckling. "I hope you don't mind a couple of flat tires. That was a lot of weight that truck was carrying. Finally had to pump up the tires with eighty pounds pressure, else they flattened right out under the load."

"As long as you got the pumps there, everything's fine," Brady said cheerfully. "We'll start right away."

Simmons, Crisp and Duncan had traveled back to Virginia with him, glad for the chance to spend the weekend with their families. Now he called Simmons and Crisp (he couldn't reach Duncan) and told them they were starting back that night.

"Boy, you *are* a pusher," Simmons said, disgruntled.

"Didn't you ever hear of *resting* on Sunday?"

"There's *work* to do," cried Brady in great good spirits. "We gotta get a move on!"

Simmons sighed. "I'll be ready."

The next day the salvage operation got back into full swing.

Deir had put the day off to good use. He had started blowing the tanks—not pumping in enough compressed air to get the tanker's forepart off the shoal, but adding just enough to lighten it considerably. He wanted to keep the forward section of the *Queen's* bottom pinned firmly to the sand for a while. That part of the tanker's belly was broad and flat and stable, and it was good to have it resting on something. He was still worried about what was going to happen as the ship started to come off the shoal where she had rested so long. The divers had reported that during the months the tanker had spent sitting in the sand she had settled into a marked trough, so that now she had a low wall all around her, holding her steady. That was fine. But once she rose up out of that depression, what would happen?

In fact, what would happen now that the tank deck was being lightened by all that compressed air? What if a storm blew up this weekend, while the *Queen* was in this partly buoyant state? All these months Deir had derived a sense of security from that brief exercise in mathematics he had performed the very first day aboard, when he and Little had stood at the rail and he had figured out that no less than forty thousand tons of water was keeping the tanker pressed against the ground. Well, with the tanks partly filled with air, the ship now held a lot less than forty thousand tons. If some of the mighty waves they had experienced in the past should strike again in this intermediate stage of the refloating process, catching the ship when she was still unstable, there was no telling what they might do to her. Capsize her, maybe. Or sweep her off the shoal entirely, and sink her in deep water.

All things considered, he was delighted Sunday morning when the rearming boat appeared in the distance and then pulled up on the port side to disgorge Brady—and the fifteen new pumps. Now they could get on with the work.

There was a great deal to be done before pumping could be resumed, and they spent the rest of the day doing it, working until one o'clock Monday morning. The new pumps, weighing a hundred and fifteen pounds each, were still in their crates. They had to be unpacked, checked carefully and thoroughly greased. Then began the long, difficult process of hooking them up—wiring them to the tanker's electrical system, connecting them to the hose, lowering them into the water at the end of long ropes. Not all of them were needed in the engine room; some were installed up forward, in those tanks that still contained water. The new pumps were best for this assignment because the tanks were filled with fumes, and the new machines were less likely than the old ones to start a fire. They did pose one problem, however. Unlike the old surplus pumps, the new ones had their switches right next to the pump mechanism itself. This meant that after a pump was lowered into place inside the tank, someone had to climb down into the poisonous fumes after it to start it going. Woody, the lay preacher, insisted on volunteering for the job. "I've been saved," he explained, with the air of a man who owns the only parachute on a wobbling plane.

At five o'clock Monday morning everybody was awake and anxious. Deir started up the big generator and at 6:00 A.M. pumping began again. He also kept the compressors feeding air into the main tanks.

They now had twenty-one pumps in action, instead of the sixteen that were operating on Friday. This battery was forcing the water out in great fountains—twenty tons of it every minute, Deir figured. There was bedlam aboard the tanker now: the roar of falling water, the racing-car racket of the generator's diesel, the thunder of the two compressors pounding away on the tank deck, the joyful shouting of the men. By 7:00 A.M., after only an hour of pumping, the water level in the engine room had dropped four feet.

The tension and excitement built up once more. Again men began to stop by the engine-room door to check the pumps' progress. Again there were leaks to patch and kinks to straighten in the hoses. And again there was the feeling of being on the verge of something momentous.

Months before they had brought aboard a number of life jackets. Now, as the water level in the engine room dropped past the ten-foot mark, Deir went around instructing everyone to keep a lifejacket handy. This reminder of danger added immeasurably to the sense of excitement. Kin Reed, who had showed up early, protested ("Darn old cartjackets never saved anyone!"), but he took his with all the rest.

All morning the tension grew. And then there came a moment when men everywhere on the ship stopped what they were doing and looked up, wondering. *Was it?* An instant later the deck under them shook again, harder, and suddenly there was pandemonium. Men began to laugh and pound one another on the back and shout from every corner of the tanker.

"She's coming off!"

Strait was standing by the engine-room door with Simmons when Simmons suddenly seized his arm, almost throwing him to the deck, and yelled, "Look at the water!" It was gently sloshing against the engine-room bulkhead—the first time it had moved since the patch was bolted on. Strait spun around and galloped down the passageway toward the stern, shouting.

He met Brady, who had been having a smoke on the fantail, and Brady yelled, wild-eyed, "Hey, Pearly!"

"What?"

"She's *floating!*"

"I know it!"

For a moment they stood there, grinning foolishly, too excited to move, and waited. There it was—it had jiggled again! They grabbed each other and cheered. Then Strait raced off once more. At last he found Deir, and the two hundred-pound Strait swept up the hundred-fifty-pound Deir in a tremendous bear hug. "You've done it! You've done it!" he roared.

Deir, laughing, squirmed loose. "We've all done it!" he said.

Henley Doughtie came steaming out of the kitchen passageway, his feet clomping on the deck, his craggy face all aglow. He grabbed Deir and dragged him toward the kitchen, bellowing. "There, by the good goddam," he boomed when Deir was inside. "Just you take a look at that plumb bob!"

It was swaying gently on its cord.

Every movement of the sea was now moving the *Queen*, shifting the great tanker in her bed of sand and batting her gently against the side of the trough. The keel forward of the tank deck was still touching bottom, but the stern was now well off, definitely afloat. With every jolt, someone would shout, "Did you feel that? Did you feel it?"

Kin Reed was trotting all over the ship, collaring everyone he could find and asking, "Is she gonna float? No kidding, is she gonna float?"

"Man," said the jubilant Deir, laughing, "what do you think she's *doing?*"

Kin still needed convincing—something he could see with his own eyes—but by now the evidence wasn't hard to supply. On the starboard side, the cables to the diving platform were alternately slacking and tightening as the ship rolled. On the port side, farther aft, the big anchor had now begun to rock slowly to and fro. Men standing on the fantail could hear the great rudder creaking in time with the movement of the ship. "By golly!" yelled Kin. "You've got her! You've got her!"

The stern was now rising noticeably, and Deir called an end to the celebration.

"Get those lifejackets on!" he called out.

This was the moment of greatest danger. The *Queen* was now touching bottom only at one point—right under the pilot-house, on the ragged plates that had once been attached to the bow. If she was ever going to capsize, this would be the time. Or, just as bad, she might even break again, somewhere between the pilothouse and the aft deckhouse. Putting on the lifejackets sobered everyone just a little.

Simmons, alone again in the engine room, found himself more deeply moved than he could have admitted. He leaned against the bulkhead and watched the water gently slopping on the steel plates. It had been such a long, hard pull, and now the *Queen* was coming alive under his feet, floating once more, a ship again at last. He had fought off any real emotional involvement with this operation from the start. He was out here for the dough; nothing else would have justified the risks, the hard life, the separation from his wife and children. Nevertheless, of all the men on the tanker when she started to come off the shoal, he was the one most affected emotionally. There was something so damn thrilling about the battered *Queen* struggling off the bottom after all these months. He felt the gooseflesh on his arms and was glad he was alone. He was being pretty damn silly, he thought.

Slowly, as the stern rose higher and higher, the *Queen* lost her list. For almost nine months she had rested partly on one side, and the men aboard her had almost forgotten what it was like to work on a level surface. Now she gradually rolled erect, to an even keel. Then, briefly, she was canted slightly to port. Deir, switching the controls on his tank deck pumps and air compressors, helped her recover her equilibrium. But after that the tanker's balance was always precarious, and Deir had to stay on the tank deck almost constantly, pumping out water or pumping in air on the low side, slowing the water pumps on the high side to keep her heavy there. A pump was kept running constantly in the one starboard tank with a hole in it.

He was on the tank deck when Henley, no longer cheerful, stormed out of the deckhouse.

"You want lunch today?" Doughtie yelled.

"Yeah, sure, Henley. What's wrong?"

"Well you goddam well better keep this damn ship even or there don't nobody eat another mouthful. You hear me? I ain't just talking to hear myself, you goddam Deir. I'll quit, damn it! You *know* that stove don't work without it's level. I've had to level the little sonofabitch four times in the last twenty minutes, and I just ain't gonna do it. Not no more. You hear? You *do* something; I don't care what. You do something, or you gonna starve!" And he turned and tramped back to his kitchen, exuding indignation.

The changing slant of the deck created other problems as well. From the beginning, the salt water that was used to cool the generator diesel had been allowed to run off onto the port deck, from which it simply followed the deck's slant back into the sea. Now it was running all over the deck, and tools that had been stored there safely for months were in danger of a soaking. The men hastily rescued the tools and rerouted the water.

During the afternoon someone looked over the side, where Kin had tied up the rearming boat, and gave a great shout. "Hey, we're pulling the barge out of the water!" The rising stern had pulled the boat's painter tight, and there was daylight under the little vessel's bow. Kin quickly untied it and gave it more line.

On the tank deck, Deir was having troubles of his own. As the *Queen* righted herself, portside hatches that had been high above the sea for months were lowered closer to the water. The rising stern dipped them down still farther. Soon swells were sweeping clear across the lower end of the tank deck, coming to within a foot of the open hatches. If the water got into those hatches and the portside tanks ever filled up, there was no telling what would happen; she might even capsize to port. He watched the hatches closely, ready to call for help, waiting for the rising tide to hit its peak. When it did so, the waves were washing to within a few inches of the hatch lips. It had been mighty near.

By now the tanker was no longer banging against the sides of the sand trench. She had risen well above it. By 1:00 P.M. the stern, which had once been within four feet of the sea's surface at high tide, towered twenty feet off the water. The bow was still touching bottom.

The lowering of the water in the engine room was creating a new problem now. As the pumps were let down farther and farther they began to outrun their hoses. There simply wasn't enough hose on the ship to stretch all that distance. They had to cut out some of the pumps and splice their hoses in to the pumps that remained.

From time to time Deir left the tank deck briefly and climbed out onto the elevator—which had been lashed to the ship's side so it wouldn't be left behind by the rising stern— and looked at the patch. Its top edge had emerged from the sea when the tanker rolled onto an even keel, and more and more of it had become visible as the ship rose. By early afternoon, some two thirds of it was above water. Rust had tanned it to a golden brown, and it was a handsome sight. Soon it would be completely out of water, and that would mean that the entire damaged area would be literally high and dry . . . safe forever.

Everybody was still working hard—Deir and Pearly Strait on the tank deck, Brady tending the three engines, Simmons watching the pumps and hoses. Sometime during the afternoon, Brady looked up and sighted the pilothouse against the horizon, and realized that the rolling of the tanker could not only be felt, and deduced from the swinging of the anchor, elevator boom and plumb bob, but it could be seen! The pilothouse was slowly rocking back and forth.

Not long after that there came one of the day's most satisfying incidents. The Coast Guard motorboat came purring up, stately and serene, for its daily visit. It circled the tanker once, as always, then approached the bow, as if something there puzzled its crew. Brady saw someone pointing to the ripples as the bow slowly rocked in the water. Men began to cluster on the boat's deck, chattering. And then, suddenly, the vessel's engine opened up in a full-throated roar, and the Coast Guardsmen raced off in the direction of Ocean City in wild excitement. Brady gave a slow smile of deep contentment. They hadn't even *asked* about progress this time!

At about the same time, the tanker's radio receiver, brought aboard by Brady some days earlier, began to pick up agitated messages from the local boatmen who were always around in good weather.

"Hey, Bill, come take a look at that old tanker! I think those guys have got her floating!"

"You're kidding!"

"Nossir, come look! She ain't listing now like she used to. Hell, I believe she's *rocking!*"

The radio discussions increased in number as the day wore on. The boatmen appeared to be about evenly divided between those who were pleased at the impending success of the long salvage operation and those who still bore the salvagers ill will. Some of the latter merely expressed doubt about the salvagers' ability to refloat the *Queen*, but others were bitter and spiteful. "I hope she slides right off there and sinks to the bottom," one man was heard to say.

By 9:00 P.M. the stern was thirty feet above the water, and the *Queen's* men once more had to get used to walking around on a sharply sloped deck—except that now it was slanted toward the bow, instead of toward the starboard side. This created problems. Henley was struggling with his stove and swearing hoarsely. One of the compressors on the tank deck was at such an angle that it wouldn't work and had to be leveled. But there were compensations. One was that it was now perfectly clear that the tanker was not going to capsize, and Deir ordered the lifejackets put aside. Another was that the tank deck had risen almost entirely out of water; for the first time since the operation began it was now possible to stroll around the tank hatches dry-shod. The only part of the deck still washed by the seas was directly under the pilothouse, where nobody was much interested in walking anyway.

Back in the aft deckhouse, the starboard cabins were out of water for the first time since December, and although it was very smelly in there, and pitch dark—there were no electric lights, of course, as there were elsewhere on the ship, and the portholes were all covered over—the men did a good deal of fascinated exploring in the rooms. Having been underwater, these cabins had never been scavenged. There was still bedding in them, and clothing and soaked books and various other odds and ends, including some small stuffed alligators which the old crew had apparently bought in great numbers in South America, and some toys which they must have been bringing home to their children. In one cabin someone discovered a pair of pants and an iron, still just as their owner had left them, with one pant leg spread flat on the table ready for pressing and the other pulled back out of the way.

Deir worked for a while after darkness fell, getting the tanks adjusted for the night. Away off in the distance were the lights of Ocean City, and he wondered how many more days he would see them from the tanker.

A short time later, while he was in the kitchen, he looked out of the porthole and frowned. What had happened to those shore lights? They were no longer visible off the port side.

"Dag*gone!*" he shouted. "We're swinging around!"

They all ran out on deck. The lights were still on the port side, but they were now farther back toward the stern. The tanker, her bow still grounded, was being swung by the wind and the tide. For all these months she had been facing northeast—in precisely the position she had been in ever since getting caught in the middle of her turn on that stormy night the previous winter. Now she was slowly drifting around toward the east.

The *African Queen* continued to move that night, and in so doing she got herself into trouble. The great March storm which had drowned Lewis Bertrand and twisted the tanker's catwalk off to one side had also swept a good deal of hardware over the side—mostly catwalk rails and light pipe that had been left lying around on deck by the scavengers. Simmons and Morris had seen it lying on the sand while they were diving but had thought nothing of it. Now the *African Queen* had changed position so that her hull was directly over this trash; as she turned with the tide she began to ride up on the metal junk with a terrible scraping sound. The men sat grimly around in the kitchen listening to the fearful *cru-u-n-nch* of rasping steel. Soon the whole ship was shaking with the impact, and they could feel the bottom plates sliding up on the stuff and then slipping off, all to the accompaniment of loud scraping and grinding. There was nothing they could do but sit there anxiously and wait for it to stop.

"She's bound to swing past it after a while," said Deir, wincing at a particularly loud grating noise from under the keel. "The tide ought to lift her over sooner or later. Worst that can happen, that junk will punch a hole in a tank—and then maybe we can still pump her full of compressed air."

After a time the noises did stop and everyone relaxed again. But Deir still kept a sharp eye on the tank deck, stepping out frequently to make sure everything was level. He stayed awake all night, sending the others off to bed long after midnight.

In the morning the *African Queen* was headed due east, facing expectantly out to sea.

21

SHORTLY AFTER DAWN on Tuesday, September 22, Deir wakened the crew, briefed Pearly on caring for the tank deck, and fell into his bunk. He had been asleep only a short time when he felt someone shaking his shoulder. He sat up, blinking.

"What is it? What's wrong?"

"Little is on board."

Deir sat there a moment, collecting his wits. *"Little?"*

"That's right. He's come back. He's up on deck talking to Brady." Several of the men were now standing anxiously around his bunk.

"Okay."

"Well . . . what are you gonna do, Lloyd?"

He looked up in surprise, then smiled faintly. From the way they were watching him they obviously expected him to march out on deck, confront Little at full height, point overboard and order him off. The fact was, he realized as he sat there on the edge of his bunk, he was not angry at Little. He didn't ever want to work with him again, didn't even want to speak to him, and had no intention of doing so. But there was no bitterness. Making an issue of Little's presence, just when they were on the verge of success, could only create trouble—and that was one thing they certainly didn't need more of. The thought of any sort of showdown was repugnant. Besides, he couldn't deny Little the right to be aboard for these last hours, to share in the triumph of the voyage to Norfolk.

"Not gonna do anything," he said, and started to put on his shoes. The Lord knew there was enough work still to do, and few enough people to do it. They could use another hand—and Little was a hard worker, no denying it. He headed out on deck.

"Don't worry about it," he said.

232

For five weeks Beldon Little had stayed in Suffolk, fretting over his enforced beaching and impatient to get back. A week after his return, Brady had left Suffolk to go aboard the tanker for good; before leaving he had promised that he would try to fix things so Little could rejoin the salvage operation. Little had helped him get together some equipment to take out to the ship, then he had settled back hopefully to await word.

Days passed, and then weeks. For a while Doris Deir continued to drop in on the Littles. "I'm sure you and Deir will work things out," she told Beldon. When the explosion occurred, Little heard about it over the radio and immediately went to the Deirs's house and offered to drive Doris to the hospital in Salisbury. She declined with thanks; her father was going to take her up. After her return from Maryland, Doris' visits to the Littles had stopped.

Little had found plenty to do at home. For one thing, the house they were renting belonged to Deir's father-in-law. That arrangement obviously was impossible now. The Littles got another place and borrowed Brady's truck for the moving. Little made frequent phone calls to Kin Reed and kept up with the progress of the salvage that way. He also called almost daily on Alvah Sadler, who was getting reports from Brady.

Once or twice Brady himself came to town—like the time the pumps burned out—but somehow Little always missed him. After a while it dawned on Little that Brady was avoiding him. He went to see Sadler. "When am I going back on the *Queen*?" he asked. "It's been a long time, and I don't seem to be getting any nearer."

"Stay away for now," Sadler had advised earnestly. "Let Paul work on Deir. Don't start trouble. It'll all come out all right; Brady will fix things."

Uneasy, Little went to see a lawyer. Could the others cut him out of his share of the tanker? "Not a chance," the lawyer said. Still Little worried.

"It isn't right, me being here while they're working on the tanker," he told his wife. "I don't know what's going on out there, even. My Lord, I helped *start* this thing. They can't keep me away. Hazel, I'm going out there."

And so he started on the long drive late Monday night, arrived in Ocean City at dawn and hired a boatman to take him out to the tanker.

His first look at the *Queen* after all those weeks set his heart to pounding. She was turned in a new direction, her stern riding high in the air—and, yes, she was bobbing! The boatman pulled up beside the ladder on the port side, and Little climbed aboard. The generator and the compressors were roaring, water was pouring out of the hoses, men were hard at work everywhere.

As he approached, each man stopped what he was doing, looked at him uneasily and exchanged vague greetings.

He stood beside Simmons for a few minutes.

"Uh, how's it going, Little?" Simmons said.

"Pretty good." They stood there a moment. "How's it going out here? Pretty good, I guess. You're getting her up."

"Yeah."

There was an uncomfortable pause. Then Little saw Brady. He walked up to him.

"Hi, Little," Brady said. They shook hands.

Little shuffled his feet, ill at ease, and then said, "I've come aboard. I'd like to help."

Brady hesitated. "Well, we can use some help," he said.

"Well. I guess if it's all right I'll go change my clothes. You let me know if there's anything I can do—if I can give you a hand with anything."

"Sure. All right."

And soon he was hard at work. He devoted the morning to repairing a bad leak in the engine room. Deir didn't speak to him, but nobody objected to his presence. Everyone was still a little strained. But he was back, and he was staying, and that was all that interested him. It felt good.

With the pumps working away steadily on the tank deck and some of the tanks filled with compressed air, it was just a matter of time before the bow, or what they called the bow —it was actually the torn midships section—came up off the

234

shoal. When it happened Pearly was the first to notice. He was working on the tank deck with Deir when suddenly he stared toward the pilothouse and said, "Hey, she's up! All the way up, I mean."

Deir looked. "Naw, I don't see anything."

"Sure," said Pearly. "Look hard at the pilothouse. Yesterday it was just rocking. Today it's rising up and down—the whole thing. Look!"

"Daggone! It *is* floating!"

There was much less excitement than there had been when the stern came off. Pearly shouted the news back to the deckhouse, and everybody came out and had a look. They were all pleased, but there hadn't really been any doubt about what would happen since yesterday. There was still a lot to do, and the men went back to work, discussing their progress cheerfully.

After a while Brady came hurrying out of the engine room, where he had been working with Simmons. "Damn, Lloyd," he called anxiously. "I think she's filling up again! The water's rising up over some of the steps that were dry yesterday. I don't know where it's coming from; there must be a hell of a leak in there someplace. It sure looks bad. The pumps are losing ground."

Deir went back to look it over. He grinned and slapped Brady on the back. "Nothing to it," he said. "Bow's coming up, water's running out of the boiler room and into the engine room. It isn't really rising. It's just running from a place up forward where you couldn't see it to a place here in the stern where you can. Forget it."

"Boy, I tell you," said Brady, shaking his head. "I'm just not thinking straight any more." He went back to the engine room.

With the bow up, the tanker began to drift almost imperceptibly toward the north and west. The day before, Kin, with great foresight, had anchored a life preserver a hundred and twenty-five feet off the port quarter to mark the vessel's position ("First time I ever found a use for one of these things," he said). During the night, as the stern had swung around toward the shore, the tanker had ridden over this improvised buoy; at daybreak the lifejacket was three hundred feet off the starboard bow. As the ship floated slowly toward shore the distance to the buoy increased, and crewmen began to urge dropping the anchor.

"Let's hold off," said Deir. "Let's get as far as we can away from all that junk on the bottom."

But he watched the *Queen*'s progress closely. At 4:00 P.M., when they were eight hundred feet from the buoy, the wind shifted and they began to drift southward—back toward their previous position.

"Okay," said Deir. "No sense waiting any longer. Let her go."

They let the anchor down from the stern davit where it had been hanging.

The *Queen*, riding at anchor for the first time in almost a year, acted as if she had forgotten how it was done. They had given her a hundred and fifty feet of cable. But instead of riding at anchor as a ship should, the tanker drifted around as if the anchor weren't even there. She floated to one side of it, and over it, and around to the other side. Never did she drift downwind or downcurrent of it and hold steady, as she should have.

"Never saw a ship behave like this before," Little said to Brady. "But as long as the anchor holds, where the ship doesn't go floating off the Lord knows where, I guess it doesn't make much difference whether she rides like she should."

But it worried them all the same. Could it be that the bow was stuck on something?

They were still debating the possibility after dark when they found something new to worry about. Out of the blackness came the lights of a boat, headed straight at them. Nighttime visitors were a rarity; who could it be? Suddenly, as the boat neared, a floodlight went on and played on the tanker's decks, blinding everyone. The intruder circled the *Queen* three times. Deir watched it closely, his face showing his concern. The radio conversations of the boatmen had unnerved everyone; it was uncomfortable to be the object of that kind of hatred, and some of those tough water-front types had talked so bitterly that the salvagers actually half feared sabotage. No one had forgotten those gun-toting visitors from Lewes months before. As the strange boat nosed around the *Queen*, Deir moved about the decks, following, never losing sight of it.

And then the suspicious-looking boat suddenly pulled up to the portside ladder, and Alvah Sadler came scrambling aboard!

"Man, we thought you were some kind of *enemy*," Deir told him.

"Brought you a fellow you'll be glad to see," Sadler said, as a stranger climbed the ladder behind him. "We were just circling around looking the ship over. I want you to meet Mr. Eugene Jaeger.

"I've hired a tug. But the Coast Guard says a 'disinterested third party' has to certify this ship's okay to enter the harbor before they can let her in. That's the law. Mr. Jaeger is the disinterested third party. He's a resident surveyor for a salvage company in Norfolk, and until he says so we can't be towed out of here."

Jaeger was a pleasant, knowledgeable man who was keenly aware of his varied responsibilities—to the Coast Guard, to all the shipping that would be affected if by some error of judgment he let a sinking or otherwise unfit ship through the Hampton Roads to Norfolk, to himself and his reputation, and, not least, to the salvagers of the *African Queen*, who, in the person of Sadler, had had to post a $100,000 bond with the Corps of Engineers as insurance against the possibility that the tanker might sink in the harbor. Jaeger would be doing no one a favor if he let the *African Queen* start for Norfolk before she was ready, and he knew it. After shaking hands with Deir and congratulating him on the salvagers' success thus far, he began to probe for weaknesses, to Deir's considerable dismay.

"We mighty near run afoul of your anchor line," Jaeger said, frowning. "It certainly seems to be in a peculiar place. Is she riding all right?"

"Oh, sure," said Deir hastily. "She's a little light, that's all."

"Yeah," said Brady. "Don't let *that* worry you."

"Well, how high is she riding, exactly?"

"Her draft is thirty-two feet," Deir said. "Same as it was when she was fully loaded with oil."

Jaeger shook his head. "She'll have to be a lot higher than that before you leave here. A lot higher."

"Well, that's no problem. We're still pumping water out of the engine room, and the afterpeak wash tank is still full of fresh water—it's never been opened because it's always been underwater, and there must be five hundred thousand gallons in there. We'll get her a lot higher. Don't worry about it."

"You heard there's a hurricane coming?"

Deir looked at him sharply. "Somebody said there *was* one, down around Florida somewhere. Is it coming up here?"

"They're expecting it to, later this week. Hurricane Gracie, they're calling it. It's a big one, and it's doing a lot of damage south of here. You don't have much time."

"It won't *take* much time. We ought to be ready for the tug tomorrow. And another day ought to see us in port."

Again Jaeger shook his head, and his face was troubled. "It doesn't seem to me that you're going to be ready tomorrow. But suppose I look around. You say the engine room still has water in it?"

"A lot less than it had. But we're still pumping it."

They conducted him into the engine room. As they entered, Deir looked at Jaeger out of the corner of his eye; he had to admit that the engine room was a pretty scary place if you were not prepared for it. Five or six electric-light bulbs had been strung in the vast room; they served not so much to light it as to make the darkness more noticeable. Everything was wet and slippery and filthy from having been underwater so long. The damaged section, with the covering tangle of pipes that had prevented the use of regular bolts on the patch, now looked more like a jungle than ever. Some kind of brown sea growth had sprouted on the metal around the great rips in the ship's side, and it hung down eerily, like long hanks of hair. The place stank. The oil fumes were so bad that they made everyone's eyes sting. In addition, there was a dank odor underlying the petroleum smell. A sludge of

238

rust, flaked paint, soaked asbestos and oil lay over everything, and here and there were bits of rotted paper and pasteboard that had once covered spare parts stored in the ship's tool-room.

Worst of all was the noise. Above the hum and gurgle of the pumps sounded the steady *slosh, slosh* of water under-foot, where thousands of gallons of brine were still waiting to be pumped out from beneath the tanker's lowest deck. It was a loud noise, and an extremely suggestive one: it sounded as if a great quantity of water were rushing into the tanker from somewhere. And it was apparent that this was exactly the thought that occurred to Jaeger—especially when a hard lurch sent a spray of water splashing up between the deck plates.

"Is there a hole under there somewhere?" he asked, staring down at his feet.

"No," said Deir flatly. "We've been getting water out of her right along for three days now. If there was a hole letting in enough water to make all that noise, all the pumps in the world couldn't get it out. No, sir. There's no hole under there. You can bet on that."

"Well, I don't like it. Sounds bad. But if you can keep her pumped out, why, I guess it's all right."

They gathered around the propeller shaft and the rudder chains. The shaft had been locked in position by the *African Queen*'s chief engineer almost nine months before, but Jaeger pointed out that the propeller might not remain locked once the ship began moving through the water again. "You'll want to tie the propeller down somehow," he suggested. "If the screw turns in the water and that shaft starts turning over those engines with no lubricant in them, they'll be ruined. And the rudder is turned to one side. It'll have to be straightened before she'll tow properly."

They climbed out of the engine room and adjourned to the kitchen for coffee—Jaeger, Deir, Sadler and Brady. Deir came right to the point.

"How soon can we get the tug out? If the hurricane is really coming this way we don't want to waste time. Now that we've got her up it doesn't make sense to sit around out here any more than we have to. Is there any reason that tug can't make it out here tomorrow?"

"I honestly don't believe you're going to be ready," said Jaeger. "That tug is going to be pretty expensive. The tug captain won't tow you until the rudder's straight and the ship's a good deal higher than it is now. If he has to wait for you to get ready it's going to run into money."

"Fifty dollars an hour," said Sadler softly.

"Let's say the day after tomorrow—Thursday," suggested Jaeger. "That will give you time to get fixed up and it should still leave time to beat the hurricane to Norfolk. If it comes."

"Well, I can't say I want to get caught in it if it does come," said Deir. Then he added thoughtfully, "Of course, I've gone this far with this job. If that hurricane comes I'm damned if I'll leave. I'm going right with it."

That night after Sadler and Jaeger left, Deir sent everybody off to bed. "The tug won't be here till Thursday," he said. "Nobody's had much sleep and nobody'll be getting much from here in. Better grab it now while you can. I'll look after things."

"*You'll* look after things!" said Simmons. "I'll bet you haven't slept six hours in the last week!"

"Well, I don't need much sleep. You know that."

"Yeah," said Strait, "but everybody needs more sleep than you've had! You go get a little rest, and *we'll* keep watch."

"They're right, Lloyd," said Brady. "You won't be any good to anyone if you keel over from lack of sleep. You go ahead to bed and we'll take care of things for a while."

"Naw," said Deir decisively. "I couldn't do it. I don't feel sleepy; if I did I'd go to bed. Go ahead, now."

It was true. He had no yearning for bed at all. He didn't feel tired or stiff. He just felt keyed up, ready for anything. He knew he couldn't keep this up forever, but it wouldn't be much longer anyhow, and there was so much to be done that he didn't dare let up. They left him, and he spent the next few hours roving around the tanker, checking the pumps in the engine room, adjusting the balance of the tank deck, trying to anticipate trouble before it happened.

When trouble came, it was something completely unexpected. There was a sudden jarring bump on the port corner, forward. Then after a moment the tanker bumped again, this time on the opposite corner, aft on the starboard side. He awakened Simmons and Crisp.

"She must have dragged her anchor to a more shallow spot," he said anxiously. "She's bumping against the bottom. We've gotta get her higher."

They began to check the pumps, some of which were now beginning to clog from the dirty water in the engine room. A little later he routed out the others. The bumps were coming faster. The seas had risen as the tide went down, and as the ship fell into each trough Deir would cringe, waiting for the impact as she hit bottom. They let out more anchor line, hoping she would drift off the hillock into deeper water. But she continued to hit.

Toward morning, with the bumping still going on, they all gathered tensely in the kitchen for coffee. Suddenly the deck dropped out from under them. The vessel swooped down and struck bottom with a resounding slam. Coffee spilled, men were thrown off balance.

"Damn!" said Deir.

They all ran out. "Get those pumps pumping!" Deir called. "I mean *pumping!*" He hurried into the engine room and ran down the ladders to the turbine deck. She had hit on the stern, and he was afraid the rudder might have been driven right up into her. It was all right. But the tanker mustn't be allowed to do that again.

He ran out to the tank deck and began pumping more air into the aft tanks. He got them up to eleven pounds, and within fifteen minutes the ship was riding a foot higher. The tide was rising now, and he felt certain that the worst of the bumping was over.

All that morning they kept working on the pumps, trying to keep them clean, fighting the water down foot by foot. The salvagers were running into a new problem now: the water level was so low that the pumps were being overworked.

They were now forced to push the water some thirty feet straight up before it could be exhausted overboard, and they simply couldn't raise that much pressure. The flow from the hoses had slowed to a trickle. There was one obvious solution: cut a hole in the ship's side and pump the water out that way; there was no need, really, to send the water clear topside when the vessel was riding this high. Little volunteered to burn the hole, but Brady, who had taken charge of the engine-room operation, voted against it.

"Boy," he said, "this place is just reeking with fumes. We don't dare bring a torch in here. Let's keep trying this way, at least for a while. Maybe the fumes'll clear out some."

The clogging of the pumps became worse hourly as more and more trash littered the water. Brady and Simmons wore themselves out running from pump to pump. As fast as they got one clean it would clog again. They didn't turn them off before cleaning them—the switches were a long way from the pumps, and in the tangle of wires that now ran through the engine room, finding the right switch for each pump was a major chore.

Pearly and Woody, meanwhile, were struggling futilely with the rudder. It was jammed hard over to port and resisted all efforts to move it. The rudder weighed many tons and ordinarily would have been turned by an electric motor. Apparently it had been jammed tight when the bottom hit the night before, and the two men, trying to pull it around with a chainfall, were unable to budge it. They decided that a couple of hydraulic jacks were called for; until they got them, nothing more could be done.

The other problem Jaeger had posed was solved without difficulty. Woody put on a mask, grabbed a steel cable, and plunged overboard; when he emerged a few minutes later the propeller had been lashed down firmly.

All this time, the men had been living with the constant roar of engines in their ears. The generator had been running for three days, and would have to be kept running until they reached drydock. If it stopped, the pumps would stop, and Deir estimated that without pumps the water in the engine room would rise so fast that the tanker would sink again in not much more than a couple of hours. This nonstop operation put a tremendous strain on the generator and its engine. Since Monday Kin Reed with each trip had brought new drums of fuel oil aboard for the diesel; it was gulping the stuff down at the rate of four drums a day.

On his Wednesday trip Kin's cargo also included a reporter from the Norfolk *Virginian-Pilot*, Gene Roberts, Jr., and a photographer, Neil Clark. The *Queen* had become big news again, not only in the tidewater region, but all over the country. The salvagers' race against the hurricane had captured national attention. Every hour or so someone would holler from the kitchen, where the tanker's radio receiver was, and the men would gather around to listen to the latest broadcast about their plight. They were fascinated and delighted. Airplanes had started to fly around overhead, and more and more boats were coming out from Ocean City. Roberts and Clark were welcomed aboard, and all the men submitted eagerly to interviews and picture-taking.

Deir paid scant attention to all this. He took time off just once: Kin invited him to hop into the boat for a sight-seeing trip around the tanker and Deir accepted with alacrity. He hadn't been off the ship for a week, and he had never really seen all of it afloat.

The sight flabbergasted him. "Man, she's a thousand feet high," he exclaimed. "Like an ocean liner. Dag*gone*, isn't she big!"

The starboard rim of the boat deck, once swept by seas, now towered high over them. The ship's side was black with oil and encrusted with mussels and other marine life, and its paint was peeling in great splotches. By design, the tanker was still riding stern-high to keep the patch clear of the water; the steel sheet hung on the hull, striped with girders, brown with rust, yet neat and trim looking.

All in all, the *Queen* was a mighty strange-looking vessel, with her torn bow, her blackened starboard plates and that big brown patch toward the stern, but she was a ship now, no doubt about that. For months Deir had been accustomed to seeing her from a distance as a couple of tall, canted white islands with the sea washing up between them. Now she was a ship again, floating at anchor, ready to move.

He took a deep breath. "Okay, Kin. Guess we better get back now."

That afternoon they got a surprise. The tugboat *Mary L. McAllister* arrived from Norfolk, chugging up to the starboard side while the *Queen's* crew lined the rail. The tug captain called out greetings. "Come to take you in," he shouted. Then he cast a doubtful look at the tanker. "You're sure drawing a lot of water. Don't think I can take you in tow like that."

"Well, hell, we didn't *expect* you till tomorrow," said Deir in some exasperation. "Maybe if we had, we'd have got her up some more. We still got quite a bit of work to do on her, straighten her rudder, pump her out . . . how come you're a day early?"

"Well, I guess they're getting worried about that hurricane coming up and catching you out here. But I can't take you like that."

For the rest of the afternoon the tug stayed in the vicinity, while the salvagers redoubled their efforts to get the water out of the tanker. Soon after the tug's arrival the Coast Guard cutter *Marion* came up, big, black hulled, powerful looking. The shoal was getting downright crowded. The *Marion's* skipper called across, "We've come out to give you an escort into Hampton Roads. We'll stick right with you until you get her there. Meantime, we're here to help you any way we can. Anything we can do for you, be sure to let us know."

The tanker's freeboard was now about sixteen feet and rising steadily, but it was apparent that it would have to go up quite a bit farther. The men were still waiting for the jacks to straighten the rudder, but there was plenty of other work to keep everyone busy. All during the afternoon and evening they kept looking out at the tug and the cutter, circling around slowly at a distance of about half a mile, first the cutter on the starboard side and the tug to port, and then the other way around. The *Queen's* crew had become accustomed to isolation and it seemed strange to have those two vessels on hand, but just the same it was comforting to have friends about—particularly with that hurricane coming.

They were now paying close attention to the radio news-casts—and not only to hear their names mentioned. Gracie had moved up the Florida coast and was beginning to pound the Carolina shore. It was a major hurricane, doing a great deal of damage farther south. If it ever struck them it would mean certain disaster. They were fairly high out of the water now, a broad target, and getting higher all the time. Their precarious balance was becoming more uncertain by the hour as all that water ballast was pumped away. If a stiff wind ever caught the *Queen* in this helpless state it would wreck her—flip her over or blow her ashore or out to sea, or simply batter her into scrap.

Despite Deir's fierce resolve never to leave the ship again until she was safely in port, all the others knew it would be foolhardy to stay aboard in a hurricane. Little wasn't saying much, but he had never regretted leaving during the previous hurricane threat. He knew what those winds could do. Deir, who had blamed him for leaving, could talk about staying, and no one who knew Deir could doubt that he meant it; he wouldn't have the slightest hesitation about pitting his courage against a hurricane. But the rest of them knew it made no sense. And yet, so great was their allegiance to Deir by this time, and so deep their desire to get the tanker safely to port, not a man for a moment considered leaving so long as he stayed.

That night no one went to bed, though some of the men dozed in corners. Deir stayed awake. He felt fine—not a bit tired. He wasn't thinking as clearly as he had been, maybe, but he was all right. They were a good crew, no denying that, but when you came right down to it there was no one a man could depend on absolutely but himself. This way if anything went wrong he'd be to blame, and no argument about it later. But nothing would go wrong—that was exactly why he was staying awake. No mistakes.

Again that night he kept on the move, checking the pumps and compressors on the tank deck, keeping the pumps at work in the engine room, walking around the decks and through the passageways, feeling a curious pride in the ship, living again after all these months. He could see the lights of the cutter and the tug a few hundred yards away. Soon, in just a few hours, the *African Queen* would be in port and they'd all be getting off her, and damned if he wasn't feeling a little sorry.

Just before daybreak he routed out the dozers. The men were finding it harder and harder to wake up; no one had had more than three or four hours of sleep a night, and it was tough to come awake and face what they had to face. Not only was the work becoming terribly laborious and unpleasant, but living conditions were deteriorating. In particular, everyone's clothes were wet. They had been living in dampness for months, but this was something different. It was almost impossible to keep hose fittings from leaking. And since about half the hoses ran through the passageway outside the cabins, that corridor was beginning to look like a small river. The water was starting to wash into the cabins themselves, and a man might go to bed at night with his pants and shirt folded carefully on a box and wake up in the morning to find them afloat.

"Let's go," shouted Deir. "Gotta get her up today. We gotta get *out* of here!"

"Lloyd," said Brady as he came into the kitchen, "why don't you pump all the water out of the tank deck? Those storage tanks still have some water in them. Damn, it doesn't seem right to leave them that way when we're trying so hard to get her up higher."

"Makes no sense," said Deir. "First of all, there isn't all that much water in the tanks anyhow. Second, if we pumped out what *is* there we'd just get the bow too high and force the stern down again. The best way is to get her all up at once. As a matter of fact, the bow is *too* high right now. I think it's about time we thought about emptying that wash water out of the afterpeak tank. Probably half or three quarters of a million gallons back in there."

The wash-water tank, as the name indicated, was where the fresh water had been stored for deck-swabbing, dish-washing and the like (a second fresh-water tank for drinking was under the pilothouse). The hatch to the wash-water tank was located on a deck that could be approached only through the engine room and had, therefore, been unreachable all these months. But now that the engine room was getting dry the tank could be drained. Brady took charge of this project. First Duncan and Crisp wrestled the cover off, then Brady lowered a pump fitted with a hose and started it going. He could see the water level start to decline.

About an hour later Deir took a tour around the decks. For a few minutes he stopped on the port boat deck to chat with Simmons, who was straightening some hose there. Then he strolled back to the tank deck, and, as it came in sight, he stopped and stared. The starboard corner, up forward, was under water. She was sinking!

Heart pounding, he raced along the deck, hurtled down the ladder to the tank deck, and frantically began turning on pumps. He realigned the compressors so that both were forcing air into the starboard tanks. As he worked he saw the *Mary L. McAllister* suddenly turn and come racing toward the tanker, apparently with the thought of rescuing the crew from what was obviously a foundering vessel.

The pumps and compressors worked like magic. By the time the tug arrived, the tank deck was level again. Deir glanced over the side and chuckled grimly at the thought of how surprised the tug skipper must be to see the forward corner high out of water once more. Well, he had to admit it had scared him, too—and needlessly, now that he had a moment to think about it.

What had happened, of course, was that he had been fooled by the same thing that had fooled Brady earlier. He shook his head ruefully. He sure should have known better. All that water coming up out of the wash tank, away back in the afterpeak, had so lightened the stern that it had risen several feet—dipping the forward end of the ship into the sea.

When he had the ship leveled to his satisfaction, Deir walked back to where Brady was working. "Man," he said, grinning, "I don't know what you're trying to do to me. You had me scared half to death." And he told Brady what had occurred.

Brady laughed. "I got to admit, that makes me feel better," he said.

Jaeger came and left that morning, looking gloomy. "You're going to *have* to get her up some more," he said emphatically. "I don't like to do this to you, but it makes no sense to get under tow before you're ready. Can't you empty her out faster? How about that wash-water tank?"

"We're pumping that out right now," said Brady.

They walked back to look, and Jaeger acted surprised. "Only one pump in there? You'll be a week with just that pump!"

By now every member of the crew knew better than to criticize those pumps to Brady. He reacted sharply. "That one pump is gonna get that tank dry today, Mr. Jaeger," he said flatly. "Not a thing wrong with those pumps. One will do it."

"I'm afraid you'll be all the way to Norfolk before you do it with just one pump," Jaeger said without rancor. "But maybe you're right.

"Now, how about the tank deck?" he asked Deir as they walked back that way. "There must be plenty of water left in the oil tanks. Can't you get rid of some of that?" They climbed down the ladder to the tank deck. "These center tanks must be loaded with water. Open them up and let's have a look."

"Can't open them, Mr. Jaeger."

"Why not?"

"They're under air."

Jaeger looked puzzled. "What do you mean, 'under air'?"

"There's air pressure in them."

"*Air pressure?*" He looked at the compressors and then, as he suddenly realized what they were for, down at the deck. "*You mean this thing's floating on a bubble?*"

"Well, any way you want to put it," said Deir. "I guess she has a few bubbles in her all right."

"How many pounds of pressure do you have in there?"

"About ten."

"Ten pounds? Good Lord, those things"—he gestured at the tanks—"they're only tested for *five.*"

Deir nodded. "There's plenty of margin," he said. "I've checked those tanks. They're good and strong. I figure they'll take up to twenty pounds before there's any danger. Not," he added with a grin as he saw Jaeger's eyebrows shoot up, "that I plan to use that much. But ten's perfectly safe. Don't worry about it."

"*Worry!* Good Lord, the whole top could blow off this thing!"

They moved off the tank deck, Deir calm, Jaeger uneasy. Neither one of them had any way of knowing that Deir's figures tallied precisely with those worked out by Merritt-Chapman & Scott engineers months before. It wouldn't have made any difference to Deir anyhow. He *knew* it was safe.

"Well," said Jaeger, "even with those tanks all pumped full of air, she's not up the way she should be. I hate to be the one to keep hammering on this, but you've *got* to get her up some more. Her draft should be no more than about twenty-five feet. It's at least two feet more than that now. Do you think you can do it? The radio says that hurricane is coming right along."

"We'll do it," said Deir.

As soon as Jaeger was gone, Deir quietly added another pound of pressure to the center tanks. The fact was that no more water could be pumped out of the tanker except in the engine room. The tanks were practically dry now: there was just enough left in the port wing tanks to balance the amount that remained in that starboard tank with the hole in it. If they were to raise the tank deck any higher it would have to be done with air. Deir didn't particularly like to add more pressure just after Jaeger had expressed doubt about the amount he already had in there, but he didn't particularly mind, either. *He* was the one who had to get the ship up, not Jaeger. And he was positive there was no danger. He wished he could say the same about the hurricane.

At that moment, Brady came down off the aft deck, looking haggard. "Lloyd, we're in trouble. I just don't know what we're gonna do."

"What's wrong?"

"Wrong? Didn't Jaeger talk to you? He says we've gotta get her up a couple more feet. I just don't see how we're gonna do it. Those pumps are a damn mess. *Nothing* seems to work!" His face was drawn, his eyes tired. "We clean 'em out

and put 'em back in the water and they're as bad as ever.
Lloyd, I tell you, you gotta lend me a hand here."

"Well, let's take a look. Don't worry about it."

"Worry?" Brady looked disgusted. "Damn it, let's take a
bomb and *blow* it out!"

They walked back to the engine room and down the slimy
ladders to the turbine deck. Deir felt the hoses. They were
soft. He went around checking the pumps.

"Turn this one off."

Simmons, working in the engine room with Brady, traced
the wire back through the maze until he found the switch.
The pump stopped, for the first time in hours. Deir knelt
down and unscrewed the cap at the end of the pump. Then
he held up the pump for Brady to see. It was solid with
sludge. Deir cleaned it and said, "Okay, start her up again."
The pump whirred and the hose jumped as a full load of
water coursed through it.

"Damn!" said Brady. "We should have been turning them
off!"

They checked the other pumps the same way. Each was
black with debris picked up from the trash-laden water. One
after another they got each of the pumps back into operation,
and soon water was running out of the engine room in a
steady stream.

After that, Brady and Simmons worked as a team on each
pump. They marked the location of every switch and the
pump it belonged to, and soon they knew them by heart.
While Simmons pulled out a pump, Brady would hurry to
the proper switch and turn it off. As soon as the pump returned to the water he would trot along to the next one. The
pumps needed constant attention; the moment the two men
completed one circuit of the pumps they had to start all over
again. They worked in silence, racing from one pump to another. But they were happy now. The pumps were working
as they hadn't worked in days.

There was just one trouble. It was still hard for the pumps
to push the water clear to the top of the engine room before
discharging it overboard. Then Brady had a thought. The
afterpeak tank, to his intense satisfaction, was now almost

dry (and just one pump had done it). Why not pump the water from the turbine deck to the afterpeak tank, about two thirds of the way to the top of the engine room, and then use another pump to raise it the remaining third? Each pump would then have much less work to do. They tried it and it worked fine—for a while. But then, as time passed and the water level got still lower, the pumps down below began to labor again.

Little came in to watch. "I tell you," he said with conviction, "there's only one thing to do. We gotta burn that hole in the hull. Right now that water has to rise twenty-five feet to reach the wash-water tank. We can put a hole in that's only ten or fifteen feet above the water level in the engine room and pump right out through the side of the ship."

"Well, I've got to admit I can't think of anything else," Brady said. "For goodness' sake, Little, be careful."

Little went after a torch and soon had cut a hole through the tanker's side. He could look right through to the sea. A couple of days before, he reflected, such a hole would have let in half the Atlantic Ocean.

That solved the problem for good. Once more the water in the engine room began to diminish perceptibly, and the ship started to rise again.

How soon could they get started now? The tension had been growing for hours. The radio was still reporting the progress of the hurricane. Sometimes it seemed to be moving toward them faster than expected, then someone would do a new calculation showing that at its present rate it wouldn't arrive until they were safely in port—if they ever got started! The tug captain was keeping close watch now. They were no more anxious to get underway than he was. He had brought a couple of walkie-talkie radios up from Virginia with him and had passed one of them up to the men on the *Queen*. They arranged for hourly communications, and the task of keeping in touch with the *Mary L. McAllister* was given to Pearly Strait. They were getting close to the critical draft now. The men on both ships agreed to that. More to the point, Jaeger, who was now aboard the tug, thought so.

There was just one thing left to do. The rudder was still

hard over, and Kin Reed had been unable to find the hydraulic jacks they needed to move it. Sadler had come aboard with Jaeger. When Jaeger left again, Sadler left with him, a purposeful gleam in his eye. Around noon he was back with two great twelve-ton hydraulic jacks, normally used for hoisting heavy earth-moving equipment. Pearly Strait and Woody Crisp joined Little, got the jacks into position and, after forty-five minutes of the most back-breaking labor, got the rudder straightened out.

They were ready.

At three o'clock Captain Raymond Rindge of the *Mary L. McAllister* had his hourly chat with Pearly. "I guess we'll take you now," he said.

Somebody whooped. There was great excitement, and men clustered on the fantail as the tug chuffed up close to the *Queen*. When the *Mary L. McAllister* was within thirty feet of the tanker the captain threw out a light heaving line to the *Queen*'s crew. They caught it and began pulling it aboard. It was bent to a three-inch manila rope, which in turn was attached to a wire cable. The actual towline was yet to come. At last they saw it slip over the tug's rail—a big eight-inch nylon hawser. Little, Crisp and Simmons were hauling away; it was tremendously heavy. Suddenly it stopped coming. One of the men ran to the rail and peered over.

"Hey, the shackle's caught on the edge of the deck."

"Well, loosen the damn thing."

"Can't reach it. We'll have to *pull* it up."

At that moment Henley Doughtie walked out on deck.

Henley at this point was far from being his usual ebullient self. Since the ship had come off the bottom he had slept scarcely more than Deir. Regular meals had ended—nobody had time to come to them. Instead the men wandered into the kitchen at all hours, exhausted. As long as there were men awake Henley tried to stay awake, ready to cook for them. He spent hours on his feet, preparing food and washing dishes. His ankles had swelled to twice their normal size, and his cursing had taken on a new edge as the demands on him increased. Much of his vituperation was directed at the two newspapermen, a couple of pleasant and innocent fellows who merely made handy new targets. "Goddam sonsof-bitches," bellowed Henley. "They drinking enough coffee to *float* this goddam ship!" But they got their food—and coffee—along with everyone else.

As Henley emerged now Crisp yelled to him. "Hey, Henley, come help with this thing!" Henley started over. "Step it up, man; we're about to bust!"

Henley perked up. He sized up the situation and his eyes gleamed. He began to rumble. "Here now, stand aside. Let Miz Doughtie's boy have a hand at that bastard." He took hold of the hawser, all signs of weariness gone now, and looked about him. "Now just how hard am I supposed to draw up on this motherlovin' rope?" He leered. "We don't want it *busted*. You got a *man* here now."

They pulled. Suddenly there was a lurch and the shackle flew up over the edge of the deck. Henley beamed. He dropped the hawser and wiped his hands on his white apron. "You need any more help," he said grandly, "you call on Miz Doughtie's boy. There are some wobble-kneed bastards around here"—his eyes swept them triumphantly—"who couldn't pull up their pants."

They made the hawser fast and began to struggle with the tanker's anchor line. It was hopeless. They couldn't drag the anchor and they couldn't pull the huge tanker anywhere near it. The *Mary L. McAllister* tried to pull the *Queen* up to the anchor so they could haul it in, but the tanker seemed to shy away from the anchor like a horse from a paper bag. And then when the tug managed to draw the crippled ship up to the anchor she rode right *over* it.

At last Deir strode up carrying a blowtorch. "Look out," he said, and in a few seconds cut away the expensive anchor line and five hundred dollars' worth of anchor.

The tug began to rumble. The water under her fantail began to churn. The hawser snapped taut. They were underway.

The men began to shout. "Exactly three-twenty!" somebody yelled. "Norfolk, here we come!"

22

WHEN DARKNESS FELL, more than four hours after they were taken in tow, Ocean City was still in sight, their progress was barely noticeable, Captain Rindge's voice over the communication system was growing more and more strained, and the elation of the afternoon had vanished completely.

The *African Queen* was proving to be an unruly tow. A gentle breeze coming up from the south, together with a tidal current from the same direction, had held her speed to not much more than one knot; after four hours they had traveled only about five miles. Moreover, she was responding to the towline no better than she had to her anchor line. Instead of following directly behind the *Mary L. McAllister* at the end of the thousand-foot hawser, the tanker was two hundred feet off to one side, blown there by the wind.

There was nothing anyone could do about this except fret, but they did plenty of that—and with good cause. It was apparent that if things didn't improve, their estimate of one day to reach Hampton Roads-Norfolk probably would have to be revised. This would add to the expense of the tow and hold them in the path of the hurricane. Worst of all, it raised the distinct possibility that the generator engine would run out of fuel. If the generator stopped, and the pumps with it, they would quickly sink. And if they sank now, there would be no convenient shelf of sand to catch them. They would sink in deep water, forever. In fact, the tug's skipper had notified the salvagers that he was taking them out to sea twenty miles, on Coast Guard orders, to make perfectly sure that if the *Queen* did sink it *would* be in deep water, out of the path of shipping.

As for the hurricane, Captain Rindge had made provision for that, too. Near the stern of the tug the *Queen*'s men had seen a hatchet, ready to be used on the hawser the instant real trouble developed. Rindge would certainly offer to take them off before using it, but at this point that seemed academic. They didn't want to be taken off. They were obsessed with the idea of getting the tanker in. It would be unbearable to lose her now—unthinkable, impossible.

"If the good Lord will just bring that wind around to the northeast, where it will blow against the broad side of that pilothouse," prayed Beldon Little, "it sure would be a help."

Little was now as oil-stained and tired-looking as if he had never been off the tanker. All of them were unkempt and unshaven, their eyes red-rimmed, their hair tousled, their clothing wrinkled, wet and dirty. They looked like a bunch of skid-row wrecks. They were beginning to walk that way, too—lurching, staggering and stumbling from lack of sleep. When they could, they limited their conversation to grunts and other monosyllables; it was too much trouble to sustain a speech longer than that. A man would start to say something requiring several words and then forget in midsentence what he was talking about.

Captain Rindge had told them that since they were now proceeding stern-first, the tanker's stern was really its bow, and vice versa. This was not too complicated, but when he added that as a consequence port was now starboard, the men gave up. It was just too much to ask of people in their condition. Unable to continue calling starboard starboard, lest it lead to confusion in communications with the tug, they began to refer to "shore side" and "sea side." It was unseamanlike, and Little flinched whenever he heard it, but it was something everyone could understand.

Despite their exhaustion, they got their work done, driving themselves with a determination that was past all reason. The pump-cleaning in the engine room was now on a twenty-four-hour basis. Deir still had to keep playing the pumps and compressors on the tank deck to hold the tanker in balance. There were still leaks to be patched. Henley was still in the kitchen serving up food on demand. He was the only man doing much talking, and he was doing it in a steady, steaming torrent. As they moved slowly out to sea the ship began to rock and pitch. This motion delighted Deir ("Man,

255

she's acting like a real ship!") but it enraged Doughtie, who found it almost impossible now to keep the kerosene stove level. He kept slipping blocks under the stove, first on one side and then on the other, and his imprecations could be heard all over the ship. "I'll throw the bastard overboard," he bellowed.

The diving elevator with its long vertical boom was still alongside the tanker, raised up off the bottom and lashed to the hull. Shortly after they got underway Deir noticed that the platform, tied to the boom with a weak cable, was dragging in the water and threatening to tear loose. He hastily called to Woody Crisp, and they ran to the edge of the deck. Just as they got there the cable snapped and the platform dropped. It lodged against a V-brace that was holding the boom to the ship. Deir and Crisp lowered a cable, then had to climb out onto the platform to make it fast. It was shaking terribly, threatening to hurl them into the sea at any moment, but they finally got the cable on and were able to climb back to the deck. They raised the platform with a davit winch and got it safely out of harm's way.

Crisp did one other thing that afternoon which gave him great pleasure. Some days before, a brand-new forty-nine-star flag, officially authorized just that July, had come aboard in a package of groceries sent by Sadler. Now Crisp dug it out, bent it onto a halyard, and sent it fluttering to the top of the pilothouse radio mast. "Now," he said. "She's an *American* ship!"

All that day Deir kept checking the generator, now the most vital single piece of machinery on the tanker. It had been running for four days without a stop, a remarkable performance, but it had to continue running, probably for a couple of days longer. It just seemed too much to hope for—even if the fuel lasted. The odds were that sometime in the next forty-eight hours the generator would break down. Every time he passed the roaring engine Deir would check it. He also took great care to keep the engine's fuel from getting too low. If the engine began drawing fuel from the bottom of the tank it might suck up sediment or water.

That night the lights of Ocean City remained in sight. Deir

sent the crew to bed in shifts. He remained awake, and there were always a couple of others awake with him. Every hour he would arouse Pearly, the only one besides Brady who seemed able to work the walkie-talkie properly, and Pearly would hold a groggy conversation with the tug skipper. Captain Rindge had reported soon after taking the tanker in tow that his engines were overheating dangerously, but now that she was moving, however slowly, everything was all right.

"Ask him what we can do about fuel," Deir said to Pearly.

"I don't know," Rindge said. "We have some that'd run your generator, but I don't know how to get it to you. You'd have to come alongside, and that's impossible."

Deir was still awake when dawn broke. He looked off toward the shore. Ocean City was still there, although considerably more distant than it had been the afternoon before. They still had perhaps a hundred miles to go. How long would the fuel last? They now had only four drums left—roughly a day's supply under normal operation.

At seven o'clock the tug skipper called in. "We aren't making any progress at all," he said. "We're doing about one and a half knots. We're sure to be another day at least."

Their plight was now the number-one news story of the day along the entire Middle Atlantic coast. The local radio stations were giving out special bulletins; if their excited reaction to the event was any indication, the *Queen* must be making black headlines all over the country. The news media were getting their information from the *Mary L. McAllister,* which was keeping them advised of the tanker's progress by radio.

The broadcasters were making much of the tanker's race against the hurricane. Gracie was still coming, and although she was being blessedly slow about it, the *African Queen* was being even slower. Food and water, as well as fuel, were beginning to run low on the tanker. If the hurricane hit and the tug cast them loose, it just didn't seem possible that they could stay aboard. Their lifejackets were certainly not adequate safety equipment in a situation like that, and there were no lifeboats and only one raft. There wasn't even an

257

anchor now. Yet no one for an instant considered leaving the ship, hurricane or no hurricane.

All that day, Friday, September 25, the unvarying routine continued until the men were able to do it in their sleep (which was getting to be precisely the ability the circumstances required). Pumps were cleaned, leaks plugged, hoses checked, over and over and over. Once an hour Pearly would pick up the walkie-talkie and check in with the tug.

By late that day they were out of drinking water. There was one container of slightly murky water that they figured could safely be boiled for coffee. Otherwise there was nothing left on the tanker to drink. That included liquor, of course. Henley had been dry for a couple of days now.

Worse than the lack of drink was the shortage of fuel. By cutting out some pumps and using the compressors very sparingly (they, too, burned diesel oil) Deir had cut fuel consumption; nevertheless, by Friday night they were scraping the bottom of the second of their four barrels.

"For God's sake," Deir told Pearly, "tell Rindge something has to be done about this fuel situation. If this generator knocks off, tell him, this boat's going under. We've gotta do something. There's no sense him dragging us halfway down the coast and then letting us sink. Tell him."

Pearly told him.

"Look," said Captain Rindge. "That cutter has all kinds of power on it. They could probably come alongside and put a line aboard you and feed you all the power you need to keep things running. It'd be tricky, sure, but there's no reason why it wouldn't work."

Deir wasn't at all sure that it would work; it might, for one thing, be the wrong kind of power. But it might be worth a try. Rindge said he had already been in touch with the *Marion,* which was patrolling about a half mile out to sea, and the cutter's captain had said that the tanker would be welcome to any assistance he could give it—power, fuel, anything.

Deir pondered. Should they try it or should they try to make their own fuel last out the trip? And if they did try it, should they do it now or wait until they really needed it?

The trouble with waiting was that the hurricane might catch them first, and then it would be too late. Yet Deir didn't want to try a difficult transfer of power between ships unless it was absolutely essential. At best it would be only a stopgap—and it could be risky.

"Let us think about it," Deir said, and Pearly passed the message on.

An hour later Rindge was back on the air, and his voice had a new sound. "I think we're getting a little luck here," he said. "First, we've just heard that the hurricane's slowing down. With any kind of break we should beat it in. And the other thing is, the weather bureau's expecting a wind shift any time now, around to the northeast. If we get a fair northeast wind behind us, we'll start moving right along."

That changed everything. "Tell him we'll try to make it without calling on the cutter," Deir said. "I think maybe we can do it now."

For one thing, the pumps had just about emptied the engine room. The *Queen* was riding plenty high now. All they needed was enough pumping to neutralize the remaining leaks. There were sixteen pumps running in the engine room. Deir cut all but six. The roar of the generator engine dropped to a throaty rumble.

As night fell they could feel the motion of the tanker change. The wind had swung around behind them. In his hourly report, the tug skipper said in a pleased voice that they were now making three knots, a respectable speed. Another thirty hours or so should see them in—if the wind held.

Not long afterward Deir, flashing a light on the seawater tank built on the port deck by Brady and Simmons while he was in the hospital, saw scum floating on the surface. He raced to the generator engine and put his hand on it. Still cool. But it must be taking dirt into its cooling system from that tank. The tank was being filled from water in the engine room, and now there just wasn't any clean water left there—just a sludge of asbestos, paint flakes and soaked cardboard. Working quickly, Deir got another pump—there were plenty to spare now—fixed it up with a hose, hooked it into the network of wires running from the generator and then dropped it overboard. He flicked the switch, and a slow stream of water began coming up from the ocean directly into the engine's cooling coils. As Brady and Simmons had suspected when they built the tank, the pump had trouble getting the water up that high, but what it drew was adequate. Deir watched the salt water running back out of the engine again, splashing on the deck and then flowing into the sea. He smiled wryly. It seemed silly to be pumping sea water *into* the tanker, even if it was running right off again. In any case, from now on that pump would have to be watched like a ticking bomb. If the pump cut out, the generator engine would overheat and conk out almost faster than you could say it.

It was around midnight. Deir couldn't remember when he had last slept. He felt pretty well, all things considered, but he was worried about the tendency his mind had to wander. Everybody else was worried about him, too; since late afternoon they had pestered him incessantly to get some sleep. His face was haggard, and his movements lacked their characteristic crispness.

He walked down the engine-room ladders to the turbine deck, where Woody and Pearly were working on the pumps. He talked to them for a minute, then stopped, puzzled.

"Where are we?" he asked them.

They looked at him sharply. "In the engine room of the *African Queen*, off the Maryland coast," said Strait, "*and you're going to bed!*"

Deir shook his head. "I'm all right. I just couldn't remember where I was for a second."

"Nossir," said Woody. "You're gonna go get some sleep if we have to carry you. We'll put you to bed and hold you there."

They closed in on him, obviously prepared to do it. Deir, appalled at the thought of being manhandled, or indeed at being forced to do anything, spoke up hastily. "Now, wait up, wait a minute," he said. "Let's talk about this. Don't do anything until we've discussed it." They looked at him.

"Now, look. Everybody else is asleep. You two fellows have the engine room to take care of. That leaves nobody to watch out for the list and correct it on the tank deck. God *knows*, we can't just leave that untended, and daggone if I want to wake anybody up. They just got to bed. Now see? I've *got* to stay up and keep going, no two ways about it."

"You don't have to do it. *We'll* do it. The engine room isn't full-time work with only a few pumps running. We'll watch out for the tank deck. But you're going to bed."

At last Deir allowed himself to be persuaded. He checked them out on the tank deck operation and finally went to his cabin and fell numbly into his bunk. He went to sleep to the sound of water sloshing on the floor.

He awakened an hour and a half later conscious that something was wrong. He lay there a few seconds, trying to clear his head, trying to figure out what was bothering him. It was still dark, but he could make out the dim outlines of the cabin. He got up on one elbow and stared around him. Everything seemed the same. He looked at the floor. The water was there, gathered in a puddle on the seaward side of the cabin. Suddenly Deir hurtled out of bed. Of course! They were listing—that's what was wrong!

His shoes were floating in the puddle. He put them on hastily and sped out. He hurried down the passageway, running in the old "one-foot-short-one-foot-long" fashion; she was tipped almost the way she had been while resting on the shoal, her original starboard side down. Damn! As he charged out onto the tank deck he hollered to Strait and Crisp for help.

There had been three pumps working steadily in that holed starboard tank. Now all three hoses were flat. The tank was rapidly filling with water, and Deir had figured out earlier that if the damaged tank ever filled up all the way with those port tanks practically empty, the added weight on one side would probably turn the ship completely over. Frantically he checked the pumps. On one the hose was merely kinked. He straightened it, and water began flowing through it once again. The other two posed more of a problem. The hose had somehow broken off one of them inside the tank; they would have to pull out the pump and attach a new hose taken from a pump that wasn't working. The third pump had simply quit; it would have to be replaced.

As he labored with Strait and Crisp, the perspiration rolling off him, Deir thought how astonishing it was that so much had happened so quickly, and that it had all waited until he went to sleep. In all the time he had been working on the tank deck there hadn't been three such near disasters as this, and here they all were at once. Pearly and Woody, thoroughly abashed, said it had all happened so quickly that they hadn't even been aware of it until Deir had started to shout.

Desperately they set about making repairs. The ship continued to go over toward her low side, and the single pump that was back in operation didn't appear to be making much headway. But at last they got another pump into action; the two together just about matched the leakage from the hole in the tank. When they finally got the third pump working the ship slowly began to right herself. By then it was almost dawn, and they got an anxious call from the tug captain, who had just noticed the list.

"Tell him we got it under control. Tell him don't worry about it," said Deir.

By the time the rest of the men were up and about, the slant of the decks was barely noticeable.

They were now in the shipping lane and were encountering substantial traffic. Some of it was regular shipping, but a huge proportion of it consisted of sight-seers who had come out to see the salvaged tanker. There were boats and ships of all kinds; even the big freighters and liners seemed to be steering as close as possible to the *Queen*. As they passed they saluted the tanker hoarsely. Captain Rindge was now doing a good deal of hooting of his own: small craft were coming so near he was afraid of running them down. During the morning the Coast Guard cutter moved in close to help clear a path for the *Queen;* after a while the *Marion* began to circle the tug and her tow, trying to keep sight-seers from coming too near. From time to time the cutter had to pull up alongside an intruding vessel and warn her away.

The Coast Guard ship was also keeping a sharp eye on the tanker. At one point Little clambered down the big boom to the diving platform to plug some rags into a leak; the cutter promptly swung around to the vessel's seaward side and stood off about two hundred feet until he had finished.

The radio now seemed to be broadcasting nothing but news of the *African Queen*. Anybody whose work took him past the kitchen would make it a point to stop a while, knowing he could count on hearing some kind of special newscast if he lingered for only a minute or two. It was apparent that people ashore were really stirred up about this whole business. Soon more newsmen began coming aboard, after making the trip out to the tanker in small boats. They were welcomed, but the crew members didn't have much time to talk to them. One photographer climbed up adorned with cameras: one in his hand and a couple more dangling from his neck. The crewmen were greatly amused, particularly after Brady saw the man hanging over the side to take a picture of the elevator, with one of the cameras around his neck hanging down in front of his lens. "I swear," said Brady, chuckling, "I never thought I'd see a photographer using one camera to get a picture of another camera."

That afternoon they started on their last drum of fuel, and Deir cut off two more pumps. That left four of them working in the engine room. But now he had something new to worry about. Jaeger, riding in the *Mary L. McAllister*, sent back word that as soon as they got through Hampton Roads and into Norfolk harbor they would have to stop pumping out the tanks. He was sure the Coast Guard and the Corps of Engineers would never permit them to dump oil-polluted water into the harbor. This posed a critical problem. That damaged starboard tank had to be pumped constantly; they dared not stop even for a few minutes. Deir didn't argue with Jaeger but he made a mental reservation: he was not going to stop those pumps. Maybe instead of pumping the water over the side, where it could be seen, he would pump it into those smashed tanks under the pilothouse, sending the water in through the deck hatches and letting it run into the sea through the broken forward ends of the tanks. Ridiculous, sure, but he couldn't help that. Somehow he had to keep those pumps running. Jaeger just didn't understand: if those pumps stopped the ship sank.

There was also one other difficulty. The black, tarlike oil in the vessel's bunker tanks, the ship's own fuel which had been in there all these months, was now starting to ooze out of small cracks in the tanker's hull. The cracks had been there all along, but the underwater pressure had kept the bunker oil inside. Now it was pushing its way out. Sometime before they got to Norfolk, Deir thought wearily, he would have to go down and take care of those cracks.

And then, all at once, it was almost over.

They were passing Cape Henry, on the south shore of Chesapeake Bay, only about thirty miles from Norfolk, and they were in the midst of bedlam. Hundreds of boats and dozens of ships were milling about in a mad crush. There were cabin cruisers and fishing boats, outboard motorboats and sailboats, rowboats and great freighters, and from all of them came a pandemonium of tooting, honking, beeping, shouting and whistling. They passed some sort of military installation on the shore and, to their utter astonishment, were accorded a three-gun salute. An aircraft carrier sailed up and circled all the way around them. People were standing up in their tiny boats and shouting; others were frantically waving handkerchiefs. On the shore more people could be seen waving. Autos honked their horns. For the first time the men on the *Queen* had some real inkling of what lay behind those newscasts. People had gone wild over their exploit. The salvagers were flabbergasted.

At this point the cutter *Marion* left, with a farewell blast of her horn, and the cutter *Cherokee* sped out from the harbor to take her place. A boat put off from the new cutter and threaded its way through the traffic jam. Soon a boarding party was on its way up the ladder, led by a man in civilian clothes. He was, he informed them, the Coast Guard inspector. Deir looked about him desperately. This was the moment he had been dreading. The water was still pouring overboard from that starboard tank; the bunker oil, black and heavy, was still hanging in great gobs from the outside of the hull. Nothing had been done to get ready for this inspection. They had reached Cape Henry so much sooner than he had anticipated. What now? Would they be made to stop here and catch up with their work? Was it possible that the whole enterprise would fail at the instant of success? His face glum, Deir shook hands with the inspector.

"I'd like to congratulate you," the inspector said briskly. "Now." He looked around the decks in a businesslike way. "What can we do to help you?"

"What?"

"We're here to do whatever we can to get you in safely. If there's anything you need, tell me now; we'll do everything in our power to get it for you. Fuel? Water? Food? Now that you've come this far we mustn't let anything stop you."

Deir stared for a moment in disbelief; then a wave of relief washed over him. He shook hands with the inspector fervently. "Man," he said, "you're a Godsend."

The inspector grinned, a little surprised. "What is it you need?" he asked.

"It isn't so much what we need; I don't think we need anything much. But there are a couple of things bothering us. Is it true that we can't pump the water out of the oil storage tanks? We got one that needs pumping all the time."

"You go ahead and pump. If you should see any oil coming out of the tanks we'd appreciate it if you'd do something about it. But don't stop. She'll sink if you stop, won't she?"

"She sure will."

"Well, then! Don't stop for anything."

He made his way around the ship, looking about him with great interest. As he approached the side with the bunker leaks Deir hastened to prepare him. "I tell you," he said a little anxiously, "we have a couple of leaks in these bunker tanks that I meant to get right at, but I haven't had time. I'll fix 'em right away."

The inspector leaned over the side. Then he straightened up. "I know you'll take care of them as soon as you get a chance," he said, and moved on.

Standing on the tank deck, he looked up at the pilothouse mast, where the flag was flapping from one side of the crossbar. He chuckled. "By rights," he said, "being a ship out of control you ought to run a couple of buckets up the mast as a warning to shipping. That's the usual thing." The words were scarcely out of his mouth before Crisp, delighted with the idea, was engaged in a feverish hunt for buckets. He couldn't find any, but there were a couple of empty five-gallon GI gasoline cans around—olive drab and rectangular, shaped to nest on the running board of a military truck. He ran those up instead. "Gotta keep everything shipshape and according to regulation," he said.

As they pushed through the water, three other McAllister tugs joined the *Mary L.* The sea was still crowded with all sorts of small craft filled with shouting, waving people. Soon a couple of familiar faces appeared: a boat owned by Duke Morris and his partner Juan Crofton showed up with Duke and Alvah Sadler aboard. They pulled up to the tanker's side and unloaded fresh water and food.

On the hour, Captain Rindge spoke up over the hand radio. "We still have another six or eight hours to go," he said. "Tide's running against us now. But we have the thing licked—hurricane's still far to the south."

The minute he got a chance, Deir went over the side to repair the leaks in the bunker tanks. They were small cracks and could be plugged with shingles, but unfortunately they were right at the water level. The only way to get at them was to rig a bosun's chair and have Woody lower him over the side. This was steeplejack work, and right in Deir's line. But no steeplejack had ever worked under conditions like these. First he had to let himself down into the water clear up to his chest before he was low enough to reach the cracks. Then he found that, this far down, the side of the ship curved away from him; to get up close to it he had to paddle himself frantically through the water, fighting the forward motion of the tanker, until he was well under the overhang of the starboard deck. The instant he stopped paddling, he began to swing back again. He had just barely time to take one whack with his hammer before the cracks were out of reach again.

While he was sitting there in the water, swinging laboriously back and forth, and pounding his hammer once at the top of each swing, a head appeared over the rail above him. It was a stranger who yelled, "Hey, what's your name?"

Deir slammed in a shingle and went flying back in a shower of spray. He shook the water out of his eyes. "Deir."

"Well, hey, I'm from the *Saturday Evening Post*. Would you give me your story in your own words?"

"Sure. But not right now."

At last he finished the patching and climbed back on board. Now everything had been done that could be done, and there was nothing to do but wait. They were sitting just off Norfolk, barely moving, waiting for the tide to turn before floating into the drydock where Sadler had arranged to have the *Queen* inspected, cleaned and, if necessary, lightly repaired. Darkness fell, but still the crowds hung on ashore. People cheered and waved, and they flashed the lights and honked the horns of their automobiles.

Late in the evening Deir fell into his bunk; there was nothing to keep him from it now. But he was too wrought up to sleep easily, and for a long time he just lay there, trying to believe that it had actually happened, and trying to decide what it felt like. Finally he dozed.

They awakened him at 1:30 A.M. They were almost in now. He slowly got out of bed and made his way out on deck. The hoses were still gushing water, but things seemed to be taking care of themselves pretty well. The men were moving around, in their cabins and on deck, their faces blank. It was really over, an experience of six months that they would be talking about for the rest of their lives and that had given most of them the greatest sense of accomplishment they would ever know. They found it hard to believe that it had reached its end; if the truth were known some of them didn't want to believe it. They were for the most part men of little education and limited prospect, and they knew there would never be another achievement for them like this one. Henley stood beside Deir for a moment on deck, obviously in the grip of emotion. "You ever do yourself another salvage, you let me know, hear?" he said suddenly, then moved off.

Some of them had shaved. Those who had clean clothes left were putting them on. Others were standing on deck, looking incredulously at the crowds that were still visible ashore. Here it was long past midnight and these people were still standing out there to greet them. And Norfolk wasn't an after-midnight town, either.

The tanker kept edging in closer and closer to the pier, the tugs pushing and panting amid great shouting and blowing of whistles. The *Queen* was an unwieldy vessel to dock. That was why they had waited out the tide. If there had been any perceptible current at this moment the task would have been all but hopeless. They moved her nearer to the shore, trying to line her up with the dock. The distance kept getting smaller and smaller. The faces of people waiting on land became recognizable.

Then the men waiting on the shore with coils of rope in their hands let them fly. Members of the tanker's crew pulled in the hawsers and made them fast. A big gangplank was moved up to the ship's side. The *African Queen* had docked.

Men came trotting up the gangplank, wearing big grins. They stepped aboard the tanker and began to fan out purposefully. On the port deck the generator engine was still pounding away. It had been running six days and six nights without a halt. Pumps and compressors were still in operation. The dockyard men began to take over supervision of them as the *Queen*'s crew watched, a little uneasy and resentful at the spectacle of strangers moving so possessively about their ship.

"Okay," said one of the newcomers. "She's our worry now."

The men walked off the ship singly and in pairs, self-consciously. Flashbulbs were popping and people were cheering and policemen were trying to control the crowd. Even the families of crew members had trouble getting through the police lines.

As Henley came down the gangplank a friend greeted him with a shout and held up a pint bottle of whisky. Henley sighed deeply and gratefully. He took the bottle, put it to his mouth and downed a long, long draft.

Little hurried down the gangway, freshly shaved, and was immediately surrounded by his family. Hazel was weeping, and his little girls were excited and proud. "You did it, Daddy.

You got the ship, didn't you?" said five-year-old Beverly Kay. "Give me the money." Little threw back his head and laughed.

Deir came down off the ship alone, walking slowly. He was wearing some clean work clothes and his narrow-brimmed Madison Avenue straw hat. It was black with grime. He had a six-day growth of beard. Under the beard his face was stained with oil. He was gaunt and haggard, with the skin pulled tight across his nose and cheekbones. His pale blue eyes stared out tiredly between red rims, and there were deep crow's-feet around them. In the last week he had averaged roughly two hours of sleep a night, and there had been several nights when he had not slept at all.

He was immediately surrounded by a noisy, happy, jostling crowd. They let Doris push her way through; behind her, a little uncertainly, came his three children, whom he hadn't seen in three months.

He took his wife in his arms and grinned wearily. Her eyes were misty.

"Well," he said, "we got her in."

23

THEY WERE recognized wherever they went. Children stared at them on the sidewalk. Adults waved to them from cars, called to them from street corners, stopped to shake hands, asked for their autographs. When they spoke, people listened so attentively that it made them uneasy, and they found themselves halting in midsentence. Friends and neighbors phoned and dropped in and were curiously grateful when they returned the visits. Strangers approached them with questions, advice and loan requests.

By the afternoon of their first day back they had encountered enough of this odd behavior to unsettle them. "Boy, I've never been so popular or so pestered in my life," Brady said when the four partners met back on the ship. A TV crew found them there and prevailed on them to make statements before the cameras for a forthcoming program about the *African Queen* exploit.

That was just the beginning. As the days passed, they began to get phone calls from magazines, radio stations, book publishers, movie companies. Reporters and photographers dogged them; the local papers, plus a few that were not so local, carried glowing editorials of congratulation. *Time* magazine devoted almost a page to the story of the salvage and the hectic voyage down the coast to Norfolk; the shotguns were prominently mentioned and the story was illustrated with one of Neal Clark's pictures showing Deir, Sadler and Strait gathered around a tank hatch. The *Saturday Evening Post* writer interviewed Deir at length for his story, which the magazine planned to run under the salvager's byline. Gene Roberts began preparing an article for *True* magazine. Representatives of the company which had manufactured Deir's versatile drill called on him for a testimonial, and an oil firm ran a pleased article in the company magazine pointing out that one of its products had been used to preserve the *Queen's* machinery after docking.

A network television show invited Deir to New York for a broadcast. The salvagers were called upon to speak before Rotary and other civic groups in Suffolk and neighboring towns, and at church meetings as well. A retired Marine Corps officer flew down from Washington to see if he could interest them in directing their talents toward the raising of a sunken dry dock in the harbor of Rio de Janeiro.

Admiration, approbation, glorification rained down on them. They were heroes, authentic heroes, acclaimed by the distinguished, cheered by thousands, esteemed by millions across the nation. It was bewildering and it was delightful.

It all culminated, after several weeks of feverish preparation, in a city-wide celebration sponsored by seven organizations, ranging from the Norfolk Chamber of Commerce and the Virginia State Port Authority to one called Youth of Tidewater Virginia. The chairman of the celebration committee sent out letters to each of the salvagers inviting them to attend, observing that the affair was "for the purpose of recognizing your outstanding accomplishment as salvors of the *African Queen.*" The wives were invited, too. So were Kin and Mrs. Reed, up in Ocean City. There was to be a parade, a speech-making ceremony in a Norfolk theater and finally a grand luncheon. The mayor would be on hand, as would the district's representative in Congress. The guest speaker would be the president of the American Merchant Marine Institute, Ralph E. Casey. Rear Admiral Hyman Rickover was invited ("to honor these other pioneers," a Chamber of Commerce official explained), but had to send regrets.

The event itself, held on a bright Saturday morning in late October, was scarcely less imposing than the preparations. The salvagers were there, thirteen of them including Howard Hill, Tom Doughty and Duke Morris, all so dressed up and clean-shaven that they scarcely recognized one another. A local automobile dealer had provided a covey of convertibles for the parading crew members to ride in, with their names hung outside on large placards. The salvagers were escorted down Granby Street, busiest thoroughfare in town, by a phalanx of motorcycle police, followed by U.S. Army units, Boy Scouts, the Norfolk Fire Division Band, an American Legion drum and bugle corps, and musical groups from the high and junior high schools, complete with high-stepping majorettes. Crowds lined the streets and cheered, and a news photographer took a picture of Pearly Strait, Jr., sobbing because he couldn't ride in the car with Daddy.

In the theater, orators outdid themselves in praise of the salvagers ("Truly a great feat," proclaimed Representative Porter Hardy, Jr.), while the principals sat uneasily onstage in a long row behind the speakers. Luncheon was served at the Hotel Commodore Maury. There was a cake in the form of the bowless *African Queen*. The high point of the ceremony was the presentation by the mayor of a framed citation and a sterling silver tie clasp (a replica of Norfolk's historic silver mace) to each of the crewmen.

Sometime during the festivities Henley Doughtie collapsed and was carried from the field sick (though not seriously), and by the time it was over all the other salvagers were reeling with exhaustion and pleasure.

There was also more important but equally pleasurable business at hand. The time had come to cash in on the long months of work.

They had scarcely reached Norfolk before Sadler received a telephone call from New York. The speaker identified himself as a ship broker and said, "I have a client who's prepared to offer you two hundred thousand dollars for your tanker, where and how she stands, cash on the barrel head. You say the word, and the money will be on deposit within an hour."

They didn't accept the offer. For one thing, it was impossible to sell the ship for a while. Legally, they had yet to establish ownership. Sadler's lawyer, a bright and able young Suffolk attorney named J. Lewis Rawls, Jr., had filed the necessary papers, but it was going to take time. They had evidence that both African Enterprises, Ltd., and Lloyd's had abandoned the *African Queen*, but even that might not be enough: newspaper stories indicated that Gifford Warner, the Connecticut salvager who had disputed their claim to the tanker, was considering suing to obtain possession of her.

The salvagers had the *Queen* in port, but they weren't out of trouble yet.

The second reason for rejecting the offer was a more obvious one. It was, they felt, outrageously low.

They held a meeting at Sadler's house and talked it over. There had been a lot of newspaper discussion about the value of their prize, and informed estimates had ranged all the way from a top of about three million dollars to a low of a hundred thousand. The low figure had all the tangy odor of sour grapes; nevertheless, it was growing apparent that the two-million-dollar figure—which, by some strange process of suggestion, had been the magic payoff number for all of them ever since the enterprise started—might be somewhat high. People were saying that the tanker market was depressed.

"Well, then we'll try the scrap dealers," said Deir. "I *know* there's a million dollars' worth of stuff on that ship, easy. Good engines, good steel, all kinds of stuff. Anyhow, we sure aren't gonna sell for any two hundred thousand dollars. *That's* no offer! No point in working out there all this time and then taking that kind of money. It's foolish to grab the first offer, anyhow. We've nothing to lose by sitting tight."

"We ought to set a minimum," said Brady. "I don't think we should even consider anything under five hundred thousand dollars."

And that's how they left it.

But it seemed clear that there wasn't going to be any problem about selling the ship. The shoppers came flocking to Norfolk—and, what was most encouraging of all, they came flocking from all over the world. To be sure, there were relatively few American customers, and for a while the reason for this had been a trifle disquieting: the *African Queen* was German-built and therefore did not meet U.S. Maritime Commission standards. To operate for an American company on the high seas, the *Queen* would have to be drastically overhauled, at great expense. The cost was enough to drive most American customers out of the market—although a Great Lakes operator, whose ships ran to Canadian ports, showed up in town and commented thoughtfully that with a blunt bow added and the tanks converted to dry cargo space, the *Queen* might be ideally adapted to lake freighting. But there was another drawback. American shippers feel strongly that U.S.-built marine engines are the best in the world and the only ones worth having. Those on the *Queen* were German.

But interest ran high among prospective foreign purchasers. Almost every day Brady, acting as the firm's sales manager, had to drive in from Suffolk and hurry out to the airport to greet a new prospect. They came so fast that he couldn't keep them straight. They came from Japan, from Formosa, Mexico, Norway, Sweden, Germany—from practically every place that had a merchant marine.

In addition, Eugene Jaeger earned the salvagers' undying gratitude by phoning dozens of his acquaintances on their behalf, just trying to spread the word.

A broker came down from New York to look the ship over, and for a while they thought of having him handle its sale. That fell through, but he did examine the tanker and give an opinion. "With the tanker business what it is, you might have a little trouble getting what she's really worth," he said, "but

I guess she'll bring, say, three hundred thousand dollars all right. You wouldn't turn up your noses at that, eh?"

Later they talked it over. "Let's not get down *too* low, here," Sadler said. "Tanker market or no tanker market, this was a six-and-a-half-million-dollar ship just three or four years ago. Well, even making allowances for a new bow and some cleaning up, we should still make a pretty penny on her. Deir and Little and the boys didn't do all that work, and Paul and I didn't do all that worrying and running around, and Paul's work out on the ship, too, just for peanuts. Let's don't get stampeded, here."

And then, as it turned out, there was no need to make a decision at all. Warner decided to take his claim to court, and that changed everything.

Gifford Warner had been hovering in the background of the salvage operation virtually from the start. A balding, articulate, bearded professional salvage operator from Essex, Connecticut, he had begun disputing the Virginians' claim to the tanker as far back as March, immediately after notice appeared in the papers that they were taking her over. He said then that he had boarded the hulk several days earlier and had posted an announcement of his claim on the pilot-house, fixing it to a bulkhead with cellophane tape. The partners had never seen the notice. Warner had ultimately taken over the ship's bow, which the Virginia salvagers no longer wanted, and he was still planning to salvage it. But he had never given up his claim to the rest of the tanker. Now, on October 16, he announced his intention of pressing his claim in court. Federal Judge Walter E. Hoffman set a hearing for December 21.

For the Virginians that posed a perplexing dilemma on top of a major problem. The problem was, of course, that it threw into question their whole profit on the salvage enterprise. The dilemma, more important at the moment, was that it left them badly in debt, with costs mounting daily and no immediate prospect of relief.

The first difficulty they found worrisome but hard to take seriously.

"I can't *believe* the judge would give the ship to that fellow now," said Deir. "It just doesn't seem reasonable. It *isn't* reasonable. There was no notice there. We didn't see any. We went aboard and did all the work getting her in. It isn't right that someone can come along and claim her now, and I don't see how a judge would let him do it."

There were now four lawyers representing the partners—Rawls, Little's attorney Henry Howell, Brady's lawyer Landon Maxey, and Hugh Meredith, member of a Norfolk firm that specialized in maritime law. All four agreed that Warner's claim seemed tenuous. Still, no experienced lawyer ever takes the opposition's case lightly, however weak it might appear on the surface. There was no telling what evidence Warner might introduce. And he was being represented by a highly reputable New York firm which presumably would not have advised him to go to court if he did not have some kind of case.

So the salvagers merely fretted about Warner's claim. But the matter of pending bills and current expenses was something else again.

Brady, who had kept the books for the salvage operation, was now spending all his evenings going over them, bringing them up to date, trying to figure out exactly what they had spent and were spending.

Their total expenses in getting the tanker off the shoal and into Norfolk were phenomenally low. It had all been done for something around fifty-five thousand dollars, a figure they could all be proud of. But within a few weeks of docking they received a staggering blow. The ship had been in the hands of the Norfolk Shipbuilding and Drydock Company for four days, during which repairs had been made to her bottom, some cleaning up and maintenance had been undertaken in the engine room and elsewhere, and various other essential tasks had been performed.

The bill came to approximately fifty-five thousand dollars.

The stunned salvagers angrily questioned the total, convinced that it was exorbitant. "It *can't* be that much," Deir expostulated. "They're charging as much for four days as we spent in six months! I'm against paying it. Let 'em sue." The others felt much the same way. A series of negotiations with the drydock company produced no solution. It now seemed likely that this claim, too, would go to court.

Meanwhile expenses were going on and on. The ship was tied up at an old grass-grown pier rented from the Norfolk and Southern Railway at five hundred dollars a month (later lowered by the line's sympathetic president to three hundred). Other expenses—insurance, additional cleaning, a full-time watchman—brought their monthly outlay to about eighteen hundred dollars. And it might be spring before there was a verdict in the Warner suit.

There was just one solution: an immediate auction, under court auspices, the money to be impounded by the U.S. marshal pending solution of Warner's claim. This would halt the mounting overhead; once the ship was sold its upkeep would become the responsibility of the new owner. The auction was suggested by the Virginians, agreed to by Warner and promptly ordered by Judge Hoffman. He made it clear that, no matter who won the suit over ownership of the tanker, the expenses incurred by the four salvagers would be paid before anyone else collected a cent.

The auction was set for November 30, and the judge, at the Virginians' request, set a minimum-bid figure of two hundred and fifty thousand dollars.

The salvagers breathed easier. In the weeks that followed, their spirits, much dampened by all their recent troubles, began to soar again. In mid-November, the court-appointed ship broker assigned to deal with prospective bidders reported that interest had been shown by ship operators from no less than fifteen countries. By November 27 the number had risen to thirty, many of whom had come all the way to Norfolk to see the vessel for themselves.

"It's gonna be nice to get it all over with," Brady said to Sadler. "The way these people are showing interest we may get up around a million yet—you watch. Maybe two million *was* a little high. Well"—he grinned—"no sense being grabby, I guess. One million will be all right, too."

"Daggone, we're gonna do all right," said Lloyd Deir. "I've got a feeling."

At noon on November 30, a cold, gray day, a great crowd gathered around the steps of the Federal Building on Norfolk's Granby Street. Hundreds of townsfolk were on hand, including a substantial number of visitors, some of whom had been out earlier to see the ship. There was an expectant bustle as Deputy U.S. Marshal Joseph A. Gilliland, Jr., advanced to the center of the crowd and stood for a moment shuffling some papers.

The four salvagers stood on the steps and looked out over the crowd. Television and newspaper cameramen clustered on the outskirts and moved among the gathering. Deir, the pepper marks of the explosion still visible on his forehead, glanced around him briefly and then settled his gaze on Gilliland, who would conduct the auction.

This was the culmination, the moment of triumph he had envisioned while sitting on that gasoline can in his workshop in March. The decision made away back then had certainly carried them along a twisted and curious path. Now they had reached its end. He supposed others had looked on the venture as a gamble; for himself there had never been much doubt of the outcome once he made up his mind. Anyhow, there certainly had been some risk, but they had won, and here was the payoff. When it all started, he had been an obscure mechanic, practically unknown outside his own neighborhood. Now his name was literally a household word in a great part of Virginia, and the various magazine pieces—including the *Saturday Evening Post* article, published just a couple of weeks earlier—had spread it across the country. It was hard to know what to think about it all. But he had tried for something that would mark a turning point in his life, and now the turning point had come—right now, right here.

He watched intently as Gilliland motioned for silence and began to read the court order.

"By virtue of a decree of sale entered by the United States District Court for the Eastern District of Virginia, on October 30, 1959, I shall proceed to sell at public auction, free of all liens, the stern section of the ex-Liberian steamship *African Queen*, her engines, boats, bunkers, tackle, apparel and other appurtenances. . . ." The reading took several minutes and included the terms of sale: "The vessel is to be sold to the highest bidder who makes bid in excess of two hundred and fifty thousand dollars, and purchase price is to be paid fifteen per cent cash at time of sale, balance within ten days, the fifteen per cent payment to be forfeited if sale is not consummated. . . ."

He finished reading and looked up. There was a brief pause, and a stir in the crowd. Then he spoke. "Gentlemen, do I hear a bid?"

There was a long silence. Obviously no one was anxious to make the first bid; the buyers preferred to wait one another out.

"Do I hear a bid?" asked Gilliland patiently.

The crowd shifted; there was a scuffing of feet and clearing of throats—and silence.

"Come on now," said the deputy marshal amiably. "We have a ship to sell here. What's the matter with you people? Don't you want to buy a ship today? Now who's going to open this bidding up?"

In the silence that followed, the four salvagers looked about them—and suddenly they knew the truth.

These bidders weren't waiting for a thing.

Nobody was going to bid.

Shocked speechless, Brady stared around at the crowd. The people standing there, all those foreign representatives, all the strangers who had been down to the dock, were so anxious to remain unnoticed that they wouldn't even look at the auctioneer lest he mistake the glance for a signal. Brady caught Sadler's eye and saw consternation written there. He himself felt sick and weak. This was disaster. A low murmur was now running through the crowd and Gilliland spoke again, more sharply.

Do I hear a bid?

There were no bids.

Gilliland raised both hands to shoulder height before him, in a brisk, helpless gesture.

"No bids, no sale," he said, and walked out of the center of

278

the crowd. Reporters began to close in on the shaken salvagers.

On December 21 court hearings opened on Gifford Warner's contention that he, and not the four partners from Virginia, owned the *African Queen*. The hearings lasted for two days and were notable mainly because they disclosed to the public for the first time the full story of the rift between Deir and Little, and because Warner testified that he could have raised the *Queen* in seven days at a cost, from sea bottom to port, of twenty-five thousand dollars.

On January 11 Judge Hoffman announced his decision. Warner's case, the judge said, brought to mind a girl who was wooed by two suitors, one of whom pursued her ardently and with vigor while the other did nothing. Warner, Judge Hoffman suggested, was like the second suitor who, having lost the girl through his own lack of effort, now stepped forward to claim her after the first man had won her. The rightful owners of the tanker, he said tartly, were the four men who had salvaged her.

That afternoon, the second auction was held. It had been ordered by the judge immediately after the first had ended in fiasco. This one would be the same as the other—except that no minimum was set, and the proceeds, if there were any, would go to the four partners—unless Warner decided to appeal, which seemed unlikely under the circumstances. Of course, if the proceeds did not cover the salvagers' expenses, which had now climbed to about a hundred and thirty thousand dollars (including the drydock bill, ultimately settled for forty-six thousand dollars) the debt would be all theirs, too.

It was an anxious foursome that showed up on the post office steps that afternoon. There was some ground for hope, still. The broker reported once again, with some puzzlement, that interest appeared to be running strong. Perhaps this time it indicated a desire to buy. In any case there were sure to be *some* bidders—and who could tell, in the heat of spirited bidding, how high the price might go?

"I'll settle for my skin," Sadler said grimly to Brady as they joined the crowd on the Federal Building steps.

There were just as many people as before. Once again there were photographers and television cameras. The crushing anticlimax of the first auction had been covered fully—and sympathetically—by the news media. All over Norfolk that afternoon there were people whose hopes, and perhaps even prayers, were riding with the four hard-pressed salvagers. Certainly the atmosphere at the scene of the second auction was different from the calm sense of expectation that had attended the first. This time the tension was almost thick enough to touch.

Deputy Marshal Gilliland read the court order—the words were the same, except that there was no reference to a minimum price. Then he looked up.

"Do I hear any bids?" he asked.

There was a moment's silence.

"Twenty-five thousand," a man called.

"Twenty-five. Do I hear thirty? Thirty?"

"Thirty."

"Thirty-five?"

Slowly the amount rose. It was not spirited bidding, but it was bidding. Three men were doing it all—only three out of that large crowd. One was a local scrap dealer, another was the president of the Norfolk Shipbuilding and Drydock Company, the third was a short, round-faced ship operator named Sam Kahn who had come down that day from New York. At sixty-three thousand dollars the drydock executive dropped out. The salvagers watched nervously as the scrap dealer and the New York bidder fought it out. The bidding was now climbing very slowly—in two-thousand-dollar raises. Kahn, smoking a big cigar, bid coolly, usually without speaking, simply gesturing to meet the marshal's new price.

"Sixty-nine," called Gilliland. "Sixty-nine. Do I hear seventy-one? Seventy-one? Seventy-one?" He looked sharply at Kahn. "Do I hear seventy-one?"

Kahn raised a finger.

"Seventy-one!" said the marshal promptly. "Seventy-one is

the bid; do I hear seventy-three?"

The scrap dealer shook his head. The salvagers had reached the end of the line. Seventy-one thousand dollars. Brady stared straight ahead, his heart pounding. Nine months before, he thought bitterly, he had been a fairly well-off small-business man. Now . . .

Deir was watching impassively. Little, off to one side, scowled. There was a meaningless sound from behind Brady, where Sadler was standing with attorneys Rawls and Meredith.

"Going once at seventy-one!

"Going twice!"

Somebody spoke behind Brady.

"Gone!"

"Wait! Wait! I made a bid. You didn't hear it! Just a minute, here." Lewis Rawls, Sadler's lawyer, pushed his way forward, and there was a great murmur from the crowd. "I'm bidding seventy-three!"

"No, no," Kahn protested. "The bidding is closed. It's my ship."

"I raised your bid," Rawls insisted. "I did it before the bidding closed, but I wasn't heard."

"No, sir," said Kahn steadily. "The only one who can reopen the bidding is the U.S. marshal himself."

A man standing beside him promptly spoke up. "I am the U.S. marshal," he said. "And I'm reopening the bidding."

"The bid is seventy-three," said Gilliland immediately. "Do I hear seventy-five?"

Brady, Little and Deir, suddenly yanked back from the abyss, turned and stared at Sadler. He was standing in the crowd, his face grim. The only possibility of preventing financial catastrophe was to risk everything—to push Kahn up to a reasonable price, and hope desperately that he, Sadler, could pull out of the bidding before the New Yorker did. If not, if his own bid bought the tanker, he was ruined. The ship would be his alone, the debts would be his alone, and the expenses would go on, and on, until he could figure out a way of ridding himself of the hulk. A faint mist of perspiration was visible on Sadler's forehead.

Rawls was now standing up front, slugging it out with Kahn.

"Seventy-seven."

"Seventy-nine."

"Eighty-one."

Kahn, calm again after his brief outburst, was bidding once more with his usual impassivity. Rawls, with an eye on Sadler and his face almost equally grim, was matching Kahn bid for bid. At ninety thousand Sadler made a move to stop Rawls, but Rawls coolly ignored him. The tanker *had* to be worth more than that. Now he was raising Kahn one thousand at a time. Kahn, imperturbable, chewing on his cigar, was letting the auctioneer call, "Going," sometimes twice, before raising.

At a hundred and fifteen thousand the raises got down to five hundred dollars.

At a hundred and thirty-three thousand, five hundred Sadler moved close to Rawls. "Any higher," he said, "and you're on your own. I've reached my limit."

"Do I hear one-thirty-four?" the deputy marshal called. "Going at one-thirty-three, five. Going twice at one-thirty-three, five. Go—"

Kahn gestured.

"The bid is one-thirty-four! Do I hear one-thirty-four, five?"

Rawls stuck out his hand to Kahn. "Congratulations," he said. "You've bought yourself a ship."

Kahn smiled and shook hands.

Sadler caught Brady's eye, and they both grinned, ashen-faced. Nine months of struggle, risk, worry, fear, were over. The four salvagers were, from this instant, quit of the *African Queen* and all her hopes and problems. The adventure was finished.

They had broken almost exactly even.

FOUR

24

PEARLY STRAIT moved to Florida. Mack Duncan shifted his family from Suffolk, his wife's home town, back to his own home town, Batesburg, South Carolina. Woody Crisp quit Duke Morris and started a deep-sea-diving service of his own. Maurice Simmons left the sheet-metal business and took a job with a major oil concern in Norfolk, starting low, but with a keen eye on the promise of advancement the firm held out to bright, fast-moving young men.

The other men returned to the work they had been doing a thousand years earlier, before they were called away by the big chance.

What they thought about the outcome of the enterprise was hard to say, even for them. Their emotions had been pulled in so many directions in those last weeks that the only distinct sensation that remained was a kind of numbness, a composite of disappointment, relief and bewilderment.

But there was no regret.

A reporter for a Norfolk newspaper who interviewed three of the partners separately the day after the ship was sold found that not one of them would say he was sorry he had been involved in the operation. Little was bitter and depressed at the outcome, but he was busy with plans to raise a sunken excursion vessel from the Elizabeth River in North Carolina.

Sadler was philosophical: "We didn't make any money, but we sure had a lot of fun."

Deir, as always, was indomitable. "I woke up this morning and found a lot of headaches I'd been having weren't there any more," he told the reporter. "I don't feel too badly about it. It's all water over the dam now."

"Lloyd," Brady asked one day, "would you do it again? I mean, would you take the chance, figuring this time you could pull it off and make the kind of money it was worth?"

Deir stared back at him levelly. "Sure," he said. "Matter of fact, I've got a plan now to raise the *Andrea Doria*. It'll work, too. The problem is to find backing. If I can get someone to put up the money I'll raise that ship. You watch."

"You know," Brady told Sadler later, "if it was anyone else but Deir you'd figure he was crazy sure enough. But I'm damned if I don't think he could pull it off—if he can find a backer. I know one thing. I'll never put another nickel of mine into something like that."

Among the news clippings of that summer that Brady's wife pasted into her scrapbook was an editorial from the Norfolk *News-Ledger*, written just before the great parade and celebration. It commented on the rumors already circulating that the vast wealth the partners had hoped for might not materialize.

"This wasn't an event to honor a clutch of brand-new millionaires anyhow," the editorial said. "It's what they did that counted, in a display of resourcefulness, initiative and bedrock courage which deeply moved this community. After today most of them may return to anonymity, but they wrote an heroic page in the annals of the sea and they illustrated an unsuspected—especially by modern, peacetime standards—dimension of the human spirit. That is what today's applause was really about."

Brady grinned when he read it. "You've heard of prophets without honor," he told his wife. "What we have here is honor without profit." They chuckled. Then he said, "I guess that isn't a bad thing to settle for after all."

EPILOGUE

The Tanker

ON AUGUST 6, 1960, the six-hundred-and-eleven-ton seagoing tug *Melanie Fair* of Hamilton, Ontario, nosed up to the great hulk of the *African Queen* at her weed-covered slip in Norfolk and heaved a line aboard. A short time later, aided by a couple of McAllister tugs, the *Melanie Fair* slowly drew the tanker away from the berth where she had lain for almost a year and headed out into Hampton Roads and the wide Atlantic. Standing at the pier as the *Queen* left were those erstwhile adversaries, Alvah Sadler and Sam Kahn; they had lunched together in the city that day and then driven down to the dock to see her off.

The tanker's destination was Antwerp, Belgium, and the tug's forty-seven-year-old skipper and owner, a lean, hard-bitten British-born sailor named William Wharton, had given himself forty days to make the journey.

Forty days later the *Melanie Fair* and her unwieldy tow were still in mid-Atlantic. It was not until early in November, three months after leaving Norfolk, that the *African Queen,* with the Virginians' patch still gleaming dully on her side, limped awkwardly into port behind the tug after one of the wildest ocean crossings of record. And at that the port was Lisbon; an eleven-hundred-mile voyage to Antwerp still lay ahead.

Almost all the lost time had been spent by Captain Wharton in trying to re-establish contact with his tow. Four times the six-inch wire tow cable had snapped; the last time Wharton had been forced to use his anchor chain as a tow line because he was running out of wire. No fewer than fourteen times it had been necessary to board the tanker at sea, often in rough weather, and once—the feat still left Wharton almost too astonished to talk about it weeks later—while tanker and tug were still attached by the tow line, an exceedingly difficult feat.

Twice the *Melanie Fair* had run so low on fuel that Wharton had been forced to cast loose from the disabled ship and head into the Azores for replenishment, leaving a crew of three aboard the *Queen*. The first time it had taken the frantic tug skipper twenty-one days to find the derelict; in that time she had drifted a thousand miles, making a speed of four knots—slightly better than she had averaged under tow! The second time Wharton had searched for her ten days, and she had drifted even faster: he finally found her seven hundred miles away.

And all the while the men left aboard the *Queen* had lived like castaways, rationing their food, fishing with hook, line and home-made harpoon, cooking their catch over an open fire built on the steel deck. Using the scraps of lumber still to be found aboard the *Queen,* they had constructed a little boat with which to visit the occasional ships they encountered. For amusement they had played chess, using pieces made of paper, on the checkerboard-tile floor of the captain's cabin. And they had lived with danger.

Their quarters in the pilothouse hung right over the water, the tanks under it wide open to the sea. ("Like living on a springboard," said Wharton later.) The noise was awful—particularly in bad weather. And there was plenty of bad weather. The winds got up to fifty miles an hour. In this furious gale the tanker, unballasted and riding high off the water, had pitched and rolled terrifyingly. After each pitch, tremors would run through her hull for long seconds. At her worst, she rolled through an almost incredible arc of sixty degrees—thirty degrees each way—and the seas that tossed her reached a height, from trough to peak, of fifty feet.

Then she sprang a leak in the engine room. Entering that dank, slippery, black, sloshing, malodorous cavern was a fearful experience, but the men aboard the drifting tanker had to go down there again and again to fight back the rising water. Slowly the *Queen* developed a marked list to port, and the men began to worry about capsizing.

The *Melanie Fair*, helped by radio messages from passing vessels, had found her charge again, had resumed the tow, and had pumped out the engine room. The three men had returned thankfully to the tug—until next time.

By the time the tug and the tanker reached Lisbon there was simply no thought of going farther—for the *Melanie Fair*, anyhow. Wharton beached the *African Queen* on a sand bank for safety's sake, and a few weeks later the *Melanie Fair* limped back to Canada. A European tug company was hired to complete the tow to Antwerp in the spring.

By now it was beginning to appear that the salvagers had got off easy. Wharton had lost money on this job. Back in New York, Sam Kahn told an inquiring newsman that, with the tanker and scrap markets both declining steadily, he stood to lose up to seventy-five thousand dollars.

In the spring the *African Queen* once again got under way. Early in May the battered tanker finally was pulled into Antwerp. She was tied up to a dock, and the tug headed back to sea.

For a few days the tanker remained at her dock unmolested. Then men began to swarm aboard her with acetylene torches. Soon great slabs of metal were being cut from the rust-flaked decks and sides. Cranes swung the steel away and loaded it for the scrap mills.

By the summer, almost two years after she had been salvaged by the four partners from Virginia, the last piece had been hoisted away, and the *African Queen* had disappeared forever.